CLOAK
AND
GAVEL

FBI Wiretaps,
Bugs,
Informers,
and the
Supreme Court

Alexander Charns

UNIVERSITY OF ILLINOIS PRESS
Urbana and Chicago

© 1992 Alexander Charns
Manufactured in the United States of America
C 5 4 3 2 1

This book is printed on acid-free paper.

Library of Congress Cataloging-in-Publication Data

Charns, Alexander, 1956–
    Cloak & gavel : FBI wiretaps, bugs, informers, and the Supreme
Court / Alexander Charns.
        p.   cm.
    Includes bibliographical references (p.   ) and index.
    ISBN 0-252-01871-0
    1. United States. Supreme Court.   2. United States. Federal
Bureau of Investigation—Corrupt practices.   3. United States.
Federal Bureau of Investigation—Political activity.   4. Electronic
surveillance—United States.   5. Misconduct in office—United
States.   I. Title.   II. Title: Cloak and gavel.
KF8742.C45   1992
347.73'26—dc20
[347.30735]   91-44533
                                                                   CIP

To my mother and father

CLOAK AND GAVEL

Whoever attentively considers the different departments of power must perceive, that, in a government in which they are separated from each other, the judiciary, from the nature of its functions, will always be the least dangerous to the political rights of the constitution; because it will be least in a capacity to annoy or injure them. The executive not only dispenses the honors, but holds the sword of the community: The legislature not only commands the purse, but prescribes the rules by which the duties and rights of every citizen are to be regulated: The judiciary, on the contrary, has no influence over the sword or the purse; no direction either of the strength or of the wealth of the society; and can take no active resolution whatever. It may truly be said to have neither FORCE nor WILL, but merely judgment; and must ultimately depend upon the aid of the executive arm for the efficacious exercise even of this faculty.

—*The Federalist,* No. 78 (Alexander Hamilton)

Contents

Illustrations follow p. 68

Preface

"The Framers of our Government knew that the most precious of liberties could remain secure only if they created a structure of government based on a permanent separation of power" between the executive, legislative and judicial branches of government.[1] James Madison concluded that unless each branch of government exercised "a constitutional control over the others," as a check and a balance, that separation alone was "not a sufficient guard against those encroachments which lead to a tyrannical concentration of all the powers of government in the same hands."[2] What Madison could not foresee was that nearly two centuries later a subdivision of one agency in the executive would wield such tyrannical power.

From the 1930s until 1972, the Federal Bureau of Investigation (FBI), initially established to investigate violations of the federal criminal laws as a component of the U.S. Department of Justice, the prosecutorial arm of the executive, accrued to itself an alarming, virtually unchecked strength. For most of his forty-eight years at its helm, J. Edgar Hoover kept his putative bosses, the attorneys general, in the dark about many of his activities. The political reality was that Hoover had no boss and no equal. Agents referred to FBI headquarters in the nation's capital as the "Seat of Government" (SOG).[3] This seat of the director's phantom government was symbolic of the bureau as an independent source of power. The director aspired to create a hybrid fourth branch of the federal government, a branch that exercised legislative, executive, and judicial powers when it suited his purposes. Hoover biographers Athan Theoharis and John Cox have concluded that Hoover, director of the bureau from 1924 until his death in 1972, "had more to do with undermining American constitutional guarantees than any political leader before or since."[4] Clark Clifford, adviser to Presidents Harry Truman, John Kennedy and Lyndon Johnson, described Hoover as "very close to being an American fascist." Clifford wrote that there was no one "who amassed and abused power more shamefully" during his reign.[5]

But there was plenty of blame to go around: a succession of presidents, attorneys general, congressmen, and Supreme Court justices either ignored or aided and abetted Hoover's unconstitutional zeal.

Despite the fact that Hoover had two law degrees and was taught that the Supreme Court was the final arbiter of the Constitution, his FBI battled for the soul of the Supreme Court in a campaign that lasted from 1957 to 1971. The goal was to push the "least dangerous"[6] branch of government to the political right on issues of criminal law and civil liberties. Though the Constitution provides for a free and independent federal judiciary, the FBI enjoyed the services of least one Supreme Court justice as its source in the conference room on a case involving illegal FBI bugging and on other cases of importance to the bureau. Abe Fortas, handpicked by President Johnson first as an associate justice and later as successor to Earl Warren as chief justice, became the only justice in history to be hounded off the Court in disgrace—but not before serving as an informer for the White House and the FBI. Other high-level Court employees had been similarly used as informers.

The FBI's anti–Warren Court program began ten years before Fortas became an associate justice. In the mid-1950s Hoover began to feel increasingly threatened by Supreme Court rulings. Chief Justice Earl Warren's Court was not blindly following Fred Vinson's approach of upholding governmental action against Communists. Although Supreme Court rulings on internal security issues in the middle to late 1950s pivoted on fairly narrow legalistic grounds,[7] Hoover heard an ominous drumbeat of "pro-Communist decisions" growing steadily louder.[8] The powerful FBI czar saw the rulings as judicial activism that impeded the work of the House Committee on Un-American Activities and state and federal administration actions against Communists and that made it impossible for the Justice Department to prosecute Communists.

Hoover also blamed the Supreme Court's desegregation cases, including *Brown v. Board of Education*, for mandating "mixed education" and spurring on violent racial turmoil in the South.[9] Here, too, Hoover believed that Communists were behind the scenes, stirring up the National Association for the Advancement of Colored People and other African-American organizations.

Believing the Supreme Court was coddling subversives, the FBI decided in 1956 to destroy the Communist party in the streets—or in the home, if need be—without such niceties as constitutional guarantees of due process. There would be no confronting one's accuser—or even the knowledge that one was accused. The FBI felt it had no choice: Supreme Court rulings, expected in 1957, would make its chief weapon against Communists—the Smith Act, which made it a crime to advocate or teach the violent overthrow of the government[10]—"technically unenforceable."[11] For Hoover, the final straw was in the spring of 1956, when the Justice Department, anticipating the Court rulings, ceased prosecuting members of the Communist party under the Smith Act: between 1949 and 1956 it had previously convicted 104 major leaders in cases the FBI had investigated.[12]

The FBI looked for another, more powerful weapon to replace criminal prosecutions. During the summer of 1956 Hoover came up with such a plan. The bureau formalized a "counter-intelligence" program, codenamed COINTELPRO, to disrupt and neutralize the Communist Party U.S.A. by reviving wartime counterintelligence techniques once used against Nazi spies.[13] As the Senate Select Committee to Study Governmental Operations with respect to Intelligence Activities (popularly known as the Church Committee after its chairman, Senator Frank Church of Idaho) noted after its unprecedented investigation of FBI and intelligence agency abuses in 1976, the COINTELPROs were not really counterintelligence programs, which were supposed to be activities to protect an agency's own security and undermine hostile intelligence operations. Since COINTELPRO targets were U.S. citizens, not foreign intelligence agents, they were more accurately described as "covert actions," "clandestine activities intended to influence political choices and social values."[14]

All manner of illegal or questionable methods were used in furtherance of the counterintelligence programs: wiretaps, buggings, breakins, informants, and disinformation. Agents were rewarded for creativity in coming up with forged letters to the wives, employers, or landlords of targets. "Snitch-jackets," papers falsely identifying someone as an FBI informer, were prepared and dropped in convenient locations or passed on to real FBI snitches.[15] There were few limits on COINTELPROs. Later such programs were directed at a broad range of individuals and organizations in eleven other categories, including "Socialist Workers Party," "White Hate Group," "Black Nationalist," and "New Left."[16] Occasionally, when the bureau successfully sowed dissension within a group or between groups, the end result was violence and death.[17] The bureau's covert war against the Black Panther party was particularly bloody.[18]

But the FBI's most important domestic covert action program was never committed to paper. To this day, the FBI denies the existence of a program directed at the pinnacle of the judicial branch of the U.S.

government itself: the Supreme Court.[19] Yet the confluence of bureau activities directed at law clerks, justices, Congress, White House, "subversives," and the general public had the effect of a long-running covert action program against the Court itself.[20] The goal of the FBI's Supreme Court program was to remake the Court in Hoover's image.[21]

Starting in 1957 and continuing over time, the FBI developed its Court program into five separate but related strategies: (1) supporting conservative nominations to the Supreme Court by influencing the nomination and confirmation process; (2) whipping up public furor against Warren Court rulings; (3) lobbying for legislation to counteract Supreme Court decisions; (4) penetrating the Court itself to gain advance knowledge of Court business and influence rulings; and (5) attempting to remove enemies from the Court.

The Court program violated Article III of the Constitution and was contrary to the bureau's function as a law enforcement agency. The FBI has only one legitimate role to play in relation to the Supreme Court: "investigating threats against court officials and providing intelligence information"[22] to the office of the marshal of the Supreme Court, who oversees the Court's police force. However, just as Hoover's FBI was a "vacuum cleaner"[23] for rumors, innuendos, and facts on those who dared to dissent in America or who espoused unconventional political or racial views, such information collection occurred around justices, law clerks, and Court workers as well.

During Hoover's directorship, the FBI had its sights on the entire federal judiciary, not just the Supreme Court. The bureau collected derogatory information on justices and federal court judges, and it used that information as a weapon against liberals on the federal bench to further Hoover's political agenda.[24] Bureau information allowed the Justice Department to "judge-shop"[25] for ideologically sympathetic federal judges. The FBI leaked information from its confidential files about liberal judges to influence policies formulated at judicial conferences.[26] Likeminded judges were enlisted by the bureau to lobby Congress and other government officials while the FBI kept tabs on judges deemed "antagonistic" to FBI interests.[27] Similarly, civil libertarian lawyers[28] and legal organizations, particularly the National Lawyers Guild, were infiltrated and disrupted by the bureau.[29] On the other hand, judges, justices, and lawyers deemed "friendly" to the bureau, including high-level officials in the American Bar Association and the American Civil Liberties Union, were cultivated; the personal favors provided to them were subtly called in when needed.[30] Such cooperative ventures between an agency of the executive branch and members of the judicial branch tended to blur the separation between branches of government.

Still, it is impossible to document the full degree of collaboration between the FBI and the federal judiciary. And this book is not a complete, unabridged history of FBI–Supreme Court relations, due to the limitations on scholarly research in this area: the FBI had set up secret filing systems and regularly destroyed records to avoid oversight and exposure. Records about the worst FBI abuses were systematically destroyed. For records that remain extant, a request under the present watered-down Freedom of Information Act (FOIA) may take from one to three years for a response. Relying upon the FOIA to learn about the FBI might be compared to reporting on the Persian Gulf war from a fallout shelter in Saudi Arabia. If any information from the government trickles out, it is censored and the answer "no records" may actually mean the opposite.

A request for FBI records under the FOIA is like any other request under the act, except that the wait is longer and one receives less—that is, if any records are determined to be "responsive" to a request. Requesters cannot trust the FBI's statements that it failed to locate records. A failure to locate records may mean that no records were located or it may mean that under the 1986 amendments to the FOIA these records are no longer subject to the FOIA, allowing the bureau to deny the existence of requested records about confidential informants, ongoing criminal investigations about which the subject is unaware and about foreign intelligence, counterintelligence, or international terrorism.[31]

For records not excluded from the provisions of the FOIA, nine statutory grounds for withholding information exist. Hundreds of pages of FBI records about individual justices, especially Justice William O. Douglas, are exempt because they remain classified to protect U.S. national defense or foreign policy. The majority of the redactions about the Supreme Court are based upon claims of privacy for informers and other sources of information.

In 1983 I began making FOIA requests for FBI records about the Supreme Court. First, I requested files on Chief Justice Warren and Justice Douglas and asked for the subject file on the Supreme Court itself. Records about Warren and Douglas were processed, but the bureau ignored my request about the Supreme Court. In 1984 I again asked about my request on the Court and was told that the request was not specific enough. In May 1984 I rephrased my request for records about the Supreme Court as a body and asked for any records about the use of justices or Court employees as FBI informers. At the end of the summer I was told that no file on the Supreme Court could be located. As a result, I systematically requested records on every deceased Supreme Court justice and subject files on wiretapping, the administrative office of the courts, and other related topics in an attempt to find references to other files about the Court. Finally, in an attempt to obtain all FBI records about the Supreme Court, lawsuits were filed in federal court in 1988 and 1989. As a result, tens of thousands of records were released during the course of the litigation. One 2,000-page file called "Supreme Court" was released during the summer of 1988. (An FBI employee had, in fact, located this file in 1984. And other employees on a FBI fee waiver committee had, unbeknownst to me, granted a waiver of copying costs for yet other documents about the Supreme Court about which I was not informed.[32] Not until I requested my own Freedom of Information Act–Privacy Act FBI file did I uncover the bureau's "search slip," which showed that records about the Supreme Court, including documents within the Supreme Court file, had been located in 1984.)

One reason that the current FBI has trouble locating records is that Hoover devised filing systems designed to thwart access by outsiders and the present administration does not care to make the information accessible now. Sleight-of-hand recordkeeping and its double-speak "Do Not File" files and other unindexed records, and "June mail" records that were maintained separately all serve to preserve secrecy by keeping evidence of illegality separate from legitimate records. And the most valuable not to be filed records that were not systematically destroyed were kept in Hoover's own office and in the offices of other senior FBI officials, such as FBI Assistant Directors Louis Nichols, D. Milton Ladd, Clyde Tolson, W. Mark Felt, and Cartha DeLoach. The particularly supersecret, unindexed office files of Hoover—the "Personal and Confidential" files—were destroyed soon after the director's death in 1972 by his personal aide, Helen Gandy. Memos documenting Justice Fortas's unethical dealings with the FBI had been transferred from the "Personal and Confidential" files to Hoover's "Official and Confidential" files, and they survived the file destruction.[33]

Those at the bureau, however, are not the only ones in the District of Columbia destroying records or making access difficult. The Supreme Court itself is not known for openness. Justice Hugo Black destroyed his Supreme Court conference notes, and Justice Byron White's papers are not yet available for research. Justice Potter Stewart's papers will not be made public until every justice with whom he served on the Court has died. Justices exercise dominion over their own Court files as if they were private citizens and not public servants. No sunshine law or freedom of information statute applies to the Court's decision-making process.[34] Neither Congress nor the president nor the public has a legal right to know what transpires in the conference room of the Supreme Court.

The end result is that the record of the FBI's interaction with the Court is uneven at best. And for this reason, I wrote this book in episodic fashion, to take advantage of what original source materials exist or are available.

Chapter one provides an overview of the FBI's Supreme Court program. Chapter two surveys FBI electronic surveillance policy vis-à-vis Supreme Court rulings from 1928 until the early 1960s and is intended to set the legal and political stage for the history that follows. The bureau's interaction with the Supreme Court on the issue of electronic surveillance illustrates the FBI's history of obeying the law when that did not interfere with bureau objectives. It also serves as an example of the unconstitutional methods the bureau—and some justices—employed to protect the FBI. The remainder of the book focuses on the period from 1966 to 1971, beginning at the zenith of the criminal justice revolution of the Warren Court and ending during the third term of the Warren Burger Court. These were the final years of the FBI's Court program and the last years of its warrantless tapping and bugging directed against domestic opponents. The Supreme Court itself had provided some of the necessary ingredients for the FBI's recipe for tyranny.

I am thankful for the generous financial support from the J. Roderick MacArthur Foundation, which made this book possible. Financial support was also provided by the Fund for Investigative Journalism, the Dick Goldensohn Fund, and the Institute for Southern Studies (special thanks to Eric Bates, David Cecelski, Bob Hall, and former Executive Director Meredith Emmett).

My co-counsel and friend, Paul M. Green, went beyond the call of duty and offered suggestions and served as FOIA pit bull. I am indebted to the work of researchers Eric Longley, Arthur Sparrow, Kay Alexander, Debbie Charns, and Lisa Balderson.

I also wish to thank Brenda Hayes, Walter Jackson, Jennifer Hawfield, and Peter Shepherd for reviewing portions of the manuscript. I have received support and encouragement over the years from Laurel Goldman, Denise Giardina, Ann and Tom Loflin, William Goldston, Michelle Robertson, Stewart Fisher, Anne Duvoisin, and a host of others, including Stella Adams, Allan Adler, Jay Asquini, Gary Bays, Donald Beskind, Paul Bien, David Birman, Kenneth Broun, Ann Mari Buitrago, Heidi Chapman, Steve Conrad, Michael Curtis, Pat DeRosa, Steve Edelstein, Miriam Eden, Marilla and Harold Feld, Esphur Foster, David Freedman, Rob Gelblum, Sandra Goldston, Patricia Guarino, Lynette Hartsell, Joan Hawfield, Joe Herzenberg, Merry Jo Hill, Tom Hosey, Al Hudson, Steve Johnson, Linda Klein, Jeff Kloiber, Gayle Korotkin, Susan Korytkowski, Bryan E. Lessley, Hal Lebowitz, Elma Longley, Valerie Lumsden, Tom Maher, Bob Mahler, Maria Mangano, Harlan and Linda Mangum, Al McSurely, Fr. Charlie Mulholland, Alexandria Nabatoff, Barry Nakell, Ilene Nelson, North Carolina Civil Liberties Union, North Carolina chapter of the National Lawyers Guild, Patrick O'Neill, Jim Overton, Polly Passonneau, Travis Payne, Jane Perkins, Phyllis Pickett, Lewis Pitts, Daniel H. Pollitt, Daniel R. Pollitt, Burnele Powell, Dan Read, Mary Rider, Betsy Riker, Rich Rosen, John Rubin, David Rudolf, Dean Shangler, Quinlan Shea, Jr., the late Bob Sheldon, William Simpson, Marianne Smythe, Steve Spreitzer, Adam Stein, Jerry Swartzberg, Thomas Trujillo, Fr. Philip Walsh, Randy Ward, Bob Warren, Linda Weisel, Shelley Weiss, Liz Wheaton, Frank Wilkinson, Peter Wood, and my professors and the staff at the University of North Carolina School of Law. Thanks also to Pam McKee, Marc Duvoisin, Robert Webb and Robert Thomason, both of the Washington *Post*, Paul Delaney at the New York *Times*, Tony Mauro at *USA Today*, and veteran newspeople Sean Bailey, Lou Bonds, Nan Chase, Katherine Fulton, Lynn Haessly, John Monk, Joan Oleck, Robert Roule, and John Stevenson.

The employees at the archives and libraries that I visited were extremely helpful. I would like specifically to thank Claudia Anderson at the LBJ Library, Dennis Bilger at the Truman Library, and Mike Klein at the Library of Congress, Manuscripts Division. Thanks also to Mrs. Carolyn Agger Fortas and Duane Vieth at Arnold & Porter.

I also thank attorney Tracy Merritt at the U.S. Department of Justice, who was an honorable adversary in litigation, and the hardworking employees of the FBI's FOIPA Section, who were hamstrung by the antidisclosure policies of the attorneys general and the directors of the FBI.

Thanks also to Professor Kenneth O'Reilly, Professor David Garrow, former Senator Robert Morgan, Professor Robert Hamilton, and Professor Dagmar Hamilton. I am most grateful to Professor Athan Theoharis, who generously offered his time for consultation and editorial input; and to Richard L. Wentworth, Harriet Stockanes, Susan L. Patterson, and the rest of the staff at the University of Illinois Press.

And special thanks to my parents, Richard and Barbara, and my brother, Lee, and sister, Debbie, Marie Barron, the late Allan Barron, and Greg Charnesky. Finally, I am indebted to Jennifer Hawfield for her advice, patience, and love during the writing of this book.

CLOAK AND GAVEL

CHAPTER 1

FBI Spying
on the Supreme Court

In decision after decision, the Warren Supreme Court has befriended the Communists and their Kremlin masters, and has weakened the defenses of the American people against this enemy. States have been forbidden to enforce their own sedition laws. The Federal Bureau of Investigation's files have been thrown open to persons accused of subversion and other crimes. The powers of Congress to investigate anything and anybody in the public interest have been cut down.[1]
— New York *Daily News*, July 1, 1957

It was easy for the FBI to penetrate the cloistered world of the U.S. Supreme Court, for the Court itself had invited the FBI in. During World War I a special agent of the Bureau of Investigation was assigned to the Supreme Court at the request of Chief Justice Edward D. White.[2] By 1924 Acting Director J. Edgar Hoover decided that at $900 a year it was too costly for the bureau to pay for an agent to guard the justices—a designated responsibility of the marshal of the Supreme Court. And Chief Justice William H. Taft, after consulting his brethren, agreed that the Court did not need the services of a special agent.[3]

Occasionally, though, the Court still called on the bureau for help with security during controversial political cases. During August 1927 Hoover ordered his agents to arrange for the protection of the Washington, D.C., residence of Justice Oliver Wendell Holmes, Jr., "against any acts of violence by Sacco-Vanzetti sympathizers."[4] Justice Holmes was spending the summer in Massachusetts and had denied a stay of execution for immigrant anarchists Nicola Sacco and Bartholomeo Vanzetti after their murder convictions.[5] And during the 1930s the marshal of the Supreme Court asked the FBI to have agents operate undercover, positioning themselves in strategic places in the courtroom, when Communists planned to picket outside the Court.[6]

FBI Informers at the Court

The FBI used contacts between Court employees and special agents to its advantage. The bureau was expert at intergovernmental public relations or, in FBI lingo, "liaison," with Court employees. Members of the Supreme Court police guard were regularly given "special tours" of FBI headquarters, where they were "accorded every courtesy." Even the wives of Court employees were given red-carpet treatment. The wife of Philip H. Crook, one of the Supreme Court police guards (who later served as an informant for the FBI), and her brother were among those given a "special tour" of FBI headquarters.

Some Court employees forgot that the chief justice, not Hoover, was their boss, which was exactly what the wily director intended. By the early 1950s virtual intimacy characterized the working relationship between Court employees and the FBI. So it is disturbing, but not surprising, to find that at least three Court employees reported directly to the FBI.[7] During the case of Julius and Ethel Rosenberg, the marshal of the Court, T. Perry Lippitt, the clerk of the Court, Harold B. Willey, and the captain of the Supreme Court police, Philip H. Crook, kept the FBI informed about the numerous legal proceedings before the Court in 1953 intended to stave off the couple's execution. Willey had even made his office and staff available to FBI agents, and suggestions were given to agents as to where to be to know immediately "what action individual Judges, or the Court as a whole, was taking." Willey and his staff also notified agents about actions "contemplated by the defense attorneys" for the Rosenbergs.

Lippitt "made arrangements for Special Agents to be . . . placed in the courtroom," to enable them to be close to phones in his office from which they called headquarters with the latest information. Crook not only made his office available for the agents use, but he also "furnished . . . all information heard by his men stationed throughout the Supreme Court Building. He kept Special Agents advised of the arrival and departure of persons having important roles in this case."[8] This presumably included any hallway conversations by justices or law clerks. That Clyde Tolson, Hoover's constant companion and chief assistant, had known Willey for many years before he was elevated to clerk was no doubt helpful in securing Willey's cooperation as a source of information.[9] These FBI informers—the clerk, the marshal, and the head of the police—were all employees of the Court;[10] Lippitt, in fact, continued to work at the Court until his retirement in 1971.

FBI Files on the "Loyalty" of Justices and Clerks

While some Court employees were on quite good terms with the FBI, others, justices as well as law clerks, were deemed politically suspect during the Cold War years: Chief Justice Earl Warren and Associate

Justices Hugo Black, Felix Frankfurter, William Douglas, Stanley Reed, and Abe Fortas were among those listed. Anyone who opposed the director or the FBI was considered subversive. Hoover himself had once suggested that conservative Attorney General Tom Clark, later the FBI's most influential supporter on the Court, might be "for" Communism.[11] Sherman Minton, a U.S. Senator and Hoover ally before being nominated to the Court, had been falsely accused of having participated in the "smear campaign" against the director, which Hoover claimed was orchestrated by radicals and Communists.[12] One can only assume that the liberal political views and friendships of Associate Justices William Brennan, Arthur Goldberg, and Thurgood Marshall are also a matter of record at FBI headquarters.[13]

At the same time, Hoover's judicial supporters were rewarded. FBI agents assisted vacationing justices by making hotel reservations, offering chauffeur services (and Christmas shopping), serving as a private detective agency, taking family pictures, arranging special FBI tours, and providing other amenities, just as Hoover did for influential people with whom he was currying favor.[14] Prior to Hoover's assuming the directorship in 1924, then FBI Director William Burns had provided similar favors to Chief Justice William Taft.

Sometimes the favors to justices paid off immediately. As Justice Harold Hitz Burton,[15] a distant relative of Hoover's, and his wife were being chauffeured by an FBI agent from National Airport in Washington, D.C., to their home, the justice told the agent that he had "considerable concern over the emergency session of the Supreme Court, as he felt that the Little Rock situation was a very grave one and that the 'issues' are certainly not clear. Justice Burton indicated he was going to go into immediate conference with those Supreme Court Justices who have already returned to Washington, and would seek a conference with Chief Justice Warren at the earliest possible time."[16] Other justices revealed even more.

The director's supporters on the Supreme Court were placed on his "Special Correspondents List" (SCL). At one time or another during their careers on the High Court, Chief Justices Earl Warren and Warren Burger and Justices Robert Jackson, Charles Whittaker, and Tom Clark were on Hoover's special list.[17] Even Justice Douglas, early in his career, received special treatment. Similarly, friendly state court judges, university presidents, congressmen, and governors were made special correspondents, and thousands of other people were placed on lesser bureau mailing lists.[18] (The bureau claims that its "Special Correspondents List" is no longer in existence, but other bureau mailing lists, for those persons "who meet established criteria" related to law enforcement or "who may be in position to furnish assistance to the FBI's law enforcement efforts,"[19] do exist. These are the very descriptions that Hoover himself might have used to describe his mailing lists.)

Most of the subversive allegations about Court personnel during the 1950s centered on Justices Douglas and Frankfurter. Some of these same allegations were dredged up in 1970, when Justice Douglas was threatened with impeachment. Today these gossip-rich accusations seem beyond belief. For example, the FBI recorded in a 1950 memo that a former State Department employee claimed that he "could prove" Secretary of State Dean Acheson and Justice Frankfurter were the "Number One and Number Two Communists" in the United States.[20] This "proof" turned out to be a suspicious man's "deductive reasoning."[21] But the FBI continued to collect such wild stories about Justices Douglas and Frankfurter.[22]

In January 1954, seven months after Ethel and Julius Rosenberg were executed, the FBI was given the chance to investigate Justice Douglas's ties to Communists. Arthur B. Langlie, Republican governor of Washington, sent a report to U.S. Attorney General Herbert Brownell, Jr., about a "colony of communist sympathizers" living in the area near Douglas's cabin. The report, prepared by the Washington State Police at the governor's request, contained information from a police investigator and various confidential informants; it was turned over to the FBI.[23]

The report listed fourteen party guests who visited Douglas's cabin in LaPush, Washington, persons the Washington State Police said were "definitely . . . not the type to be associated with any real American."[24] One Douglas friend of "doubtful loyalty" named in the report was Owen Lattimore, who had been accused by Senator Joseph McCarthy of being Alger Hiss's boss in an alleged State Department espionage ring. Lattimore reportedly used the Douglas cabin for two weeks after testifying before the Senate Subcommittee on Internal Security—and was represented by attorney Abe Fortas, Douglas's protege.[25]

The State Police feared that the area around Douglas's cabin might make a good landing base for the Soviets. As a "matter of National Security," the police noted that the cabin was located within two miles of a U.S. Navy air station. Nearby Rialto Beach was believed to make a "perfect landing area" on the Pacific Ocean, and a large flat section of ground was close, "which would allow an estimated 100,000 soldiers to camp."[26]

Even though FBI Agents in Seattle did not believe there was any Communist activity of importance in the area, a twelve-page summary was prepared, listing Douglas's alleged connections to Communists or acts tending to show such sympathies.[27] The FBI scoured its files for subversive information on the individuals named in the Washington police report.[28] The "subversive" friends of Douglas were then investigated. After two and one-half months, the FBI determined that the Washington report was a poorly veiled attempt by the governor to impress Brownell with his anti-Communist credentials in order to obtain a judicial appointment. Despite this finding, the FBI continued to refer to this report in FBI memos written about Justice Douglas.

In 1954 the FBI also interviewed a so-called friend of Justice Douglas's, who claimed that he had been told by Douglas himself that the justice "had been approached . . . by Irving Kaplan of the United Nations who asked that [Douglas] replace Alger Hiss in the Communist underground." Kaplan had been named as a member of the Communist espionage network by Whittaker Chambers, the former Communist now turned informer. According to Chambers, Kaplan was the man Chambers had contacted to find employment with the government while still a Communist. Chambers's accusations against Hiss led to Hiss's perjury conviction in 1950 for denying that he passed official secrets to Chambers for delivery to the Soviets. The confidential source also said that Justice Douglas was angered about being approached by Kaplan, feeling that his Court opinions had been misinterpreted as pro-Communist. According to Douglas's "friend," the justice was "a bitter anti-Communist and . . . Douglas had stated to him in his opinion Justice Felix Frankfurter was probably a Communist." Hoover ordered the agent in charge of the Washington field office to interview Douglas about the Kaplan story, but not to mention the alleged comment about Frankfurter, since both men served on the Court together.[29] The FBI files on Justice Douglas show no record of such an interview. Justices Frankfurter and Reed both found their way into the FBI's files because they had been character witnesses for Hiss.[30]

Hearsay, speculation, and rumors from the mighty as well as the unheralded carried the day and were duly recorded. In 1954 General Douglas MacArthur told the FBI that his "best bet for the real brains of subversive leadership in the country is [J]ustice Felix Frankfurter."[31] The following year federal Judge William T. McCarthy of Boston complained to the Boston office about the "insidious influence that has been exercised by Justice Felix Frankfurter in our Government for many years." The agent wrote to Hoover: "Judge McCarthy, who has been a vigorous and outspoken opponent of Frankfurter and Communism, has been a long time friend of the Bureau, and has the deepest respect and regard for you." Later, the Boston office wrote Hoover that an informant overheard a labor organizer praise Frankfurter's past activism, explaining that they (Frankfurter and the organizer) had marched together protesting the Sacco and Vanzetti verdicts.[32]

The justices' law clerks came under suspicion as well. During 1957 the High Court issued numerous rulings that were perceived by the bureau as pro-Communist.[33] Though the law clerks that year were generally less liberal than many of the justices,[34] the FBI took seriously an allegation in May about a "ring of left-wing law clerks." The clerks were said to "have pretty well established a hierarchy in certain instances" at the U.S. Supreme Court and the Circuit Court of Appeals in Washington, D.C. The FBI apparently believed that the law clerks were the unseen hands writing the pro-Communist decisions of the Supreme Court.[35] The bureau checked its files for subversive references on all law clerks of the U.S. Supreme Court and of the U.S. Court of Appeals for the District of Columbia. In its own memos the FBI acknowledged the impropriety of checking their files in response to an allegation about the political beliefs of the clerks. The original informer had been important enough to have direct telephone access to a high-level assistant to Hoover. Another ranking informer was federal Judge John H. Druffel of Cincinnati, Ohio. The bureau described Druffel as "an extremely friendly federal judge [who] regard[ed] himself as the 'godfather' of the FBI."[36] Druffel's information about the clerks was reported to headquarters and ended up in the FBI's massive subject file on the Supreme Court.[37]

To Hoover, any perceived liberal or leftward tendencies, even those of a relative, tainted a person.[38] And in such an environment sometimes law careers were saved by quirks of fate. Robert Hamilton, now professor of law at the University of Texas, clerked for Justice Clark during 1955 and 1956. Hamilton's natural father, Harold Glasser, had worked with Harry Dexter White at the Treasury Department. After Whittaker Chambers accused Glasser and White of having Communist ties, Glasser lost his job.[39] It was fortuitous for Hamilton that his surname had been legally changed: if he had used his natural father's name, he would not have been offered a clerkship with Justice Clark, for in May 1955 Justice Clark's secretary, Alice O'Donnell, telephoned Cartha DeLoach at FBI headquarters. She explained that Justice Clark had on several prior occasions submitted the names of prospective law clerks to the director on a confidential basis and that Hoover had ordered FBI files searched for information about the applicants. O'Donnell requested file checks on two current applicants, one of whom was Hamilton. No derogatory information was found.[40] According to O'Donnell, it was standard procedure for her to ask the FBI for a "name check" on a prospective law clerk if there was a reason. "We [Clark and I] were the only ones at the Court who did that because of [his] contacts [at FBI headquarters]." Aside from Clark's FBI connections, O'Donnell had acquired contacts of her own during her years as Clark's secretary when he was U.S. attorney general.[41] As Clark's secretary, O'Donnell said, when she wanted something from the FBI she went to headquarters, not to the Washington field office. Unbeknownst to O'Donnell, the FBI had provided the same confidential services when Fred Vinson was chief justice. For both Clark and Vinson, the FBI searched its files and provided confidential information without first obtaining Justice Department approval.[42]

The original allegations against law clerks led to other investigations. In late 1957 a man said by the FBI to be psychotic confidentially told the bureau that the father of one of the Supreme Court law clerks was a Communist. Though the Washington field office said the accusations should be disregarded, Hoover ordered them to "discreetly ascertain identities of newly appointed law clerks" of one of the justices, apparently Associate Justice William Brennan. Hoover also ordered an investigation of a former Supreme Court clerk, whose father was allegedly a Communist, in order to determine if this person was working for the federal government, and if so, to have him removed.[43] Even Justice Minton (who was off the Court by 1957), whose view of internal security was often in line with Hoover's, was critiqued in an FBI memo. The memo said his writing was "sound" while on the Court of Appeals but his Supreme Court decisions "stunk"—presumably due to the influence of his liberal law clerks. In addition to political beliefs, the FBI noted the sexual preference of judicial employees (as it did with other federal workers). "A specified individual was designated to receive information concerning sex deviates among employees of the Judicial Branch of Government."[44]

The FBI as Lobbyist

In addition to keeping tabs on justices and law clerks, the FBI stretched constitutional propriety in other ways. On June 3, 1957, the Supreme Court issued the controversial *Jencks* decision, which gave criminal defendants the right to obtain statements that government witnesses, including informants, made to the FBI.[45] Clinton E. Jencks, president of an International Union of Mine, Mill & Smelter Workers Local, was charged with falsely swearing in an "Affidavit of Non-Communist Union Officer" with the National Labor Relations Board that he was not a member of, nor an affiliate with, the Communist party. The government's principal witnesses were two FBI informers within the Communist party, who had made contemporaneous notes of their activities and submitted them to the bureau.

Justice Brennan, writing for the Court, held that criminal defendants had the procedural right to inspect and use FBI informant reports once the witness testified on direct examination. Brennan wrote that a criminal prosecution must be dismissed when the government refuses to provide the accused with relevant statements or reports in the government's possession that concern the informant's trial testimony. *Jencks* posed a direct threat to the FBI's informers in criminal cases as well as to its political information gathering. Justice Clark, convinced that the Court's position was motivated solely by the fact that the defendant was alleged to be a Communist,[46] wrote a blistering dissent, the centerpiece of which was a lengthy quotation from Hoover. Justice Clark wrote: "Unless Congress changes the rule announced by the Court today, those intelligence agencies of our Government engaged in law enforcement may as well close up shop, for the Court has opened their files to the criminal and thus afforded him a Roman Holiday for rummaging through confidential information as well as vital national secrets."[47]

The day after the *Jencks* ruling, federal Judge Edward A. Tamm telephoned Hoover to complain. Tamm, a former FBI assistant to Hoover, said that the "potentials of such a ruling were tremendous." Hoover assured Tamm that he had received "several calls from various Congressmen and Senators and also that some articles were to appear in the press concerning" the case. Hoover also let Tamm know that legislation was being discussed that "would take care of the matter." Tamm, believing that the bureau was fighting a holy war against Communism, suggested that the FBI's relationship to its informers was like that between priest and confessor.[48] So serious was the threat to bureau interests posed by the *Jencks* ruling that a memo about *Jencks* was placed in an FBI subject file along with memos about the bureau's "Burglar Alarm and Intrusion Detection System."[49] Hoover considered the *Jencks* decision tantamount to a "burglary" of FBI offices; the day after the ruling another file was opened to track proposed legislation to remedy the problem. The Supreme Court was intruding upon the FBI's domain, and the bureau was going to enter the political fray to counteract the ruling.

The FBI's friends in Congress were quick to respond to the *Jencks* decision—with the bureau's assistance.[50] The day after the ruling, eleven House bills were introduced to counteract the decision.[51] Congress eventually enacted the Jencks Act,[52] on September 2, 1957, which established procedures for the release of government witness statements, including those of FBI informants, to criminal defendants, along with other pretrial discovery information.[53]

FBI and the Media

Hoover followed and encouraged media attacks against the Warren Court. This was particularly true two weeks after *Jencks v. U.S.*,[54] when, on June 17, 1957, the so-called Red Monday decisions were handed down: *Yates v. U.S.*,[55] *Service v. Dulles*,[56] *Watkins v. U.S.*,[57] and *Sweezy v. New Hampshire*.[58] The *Yates* decision, written by Justice John Harlan, reversed the convictions of "second-string" Communist leaders and effectively overturned much of the 1951 ruling in *Dennis v. U.S.*[59] by holding that the Smith Act did not prohibit theoretical advocacy and the teaching of the principles of violent overthrow of the government unless there was a specific plan of action. Theoretical advocacy was not sufficient to convict. *Yates* was viewed as the last nail in the coffin of Justice Department prosecutions of Communists under the Smith Act.

Hoover's personal views about the Red Monday decisions were sometimes written on the margins of newsclips, which were later placed in the bureau's files on the Supreme Court. "What a travesty upon 'blind justice' the U.S.S.C. has become," Hoover wrote beneath one news article.[60] David Lawrence, editor of *U.S. News and World Report*, a Hoover friend, and a beneficiary of leaks, wrote in a newspaper column that Supreme Court justices should be elected to the bench as a way to stop their liberal rulings. Hoover agreed, scratching this note in the side margin of the article: "Not a bad idea. At least the courts wouldn't get any worse type than are on the bench now thru presidential appointment."[61] After Lawrence wrote another column entitled "Recent High Court Rulings Called Damaging to Nation," Hoover thanked him for "alerting [his] readers to the difficulties facing law enforcement, especially in the internal security field, if the [*Jencks*] ruling is allowed to stand."[62] Reacting to another news article that claimed that "10 major decisions handed down in a little more than a year greatly weakened the Government's drive against communists and subversives," Hoover scribbled: "An excellent round-up of U.S.S.C. plague of decisions thru June 10."[63] After William Randolph Hearst wrote an editorial blasting the *Jencks* case and supporting legislation to counter it, Hoover thanked him for the support.[64]

The bureau also pushed the anti-Communist forces at the 1957 American Bar Association (ABA) annual conference in London. The ABA's Committee on Communist Tactics, Strategies and Objectives issued a report, blasting the Supreme Court's decisions in the national security area.[65] In 1959 former FBI assistant to the director Louis Nichols authored the ABA report about Communism.[66] The ABA reports were given extensive news coverage. In response to the ABA's lambasting of Supreme Court rulings, Earl Warren resigned from membership.[67]

As was true of the ABA report, the public's outrage personally affected the justices. "The Court was aware that its 1956 Term record—an unblemished record of reversals in cases involving Communist defendants—would produce an outcry," said William Cohen, who served as Douglas's law clerk from 1956 to 1957.[68] The public furor created by the Red Monday decisions caused the justices to snipe at each other. Black and Douglas had been warring with Frankfurter since the early 1940s, and the acrimony between Frankfurter and Black continued into the 1950s. Frankfurter viewed Black's decisions as result-oriented and political. Black, Douglas, Warren, and Brennan resented Frankfurter's method of lecturing the other justices during the conference discussions that occurred before a vote. Douglas, saying over his shoulder, "Call me when he's finished," would walk out of the conference room when Frankfurter pontificated during conferences.[69]

At the start of the October 1957 term, Justice Frankfurter circulated a memo that accused the chief justice of "massing important adjudications toward the end of the Term," which Frankfurter claimed was "bad for the Court, internally and externally." Warren denied that cases were massed at the end of the term and circulated his own memo, listing "the cases decided last June which were most controversial, together with the date of argument, date of the first circulation of the opinion, and the date it was handed down."[70]

Even two months before Red Monday, during April 1957, the Court was aware of the anti-Court sentiment generated by its rulings in such cases. In a case involving an illegal search and seizure by the FBI, Justice Harlan wrote to Douglas explaining why he wanted to attach an eight-page appendix to the opinion he was writing in *Kremen v. U.S.*[71] This appendix was a list of more than 800 items that agents removed from the defendant's home. Its only purpose was to educate "readers who are always ready to criticize the Court for setting aside convictions, particularly in Commie cases."[72] Harlan also said that issuing a *per curiam* —unsigned—opinion "cover[s] up . . . our differences [and] offends my professional instincts, but I do recognize the problem at hand is part of a larger picture." The "problem" was the accusations of "pro-Communism" generated against the Court by President Dwight D. Eisenhower, Congress, the press, and the FBI. The Court ultimately issued a one and a half page *per curiam* in *Kremen,* along with an eight-page inventory of the hundreds of items seized by overzealous government agents without a search warrant.

The FBI subtly encouraged the hundreds of people who wrote to the

FBI professing anti–Warren Court sentiments. Hoover, through form letters, thanked each writer for the kind comments about the bureau, enclosed one of his anti-Communist tracts, and said that unfortunately the FBI, a fact-finding law enforcement agency, could not comment on Warren or his Court.[73] The bureau's own propaganda campaign against the Court may have served to encourage others, such as the John Birch Society.

The FBI tracked the John Birch Society, though the Birchers generally agreed with Hoover's view of the Warren Court. Billboards went up across the country attacking Warren, accusing him of being a Communist and a race-traitor. A poster was anonymously distributed with a mug-shot type photo of the chief justice: "WANTED for Impeachment— EARL WARREN." The poster described the chief justice as "a dangerous and subversive character. He is an apparent sympathizer of the Communist Party and has rendered numerous decisions favorable to it. . . . Warren is a rabid agitator for compulsory racial mongrelization. . . . Persons wishing to aid in bringing him to justice should contact their Congressmen to urge his impeachment for treason."[74] But impeachment was harder to accomplish than helping to nominate and confirm conservatives in the first place.

FBI "Special Inquiry" of Court Nominees

Possibly Hoover's most enduring legacy is the FBI background investigation of Supreme Court nominees, dubbed "special inquiry" or "SPIN," which is now conducted on every nominee to the High Court. Ironically, the practice of FBI involvement in the Supreme Court confirmation process was not a role originally sought by Hoover. It began after President Eisenhower's and Director Hoover's great "mistake"—the confirmation of Earl Warren as chief justice. Neither the president nor the Senate knew that California Governor Warren, the man Senator McCarthy would later accuse of following the Communist party line, had had a long-standing political alliance with Hoover.[75]

The members of the Senate Judiciary Committee had complained about the absence of a FBI report on Warren.[76] Senator William Langer (R–North Dakota), chairman of the committee, had accused the FBI of withholding the report.[77] Hoover ordered Nichols to "straighten Langer out" by telling him that the FBI had never done a full background investigation on Warren and thus had no report to give him. It was true that the bureau never conducted a background investigation on Warren, but its files contained 600 references to Warren, constituting more than one thousand pages of documents. That same day—February 8—Deputy

Attorney General William P. Rogers called Nichols at FBI headquarters to tell him that "we have no other choice but to make a quick investigation of Earl Warren. . . . [It] does not need to be widespread; . . . it appears that the thing in issue is the principle of requiring an FBI report." Rogers said that he would leave it up to the FBI to use its best judgment about what to do.

Initially, Hoover was adamant that it was *not* up to the FBI: it was the attorney general's job to set the parameters of the investigation. Eventually he relented and ordered a "restricted" investigation, and the resulting report was prepared after information in FBI files was sanitized, omitting Warren's close relationship to the bureau and certain information that was of "unsavory origin" and "improbable." The report did contain a reference to Warren's public position against loyalty oaths and an allegation linking him to subversives.[78] While the report was being prepared, an FBI source on the Senate Judiciary Committee told Nichols that Senator Langer was now calling for a full and complete field investigation.[79] After learning of Langer's plans, Hoover ordered a "thorough" investigation on February 10. On February 11, confronted again with time constraints, Assistant Director Clyde Tolson reiterated Hoover's admonition: "We must not be stampeded in our investigation."

Some criticisms of Warren were initially excluded from the FBI's report, but it was decided that "[i]n view of the possible embarrassment . . . in not going to persons who obviously were opposed to the appointment of Warren to obtain their comments concerning him," one opponent was specifically sought out for any comments he desired to make.[80]

The FBI's investigation was completed on February 16, 1954. A twenty-seven-page report was sent to the attorney general and passed on to the Senate Judiciary Committee: it was shoddy, biased in favor of Warren, and restricted by time constraints and Justice Department instructions.

The Department of Justice and Hoover were not the only ones unhappy that the FBI had been forced to investigate Warren. Max Lerner wrote in the New York *Post:* "The news that the Chief Justice of the United States is being investigated by the FBI, at the request of a Senate Judiciary subcommittee, sounds as if it came out of a surrealist history of America or a *Pravda* editorial whimsy. But it is, alas, a fact, not just a bad political joke."[81] Lerner would continue to be displeased with the FBI investigating Court appointees. Hoover, however, came to appreciate the new opportunities such investigations gave him to help frame the debate about the men who were nominated to sit on the High Court. The director continued to exploit the background investigation of Supreme Court nominees to further his political agenda.

During the FBI's investigation of Warren, the FBI did much to assist the chief justice–designate. Agents in Los Angeles kept tabs on the friends of Warren's daughter Nina, advising her father about the "bad crowd" with which she was hanging around.[82] The FBI passed on political intelligence to Warren's supporters about right-wing opponents of his confirmation. At the request of Warren Olney III (assistant attorney general in the Criminal Division of the Department of Justice, a longtime friend, and a former California assistant attorney general under Warren), the FBI searched its files for information on individuals and organizations who were opposing Warren.[83] On March 1, 1954, the Senate by voice vote unanimously confirmed Warren as chief justice of the Supreme Court.[84]

After the Warren Court's "left-turn" in the mid-1950s, Hoover began to look to the FBI background investigation to change the make-up of the Court. During 1957, the Warren Court was almost evenly divided into two camps on criminal and constitutional law issues. Both factions wooed the swing-vote, often Associate Justice John Marshall Harlan (who would later swing more often to the right). The liberal faction was the one-two punch of William O. Douglas and Hugo Black, joined by Warren and William Brennan. The Court's "right" was made up of Felix Frankfurter, Tom Clark, Harold Burton, and Charles Whittaker.

Whittaker had arrived at the Court with Hoover's blessing. After Justice Stanley Reed retired in 1957, the organized bar, stung by the increasingly liberal Warren, pressured Eisenhower to nominate lawyers with judicial experience to the Supreme Court, so that the nominee's judicial voting record could be assessed. Both the president and Attorney General Brownell were looking for a conservative Republican. Brownell suggested Whittaker, a Republican, whose nomination to the federal district court and later to the federal circuit court of appeals had been met with widespread praise. The attorney general had probably already asked Hoover for an FBI file check on Whittaker.

On March 1, 1957, Deputy Attorney General Rogers called Hoover to bring him up to date on Whittaker's nomination. Rogers said "that the President had just about decided on Whittaker who "would probably vote all right," was "probably a conservative," and who had made the right decision in a recent Fifth Amendment case.[85] Rogers was referring to *Davis v. University of Kansas City,* [86] in which Dr. Horace B. Davis was fired from Kansas University for invoking the Fifth Amendment during a congressional investigation. Whittaker upheld the dismissal, writing that a professor did not have a right to refuse to answer whether he is "a member of a found and declared conspiracy by a godless group to overthrow our Government by force." Neither Hoover nor Rogers mentioned the fact that in *Slowchower v. Board of Education*[87] the

High Court had overruled Whittaker's overly narrow interpretation of the Fifth Amendment's protection against self-incrimination.

Hoover had every reason to believe that Whittaker would make a good law-and-order justice, considering his past cooperation with the Kansas City FBI field office. In 1954, when Whittaker was appointed to a federal judgeship, the agent in charge of the Kansas City FBI office wrote to Hoover: "Judge Whittaker is very influential in the Kansas City area.... He is friendly towards the Bureau and is believed to be fully cooperative.... It is recommended that he be approached as an SAC [special agent in charge] Contact." FBI headquarters turned down this request due to the type of "services" these contacts could render.[88] On March 4, the president announced Whittaker's nomination.

In 1958 Hoover instructed his assistants to dig into his massive subject file on the federal judiciary to compile a list of "outstanding jurists" to be used as an all-star list of pro-FBI judges for speaking engagements, special judicial commissions, and apparently for placement on the High Court.[89] The information in the bureau's files, including that in a file entitled "Federal Judges," was valuable to Hoover when he made suggestions to the attorney general and the president about judicial nominees. As far back as 1939, the FBI had maintained this compilation of personal and political information about the nation's federal judiciary.[90] Hoover's 1958 FBI "wish list" had eighteen names on it, including Judge Potter Stewart and Judge Warren Burger.[91]

According to Rogers, who from 1953 to 1961 was in the Justice Department as deputy attorney general and later as attorney general, Hoover did not influence the selection of nominees; he was simply given the names of prospective nominees so that he could conduct FBI file searches.[92] According to FBI records, however, Rogers and the bureau kept each other current on the status of nominees. And, of course, it was Hoover, not the attorney general, who controlled the FBI files (and selected what went into those files) that everyone relied on when deciding whom to nominate.

In the fall of 1958, six months after Hoover's wish list was prepared, Justice Burton retired from the High Court. President Eisenhower, as he had done since 1954, directed the attorney general to have the FBI investigate prospective appointees.[93] Agents in Cincinnati reported to Hoover that Judge Stewart "is a Conservative [and] his acquaintances are believed to be conservative" with no "known Left Wing connections." "He certainly has not rendered any opinions which can be construed as anti-law enforcement or anti-Bureau."[94] The Legal Research Desk at FBI headquarters also reviewed Stewart's appellate opinions in criminal cases while he was on the U.S. Sixth Circuit Court of Appeals. They showed a "clear appreciation of the problems of law enforcement," with "no evidence of a 'sob sister' attitude toward the criminal." Mention was made of Stewart's "extremely friendly" attitude toward FBI personnel of the Cincinnati office, which was on the same floor as Judge Stewart's office. One agent had known Stewart for thirteen years, and both men attended the same Episcopal Church. According to this agent, Stewart had "frequently commented . . . that the FBI and John Edgar Hoover were doing a grand job." Hoover reported his favorable findings about Stewart to Rogers. Rogers told Hoover that Judge Stewart was coming in that night.[95] The next day Potter Stewart was appointed to the Supreme Court by President Eisenhower.

Politicized FBI background checks had been going on since 1930 with respect to federal judges, but background investigations did not begin in earnest for Supreme Court justices until 1954. Information about judges and justices included whether the judge was a friend or foe of the FBI. For example, federal Judge Matthew M. Joyce was said to be "one of the fairest and most sincere" with whom the agent had come in contact. "Joyce is one of the friendliest of the judges to the FBI. [H]e seems to have a high degree of confidence in the agents, often calling them to his chambers for information on a specific point. [J]udge Joyce is eminently qualified and eminently satisfactory." The bureau also critiqued judges' sentencing trends, whether they had a sense of humor, and their views about Hoover.[96]

The FBI's files on the federal judiciary, like its final reports summarizing the background investigations of judicial nominees, have always reflected the political realities of the day. During Prohibition, for example, Hoover ordered his men to make a "discreet very thorough investigation" about the qualifications of a number of men for a federal circuit court judgeship, including whether the applicants drank alcohol or otherwise opposed the Eighteenth Amendment.

In 1965 the Justice Department sent a memo to the FBI requiring that all background investigations for federal judges include information about the prospective nominee's position on civil rights. African-American leaders were to be sought out for their comments about the nominee so that President Lyndon Johnson might avoid criticism later.

On the other hand, ethical improprieties by "firm supporters and good friends of the FBI" were often excluded from FBI reports. For example, information in FBI files pertaining to the impeachable ethical violations of Justice Fortas were not made available to the Senate in 1968 when he was nominated to be chief justice.

In the 1990s FBI background investigations are also a reflection of

White House desires. The president asks *his* law enforcement agents to investigate *his* nominee. These investigations still include a check into "loyalty," which necessarily involves a subjective element. Today loyalty entails a shared set of values about the "war on drugs" and terrorism rather than the single litmus test of anti-Communism.

During the Hoover years, one of the most potent and invasive of the FBI's techniques used to investigate those who lacked loyalty had silently and illegally altered the careers and fortunes of thousands of Americans, including Supreme Court justices. Sometimes what came indirectly into the FBI's hands about a justice was much more valuable—and more politically damning—than a background investigation.

CHAPTER 2

Wiretapping and Bugging: "Instruments of Tyranny and Oppression"

Whenever a telephone line is tapped, the privacy of the persons at both ends of the line is invaded and all conversations between them upon any subject, and although proper, confidential, and privileged, may be overheard. [T]he tapping of one man's telephone line involves the tapping of the telephone of every other person whom he may call, or who may call him. As a means of espionage, writs of assistance and general warrants are but puny instruments of tyranny and oppression when compared with wire-tapping.[1]

—Justice Brandeis, dissenting in *Olmstead v. U.S.* (1928)

Beginning with the administration of President Harry Truman and continuing into that of Richard Nixon, the FBI secretly listened in on the conversations of a number of sitting Supreme Court justices. As early as 1946, warrantless FBI wiretaps captured a number of Associate Justice William O. Douglas's conversations[2] and may have helped convince President Truman to abandon consideration of Douglas as chief justice and nominate his friend Fred Vinson instead.

Justice Douglas certainly was not alone. Following the implicit or explicit go-ahead from a succession of attorneys general, from 1941 to the mid-1960s, the FBI tapped and/or bugged at least 13,500 individuals and organizations, including almost every civil rights group and labor union with any left-liberal tendencies.[3] And for every electronic surveillance (referred to as ELSUR) target, there might be tens or hundreds of nontargeted people whose voices were caught "walking-in on" the tap or bug, not to mention each person mentioned during conversations. Close to a half-million conversations might have been overheard by the FBI during those years. In 1945 alone the FBI conducted 519 wiretaps and 186 buggings.[4] From 1943 to 1963, in its investigation of the Socialist Workers party, the FBI had "wiretaps in place for a total of about 20,000 wiretap-days, and bugs in place for about 12,000 bug-days."[5]

Supreme Court justices were not immune from the bureau's penchant for electronically facilitated listening. (When Tom Clark arrived on the

Court in 1949 from his post as attorney general, he asked the other justices if the conference room had been recently swept for electronic listening devices.[6] From 1945 to 1974, at least twelve justices were overheard talking or were mentioned on over 100 occasions—including Chief Justices Vinson and Warren and Associate Justices Douglas, Hugo Black, Felix Frankfurter, John Harlan, Stanley Reed, Robert Jackson, Frank Murphy, Harold Burton, Potter Stewart, and Abe Fortas.[7] The government continues to claim that many of these ELSUR records remain classified to protect U.S. national defense or foreign relations. For the most part, transcripts of the wiretapped conversations (referred to as logs by the FBI) are publicly available for only two of these taps. But it was these two taps that gave Hoover and Truman unprecedented access to the behind-the-scenes lobbying among members of the High Court and among influential New Dealers. Ironically, the Supreme Court had itself paved the way for the FBI to penetrate American homes, offices, and Supreme Court chambers.

The Supreme Court Gives the Constitutional
Go-Ahead for Wiretapping

In 1928 the Supreme Court ruled in *Olmstead v. U.S.*[8] that neither English common law, developed case by case over the centuries, nor the Fourth Amendment to the Constitution prohibited federal agents from wiretapping. Prohibition officers had inserted wires in the telephone lines in the basement of the 1025 Henry Building in Seattle, Washington, where Roy Olmstead and others had maintained an office out of which they engaged in "a conspiracy of amazing magnitude to import, possess and sell liquor unlawfully."[9] Other phone taps had been placed on phones in the homes of Olmstead as well as four other defendants in the case.[10] For nearly five months at least six federal agents took turns listening to telephone conversations and recorded 775 pages of typewritten notes.[11]

It was not only the criminal defendants who had something at stake in *Olmstead*. The privacy rights of all Americans were at issue. It was for this reason (as well as the fact that the government had tampered with phone lines) that AT&T and three other phone companies filed friend-of-the-court briefs arguing that wiretapping was a violation of the Fourth and Fifth amendments. Despite the arguments of the lawyers for the defendants and the phone companies, Chief Justice William Howard Taft wrote for the 5–4 majority that "the [Fourth] Amendment itself shows that the search is to be of material things—the person, the house, his papers or his effects."[12] A divided Court sanctioned the government's invasion of privacy since agents did not physically touch or take anything. And in so ruling, the High Court relinquished an important victory won during the Revolutionary War.[13] The colonists had fought against "general warrants" and "writs of assistance" that had allowed British customs authorities to conduct sweeping, general searches for contraband.[14] In 1761 a young patriot, John Adams, listened to the magnificent courtroom oration of attorney James Otis, Jr., who argued against general warrants and the hated writs. Adams wrote, "Every man of a crowded audience appeared to me to go away, as I did, ready to take arms against Writs of Assistance. . . . Then and there the child Independence was born. . . . [H]e grew to manhood, and declared himself free."[15] It would take the Revolutionary War and fifteen more years before the excesses of the general warrants and writs of assistance led to the ratification of the Fourth Amendment[16]: "The right of the people to be secure in their persons, houses, papers and effects, against unreasonable searches and seizures, shall not be violated, and no Warrants shall issue, but upon probable cause, supported by Oath or affirmation, and particularly describing the place to be searched, and the persons or things to be seized."

The majority in *Olmstead* held that the right of the people to be secure in "their persons" and "houses" did not mean security against unreasonable searches and seizures of one's *words,* even if spoken in the security of one's own home. The majority opinion also suggested that the "uninvited ear"[17] of the government was not prohibited by the Fourth Amendment because the wiretap had not been installed by trespassing on the *criminal defendant's* property. Justice Louis Brandeis passionately disagreed: "Can it be that the Constitution affords no protection against such invasions of individual security?"[18] The Constitution included a "right to be let alone" and "[t]o protect that right, every unjustifiable intrusion by the government upon the privacy of the individual, whatever the means employed, must be deemed a violation of the 4th Amendment."[19]

As for the Fifth Amendment's prohibition against compelled testimony and self-incrimination, Taft wrote that Olmstead and his co-defendants were not aware that the government was listening in on their calls and, therefore, their conspiratorial conversations had not been compelled, but were voluntary.[20]

Still, four Supreme Court justices and many others considered wiretapping a "dirty business."[21] Even the solicitor general in his *Olmstead* brief claimed that the government was "not defending wire tapping as a method proper generally to be used for detection of crime."[22] And Hoover vowed that wiretapping "would never be done in this Bureau while he is Director" because government agents had "no ethical right" to tap, even though the *Olmstead* ruling had given them that right.[23] For three years after the *Olmstead* decision, the FBI's *Manual of Rules and Regulations,* under the heading "unethical tactics," banned wiretapping and provided for the dismissal of anybody who engaged in it.[24] "Wire 'tapping,' entrapment, or the use of any illegal or unethical tactics in procuring information will not be tolerated by the Bureau."[25] This rule had been in effect for "many years" prior to 1929.[26] As with the temporary prohibition against gathering political information, the wiretap ban may have resulted from the housecleaning conducted in the wake of the Teapot Dome scandal, under orders issued by Attorney General Harlan Stone in 1924 before he was nominated to the Supreme Court.[27]

But the FBI regulation had not stopped the agents in the Indianapolis office from tapping phones with the help of federal court employees. Agents had talked court personnel into allowing them to set up their headphones and recorder "in a vacant Grand Jury room . . . in order to save the expense of renting a room" when they listened to wiretapped conversations. This particular tap was designed to catch people who were believed to be fixing the price of hogs. The use of the grand jury room by the bureau was given without the knowledge or permission of federal Judge Robert C. Baltzell who was opposed to wiretapping and whose chambers were in the building. Angry when he learned about the use of the grand jury room as a listening post for wiretappers, the judge told the head of the local bureau office that he did not even "know whether his own telephone wire had been tapped or not."[28] After learning of the incident in 1928, Hoover called the tapping "unwarranted, unethical, improper and perhaps unlawful"[29] and chastised the agents responsible for the tapping; the federal judge was told it would not happen again. But, of course, it did, thousands of times, though presumably not *inside* the federal courthouse in Indianapolis.

In 1931 Attorney General William D. Mitchell (in office, 1929–1933) reversed rulings of his two predecessors and allowed bureau wiretapping in certain, limited circumstances.[30] The Prohibition Unit at the Justice Department had been wiretapping for years, though this policy was hotly debated.[31] In the spring of the next year, a congressional appropriations bill prohibited the use of funds for wiretaps in prohibition cases. Congress repealed the Eighteenth Amendment in 1933 contingent upon ratification by the states.[32] Soon after, President Franklin D. Roosevelt signed an executive order that combined the three Justice Department bureaus, Prohibition, Identification (fingerprint), and Investigation into one new division, which would later be named the Federal Bureau of Investigation with Hoover as its director.[33]

Attorney General Homer Cummings (in office, 1933–1939) permitted phone taps in kidnapping and gangster cases. The bureau used wiretaps to catch the gangsters responsible for the Kansas City massacre, which had left FBI Special Agent Raymond J. Caffrey and three police officers dead after a machine-gun ambush by Charles "Pretty Boy" Floyd and others.[34] During this time the Chicago, Kansas City, and New York FBI offices had the most taps going, and, though most of the wiretaps concerned racketeering and kidnapping, there were also national security–related taps.[35] Twenty-four of the phones being monitored by the FBI were related to the Kansas City massacre investigation. No phone appeared to be off limits to bureau tappers, as attorneys' offices, post offices, taverns, and homes were tapped.[36]

Even the attorney-client relationship did not deter Hoover. The director authorized agents in Chicago to tap the phones of an attorney "in an effort to determine the whereabouts of John Dillinger," Public Enemy Number One, who had escaped from custody on a murder charge and was on the run with Lester Gillis, better known as "Baby Face" Nelson.[37] Taps were placed on phones of innumerable Dillinger friends and presumed associates and on phones in places frequented by them.[38] In the end, it was brothel owner Anna Sage, wearing a red dress, who led the bureau to Dillinger and Dillinger to his bloody death outside the Biograph theater in the Windy City.[39] A human informant succeeded in finding the infamous outlaw after ELSUR came up empty.

Wiretapping Takes a Licking in Congress
(but the FBI Keeps on Tapping)

Justice Taft had written in *Olmstead* that "Congress may . . . protect the secrecy of telephone messages by making them, when intercepted, inadmissible in evidence in Federal criminal trials, by direct legislation." On June 19, 1934, Congress enacted the Federal Communications Act,[40] which prohibited the interception and divulging of telephone-wiretapped information by any person. The Federal Communications Act did not cover microphone surveillance, nor did it deter the FBI from wiretapping people suspected of wrongdoing, even if those persons were Supreme Court employees.

On October 9, 1936, the marshal of the Supreme Court reported to the Washington FBI field office that he had heard that some Court employees were trying to obtain advance copies of Court decisions in order to sell them.[41] The marshal did not first notify Chief Justice Charles Evans

Hughes but went to the FBI. After the attorney general and eventually the chief justice were consulted, the FBI set up a sting operation to see if an undercover FBI agent could buy an advance copy of a Court decision. Supreme Court employees participated in the FBI sting against other employees.[42] As part of the investigation, the home phone of William J. Cox, clerk and storekeeper at the Supreme Court, was tapped. It is not clear whether the chief justice was told of the wiretap, but he had specifically authorized FBI surveillance of other Court employees.[43] The bureau's undercover operatives tailed the suspects and photographed their meetings. A sensitive microphone was also installed by the FBI in a Buick to record the conversations of the suspects during an arranged meeting.[44] Despite all of the intrigue, no advance copies were procured by the FBI.[45] Three Court employees were fired on November 25, 1936, and Chief Justice Hughes mailed a letter of commendation to the bureau for a job well done.[46]

The sting operation occurred at the height of President Roosevelt's anger at Supreme Court decisions overturning his New Deal legislation and was only months before the president unveiled his "court-packing" plan. During the sting operation, the chief justice came to believe that an electronic bugging device might have been placed in the conference room at the Supreme Court.[47] Evidently, Hughes did not believe the bureau would bug the justices' conferences, and he asked the FBI to sweep the room for microphones.[48] The FBI's censorship of the file about this incident makes it impossible to determine whether a bug was found and, if so, who put it there. Justice Douglas, who joined the Court three years later, claimed in his autobiography that a microphone bug had indeed been found in the conference room and that it had been planted by two Court employees at the behest of D.C. police officers.[49]

In 1937, the Court ruled in *Nardone v. U.S.*[50] that the words "any person" in the antiwiretap law included federal agents. This meant that information obtained by phone taps was inadmissible in court. Justices George Sutherland and James McReynolds dissented. Sutherland wrote that his "abhorrence of the odious practices of the town gossip, the peeping Tom, and the private eavesdropper is quite as strong as that of any of my brethren. But to put sworn officers of the law, engaged in the detection and apprehension of organized gangs of criminals, in the same category, is to lose all sense of proportion."[51] Hoover agreed with the dissenters—so did the Justice Department.

The Federal Communications Act prohibited intercepting *and* disseminating any information overheard in the taps. It was this "and" that the Justice Department would seize upon to disregard *Nardone.*[52] Hoover had one of his top assistants, Edward A. Tamm, later a federal judge, seek the advice of Assistant Attorney General Alexander Holtzoff about the "significance . . . of the Supreme Court decision" in *Nardone*.[53] Holtzoff said that *Nardone* did not apply to the FBI because agents were not disseminating the information outside the government. Section 605 of the Federal Communications Act "penalizes the intercepting *and* divulging" the intercepted wire communication.[54] According to the Justice Department, the FBI could wiretap if it did not divulge, that is, attempt to use the fruits of the interception as evidence in a court of law. Holtzoff told Tamm that "the Bureau was at liberty to act in an investigative capacity upon any information which was developed over a telephone tap." In any event, Tamm was assured that the Justice Department would not prosecute agents for wiretapping. In the future all FBI taps were for "intelligence purposes." Eleven days after the *Nardone* ruling, Hoover sent out a memo to agents in charge of his forty-seven field offices across the country and advised them that "the Bureau's policy with reference to the use of telephone taps will not be changed in any regard by this decision."[55] As always, FBI taps were to be authorized by Hoover alone. Two years later, in *Nardone II*,[56] the Court held that any evidence discovered through the wiretaps was inadmissible as evidence. Holtzoff again advised the FBI that "the Bureau was under no legal or implied prohibition from utilizing telephone taps for investigative purposes . . . in cases of major importance."[57]

On March 15, 1940, apparently in response to press allegations that the FBI had wiretapped members of Congress, Attorney General Robert Jackson banned the bureau from using wiretapping, even in extortion, racketeering, or kidnapping cases.[58] But World War II was raging in Europe, and on May 21, 1940, President Roosevelt secretly issued an executive order that said the nation's defense required electronic surveillance against saboteurs and "fifth columnists." The president wrote, "I am convinced that the Supreme Court never intended any dictum in the [*Nardone*] case to apply to grave matters involving the defense of the nation."[59] Jackson was ordered to approve listening devices directed against "subversive[s]" and spies, limited as much as possible to aliens.[60] Yet Jackson did not even keep his own record of the taps he approved. In fact, from 1940 to 1964, neither Attorneys General Robert Jackson, Francis Biddle, Tom Clark, J. Howard McGrath, Herbert Brownell, William Rogers, nor Robert Kennedy kept detailed records of wiretaps approved in their Justice Department offices.[61] Oversight was virtually nonexistent, and Hoover was the attorney general in charge of wiretapping.

Inside the bureau, agents had no qualms about wiretapping. "It was very clear in my mind," said FBI veteran Edward Scheidt, looking back over his years as agent in charge of FBI field offices during the 1940s and early 1950s.[62] "The President of the United States had issued instructions that the Attorney General could authorize the FBI to wiretap. . . . Everybody [in the bureau] thought that it was strictly legal. . . . In fact, [we] thought that [we were] defending the country . . . [and] doing something noble."[63]

The Supreme Court appeared to give the constitutional go-ahead for bugging accomplished without trespass. In 1942, in *Goldman v. U.S.,*[64] the Court said evidence obtained by eavesdropping—placing a detectaphone voice amplification device against the wall of an adjoining room—was admissible as long as there was no physical penetration into the defendant's premises. It was irrelevant, the Court noted, that the federal agents had earlier burglarized the room to install a microphone that later was found to be inoperable. The burglary did not assist the detectaphone listening. Issued on the same day as *Goldman, Goldstein v. U.S.* held that wiretaps could be used to prod witnesses whose conversations had been overheard by wiretaps to testify against a defendant on trial whose conversations had not been overheard in the taps as long as the wiretapped conversations were not admitted into evidence.[65] Dr. Maximilian Goldstein, one of four co-defendants convicted of mail fraud and conspiracy to present false claims to insurance companies, had not been the victim of the government's violation of the Federal Communications Act, and thus he had no legal "standing" to object to the testimony of other co-conspirators who testified after they were told: "We have watched your telephone; we have watched all these lawyers' telephones; we have had rooms tapped. . . . If you want to hear your voice on a record we will be glad to play it."[66] *Goldstein* weakened *Nardone.* By not declaring *all* evidence directly or indirectly derived from wiretaps inadmissible under the exclusionary rule (which makes the fruits of illegal government conduct tainted as evidence), the Court encouraged further wiretapping.

The Supreme Court had made it clear that wiretapping was not a violation of the Fourth Amendment rights of criminal suspects. But could the White House and the FBI listen to the conversations of Supreme Court justices who were talking on the phone with bureau targets confident that they were not violating the Fourth Amendment (even if they might be violating the separation of powers between co-equal branches of government)?

Altering the Court's History with FBI Wiretaps

Chief Justice Harlan Stone, who as attorney general installed Hoover as director of the Bureau of Investigation, died in the spring of 1946, almost a year after the death of President Roosevelt. When the Truman White House made its decision about whether to elevate one of the sitting justices to position of chief justice, it had the benefit of valuable political intelligence derived from warrantless wiretaps. Summaries from FBI wiretaps on influential Washington lobbyist Thomas G. Corcoran were regularly sent to the Truman White House, and they included intercepted conversations with Corcoran's friends on the Supreme Court, Associate Justices William Douglas, Stanley Reed, and Hugo Black.[67]

"Tommy the Cork" Corcoran, a Harvard Law School graduate, former law clerk to Justice Oliver Wendell Holmes, Jr., and adviser to President Roosevelt, was influential in political circles and a thorn in Truman's side. Truman despised the charming and clever Corcoran. Anyone who maintained a close relationship with Corcoran was viewed by Truman as tainted.[68] Corcoran had been assistant to the attorney general from 1933 to 1940, and he had maintained his friendships at the Justice Department. The White House perceived Corcoran to be so powerful that he was said to be acting as de facto attorney general.[69] It was, in fact, Hoover who acted as if he were attorney general.[70]

Truman apparently had asked his chief aide and friend Edward McKim to have the FBI tap Corcoran; Hoover installed the taps without authorization from Attorney General Clark.[71] It was not until November 15, 1945, five months after the taps had been installed, and after Clark's own conversations had been intercepted (probably unbeknownst to him), that Clark authorized the eavesdropping.[72] Clark's avowed purpose in making the after-the-fact "request" was to make sure that Corcoran's activities "did not interfere with the proper administration of justice" and to see if there was any "violation of law."[73] The real purpose was protection: the FBI had been warned by White House military aide Harry Vaughan, the president's "old and treasured" friend, that if the taps on Corcoran ever became public, Vaughan "would deny any knowledge."[74] Vaughan served as the "liaison between Truman's desk and Hoover's. Every report from Hoover came across [his] desk."[75]

Corcoran was not the only close friend of a justice to have his phone tapped. Earlier, the FBI had tapped the phone of Edward F. Pritchard, Jr., an assistant to Treasury Secretary Fred M. Vinson. As with the Corcoran taps, the bureau had been advised by McKim that if the Pritchard taps were exposed "it would be incumbent upon the President" and White House aides to "deny that any such investigation had been ordered."[76] Pritchard had served as law clerk to Justice Felix Frankfurter, and he talked on the phone frequently with the justice. Pritchard was also a friend of Corcoran. The tap on Pritchard snagged a number of conversations with Frankfurter, including those that showed Frankfurther was discreetly providing material to Drew Pearson for his newspaper columns.[77] As a result, White House aides also requested FBI taps on Pearson. The Corcoran, Pritchard, and Pearson taps were requested as a result of Truman's excessive concern about the loyalty of those working under him, as well as concern about the leaks about meetings with Joseph Stalin that showed up in Pearson's newspaper columns.[78] Truman also learned from the taps of Corcoran's low opinion of him.[79]

On April 22, 1946, Chief Justice Harlan Stone, then seventy-three, lost consciousness while listening to an oral argument. He was taken to the hospital and pronounced dead at 6:45 P.M.[80] FBI wiretap summaries record that at 7:55 P.M. Justice Douglas phoned Corcoran to tell him about Stone's death.

TC: Oh Lord, does the world know that?

WD: You're the first one. . . . I just got a flash from his house. His secretary just called me. . . . Cerebral hemorrhage. He passed out on the bench at 2 o'clock and we carried him out. . . .

TC: Well the lightning is striking isn't it?

WD: Another great oak has fallen.

TC: He really was a great guy. He was an awfully good friend of yours.

WD: O.K. Tom.

TC: Can I see you in the morning?

WD: Yes, I'll drive by and get you.[81]

Corcoran may have learned of the chief justice's passing before President Truman did. Vacationing aboard the presidential yacht *Williamsburg*, Truman did not get a press release out until the next day.[82]

Soon FBI wiretaps were picking up conversations about the vacancy for chief justice. Initially, speculation about a successor focused on Justices Jackson, Black, and Douglas, with Secretary of the Treasury Vinson and Secretary of State James Byrnes also mentioned.[83] Justice Black, as the senior associate justice, temporarily assumed the duties of chief justice. Black's nemesis, Justice Jackson, was in Europe serving as U.S. chief prosecutor in the Nuremberg war crime trials. According to Justice Jackson, President Roosevelt had promised him the chief justice-ship. But Roosevelt was dead, and President Truman had to deal with a Court that was sorely divided by personal and political bickering. The personal animosity between Justices Black and Jackson had begun years before, during Charles Evans Hughes's chief justiceship,[84] and the bad blood between Jackson and Black continued for years. The battle within the Supreme Court in 1946 lined up thusly: Stanley Reed, William Douglas, Frank Murphy, and Wiley Rutledge were siding with Black; Felix Frankfurter and Harold Burton were allies of Jackson.[85]

On April 28, 1946, the wiretaps record that Corcoran talked to Ernest Cuneo, attorney and president of the North American Newspaper Alliance, about the battle between Black and Jackson for chief justice.

TC: What's going on down here is . . . a real struggle for the Chief Justiceship in which it's [Justice Robert H.] Jackson against [Justice Hugo] Black, with the chances out of it will emerge Jimmy Byrnes [Secretary of State].

EC: Jimmy may emerge huh?

. . .

TC: [I] don't think either man [Jackson or Black] frankly, will accept the appointment of the other. I think either of them will resign and quit if the other man went in, but that isn't because of Jackson. . . . Jackson is . . . Frankfurter. . . . It's the old, old struggle, the guy [Frankfurter] can't keep out of it. It's Frankfurter against Black. That's what it is. . . . And Bob Jackson is being hurt enormously by that factor.[86]

Both Cuneo and Corcoran said they were pulling for Justice Black.[87] The next evening, April 29, a caller identified as Harvey told Corcoran that Justice Reed is "plugging strong for Bill" Douglas and that former Chief Justice Hughes had been in with President Truman that day.[88]

Harvey was correct. Hughes had visited the White House earlier that afternoon and had talked about the chief justiceship at the invitation of the president.[89] They discussed the "difficulties" between Black and Jackson. Truman had met that morning with Vinson about the field of candidates.[90]

The press reported that the choice had been narrowed to Jackson and Douglas and that the president would be seeking advice from Attorney General Clark and Senator Alben Barkley, in addition to Vinson.[91]

Truman was getting unsolicited as well as solicited advice. White House insider Irving Brant wrote the president that elevating Justice Jackson would be a "demoralizing blow to the Court." On the contrary, according to Brant, selecting Justices Black or Wiley Rutledge would "make history." Or Douglas could "fittingly" be named chief justice.[92] Brant followed up with phone calls and a visit to the White House.

Rumors about the Court came over the tapped wires, and government agents were there to record them. On April 30, 1946, Corcoran called Justice Reed at home and told Mrs. Reed that he had heard at a party that the "new chief justice was Bob Jackson." Corcoran said that he would stop by to see Reed.[93] The FBI agent transcribing this conversation must have perked up. Early the next morning, presumably before the transcripts of the previous day's conversations had been typed, Hoover summarized this conversation in a letter he sent by special messenger to White House military aide Vaughan.[94] Corcoran subsequently called Mrs. Reed to say that the rumor was wrong and that Jackson would not be the next chief justice. The press was still speculating that Truman was going to nominate Jackson or Douglas.[95]

On May 2, former Justice Owen Roberts talked to President Truman[96] and gave him his list of nominees for the position. Vinson was one. The others, like Vinson, were former or current federal judges, but no sitting justice was recommended.[97] Once again the wiretaps revealed that Corcoran had his sources inside and outside the White House. A caller identified only as Rowan called Corcoran that evening. Corcoran told Rowan that Justice Douglas believed that Rowan had accomplished his "minimum objective," but that "there was a counter-attack [by former Justice Owen Roberts] this morning to knock off [his] maximum objective. . . . [T]he situation had been left so confused." Rowan described the battle for the chief justiceship as "bloody."[98] While on the bench, Roberts had subscribed to Frankfurter's negative view of Black and had no love for Douglas either. After Roberts retired, Black and Douglas refused to sign a farewell letter to him, and so no letter was sent from the Court.[99] Roberts knew firsthand of the backstabbing among the justices.

Other information provided by the wiretaps on Corcoran made it clear that neither Douglas, Jackson, nor Black could be elevated by Truman without damage to the Court. The taps kept Hoover and the White House apprised of Corcoran's frequent contacts with Justices Reed, Douglas, and Black. On the morning of May 1, Corcoran called Justice Black's home and talked to Mrs. Black. He arranged to pick up Justice Black at a set time, presumably because he was already distrustful of speaking freely on the phone. When Corcoran called Justice Douglas at his chambers later that day, he tapped the phone receiver with his pencil and said: "I'm doing my own tapping now." Douglas and Corcoran both laughed. Later, Corcoran would comment to his callers that he was "awfully afraid of this wire." Corcoran told Douglas that the postmaster general was pulling for Justice Jackson.[100]

That evening Senator Burton Wheeler called Corcoran. Wheeler told Corcoran that he tried to put in a good word for Black with Truman. Wheeler had heard that Black had threatened to resign if Jackson were appointed chief justice. According to Wheeler, the president had not yet made up his mind.[101] The Corcoran wiretaps show that Corcoran began lobbying for Douglas as a compromise candidate for chief justice, with support from Reed.[102] Corcoran told one caller it would be the kiss of death for him to support Douglas publicly. On the other hand, the taps showed that when Corcoran asked Vinson for special help, Vinson generally turned him down. Corcoran's callers repeatedly mentioned that behind the scenes Justice Frankfurter was flexing his political muscle on behalf of Jackson.

In a wiretapped conversation prior to Chief Justice Stone's death, Corcoran had alluded to Douglas's presidential ambitions: "[I]f there is a Chief Justiceship, [President Truman] ought to make Douglas the Chief in order to make Douglas a captive for political purposes. . . . [It] would keep him out of the political arena."[103] Truman possibly had this in mind when he offered Douglas the post of secretary of the interior only months before Stone passed away. Douglas had turned the president down, saying that he wanted to make the Court his life's work.[104]

Three months later, the question was whether Douglas's title would be chief rather than associate justice. FBI wiretap summaries on May 4, 1946, record that Drew Pearson called Corcoran and told him Douglas had been in the lead for the chief justiceship, but Frankfurter had started lobbying against him. Corcoran said that the president had decided on Jackson until the left wing of the Court objected. According to Corcoran, the next chief justice would be someone outside the court, possibly Vinson or Byrnes. "Is it lost for Bill?" Pearson asked Corcoran.

It was lost. In addition to the wrangling between the justices, the wiretap summaries may have raised enough questions about Douglas's allegiance to Truman to turn the president against Douglas. (Yet, two years later in 1948, Truman offered Douglas the vice-presidential slot, and he turned it down. Truman referred to Douglas as a "professional liberal" in his memoirs, writing that "[Douglas] belongs to that crowd of Tommy Corcoran, Harold Ickes, Claude Pepper, crackpots whose word is worth less than Jimmy Roosevelt's." All of the people Truman named were overheard in the Corcoran wiretaps.) In addition, President Truman's previous judicial selections were driven by his desire to appoint men loyal to him personally, often his poker-playing buddies, rather than concerns about ideology or legal excellence.[105]

According to Truman, both former Chief Justice Charles Hughes and former Associate Justice Owen Roberts had suggested that someone from outside of the Court be nominated to try to mend fences inside the Court.[106] The wrangling at the Court became public knowledge on May 16, when the Washington *Evening Star* printed an article about the feud between Jackson and Black.[107] Still, lobbying on behalf of Douglas continued. On May 19 Leo Crowley, who had been administrator of the Lend-Lease Program, called Corcoran and told him that Byrnes "is not sympathetic to . . . Black. . . . I asked him to put in a plug for Bill. . . . He's very friendly to Bill now."[108] FBI taps not only provided the latest lobbying about candidates for chief justice but also let Truman and Hoover find out that "Tommy the Cork" was the ghostwriter and editor of some of Douglas's speeches.[109]

In the end, the internecine battle at the Court doomed the chief justiceship for Douglas. Today, no one can be certain why Truman made his selection or whether the taps on Corcoran swayed either him or his advisers.[110] In the six weeks between Stone's death and Truman's nomination of Vinson as chief justice, Douglas was a party in ten FBI-wiretapped conversations and discussed in another eighteen.[111] Information from the wiretaps provided one more solid reason for Truman to select someone outside the Court. But Truman did not wish to offend Douglas either. On May 31, a week before his public announcement, Truman met with Vinson at the White House. One hour later President Truman phoned Douglas at his Supreme Court chambers.[112]

On June 6, 1946, Truman appointed Fred Vinson, his close friend and favorite poker companion, to be chief justice. Truman hoped the appointment might heal the wounds at the Supreme Court.[113] Instead, it caused further infighting. When Justice Jackson learned of the nomination in Germany, he went on a verbal rampage in which he blamed Black for Truman passing him over as chief justice.[114] The president called Justice Black at home to counsel against retaliating in the press, which would only further damage the Court.[115]

The Corcoran summaries were so valuable and politically explosive that Hoover kept them in his office. And the wiretaps continued, with one major interruption, until 1948. A short list of the non-Court luminaries picked up in these taps during the spring of 1946 include Abe Fortas, Congressman Lyndon B. Johnson, Senator Robert La Follette, Fiorello La Guardia, Senator Claude Pepper, Senator Burton Wheeler, Speaker of the House Sam Rayburn, Secretary of Treasury Fred Vinson, Secretary of the Navy James Forrestal, former Secretary of Interior Harold Ickes, as well as attorneys David Bazelon, Joseph Rauh, Jr., and Paul Porter.

FBI electronic eavesdropping continued to provide Hoover with important intelligence about Court-related politics. In 1948 Hoover was tipped off that someone had mentioned him as Douglas's running mate should Douglas decide to run for president. Hoover also learned that Fortas and other Douglas advisers were cool or openly opposed to the idea. "Abe Fortas, in whom Douglas appears to have complete confidence, was completely indifferent to the suggestions of [Hoover's] name as Douglas' running mate, and indicated . . . that a more desirable candidate could be found." Some Douglas advisers said such a ticket smacked of a police state. This memo, dated April 14, 1948, from Tamm to Hoover was marked: "This memorandum is for administrative purposes. To be destroyed after action is taken and not sent to files."[116] Obviously, since Hoover was mentioned, this information could not be passed on to the Truman White House.

"June Mail," "Do Not File" Files, and Other Un-Due Processes

The only time the FBI created a problem for itself by wiretapping was when the ELSUR target was subsequently prosecuted for a violation of a criminal law. Electronic surveillance and the leads it provided were inadmissible in court. Either the Justice Department was precluded from prosecuting or the existence of the wiretaps had to be concealed from a court. To shield its illegal conduct, the FBI set up a separate filing system.

In 1940 Hoover ordered that when other FBI officials submitted memos to him concerning illegal or embarrassing activities, they were to use blue (later pink) paper, and the records were to be stamped with the notation that the records were for administrative purposes only. If Hoover did not retain these records in his own confidential office files, they were destroyed.[117] Regular records were typed on white paper and serialized. The "Do Not File" procedure was revised to cover requests and authorizations for burglaries to be committed by FBI agents.[118] Similarly, on December 21, 1949, all bureau records that were not required to be destroyed and that authorized illegal acts or were the fruits of illegal buggings, wiretappings, or burglaries were ordered to be designated as "June Mail." "June Mail" was sent to a high-security safe called the Special File Room.[119] These parallel filing systems were designed so that agents could deny knowledge of illegal tactics.[120] The "June" system "reduc[ed] the possibility of disclosure through testimony in court or through inadvertence to outsiders."[121] This was somewhat similar to the agent 007 "For Your Eyes Only Then Destroy" procedure, except that these not-to-be-filed records were filed but kept out of regular FBI files. Other records of the highest sensitivity continued to be maintained in Hoover's own office, listed as "Official & Confidential" or "Personal & Confidential." As far as the rest of the world knew, "Do Not File" records did not exist.[122] Hoover ordered the regular destruction of all "Do Not File" records at field offices and among his top assistants. Only Hoover's and Louis Nichols's office files and portions of the files of Clyde Tolson and D. Milton Ladd survived destruction. And it appears that former Assistant Director Cartha DeLoach took some or all of his office files with him when he retired from the bureau.[123]

No Means Yes in the World of Microphone Bugs

Although Hoover effectively destroyed or hid ELSUR records at his headquarters, his warrantless wiretapping had already become a matter of public record in the prosecution of a Justice Department employee, Judith Coplon. On March 4, 1949, Coplon was arrested, without a warrant, by Special Agent in Charge Edward Scheidt.[124] Coplon was carrying twenty-eight FBI documents that the bureau said she was about to deliver to her Soviet contact, Valentin Gubitchev, a United Nations staffer. She was charged with illegally possessing secret government records. During Coplon's two trials, one in New York and one in Washington, D.C., her defense lawyers doggedly tried to get the government to admit it had wiretapped their client and to produce the phone logs. Coplon's lawyer was unsuccessful in the first trial. In the second, the judge held a hearing on the wiretapping issue and found that not only was Coplon's phone tapped before and after her indictment but also that her conversations with her attorney might have been overheard and that Hoover ordered notes about the phone taps destroyed. On appeal, based on the illegal arrest and the evidence of illegal wiretapping, Coplon was granted new trials in both cases.[125] Chief Judge Learned Hand wrote the decision for the Second Circuit Court of Appeals. After the ruling, Scheidt was in Judge Hand's chambers, and the judge told Scheidt, "See what I did for you [FBI] boys. I put the [blame for the] wiretap on the Attorney General [in my opinion]." Judge Hand did write that "all the 'taps' were made at the personal direction of the Attorney General," but he also ruled that Scheidt's arrest of Coplon without a warrant was unlawful.[126] The D.C. circuit court also ruled that the arrest was unlawful. Coplon was never retried.

As a result of *Coplon,* Congress again considered legislation that would allow the use of legally obtained ELSUR evidence in court.[127] The Milwaukee *Journal* and other newspapers editorialized for wiretapping legislation. When agents "resort to wire tapping, the evidence gained by it is not admissible. This has seriously embarrassed the prosecution of traitors. The Judith Coplon spy case dramatized this fact." The *Journal* called for the passage of Representative Kenneth Keating's bill,[128] which would have allowed wiretap evidence after a judicial warrant had been obtained.[129]

The bureau opposed the restriction of its activities[130] through legislation that would grant judges the authority to approve technical surveillances. The only legislation acceptable to the FBI would give the U.S. attorney general authority to order wiretapping. To that end the Justice Department sponsored its own wiretap bill. To assist in lobbying efforts, the FBI prepared a blind memo "setting forth [FBI] views on wire tapping" to provide "some ammunition" for Judge Jerome Frank's "use in discussions with Congressman Celler" and others.[131] Representative Emmanuel Celler's bill was "sponsored by the [Justice] Department" and allowed "the introduction in evidence of information obtained by wire tapping" if the tap had been approved by the attorney general.[132]

If federal judges had to approve wiretaps, Hoover "would prefer no legislation at all." This had been Hoover's position in both 1940 and 1941 when wiretap legislation had been introduced.[133] Bureau officials believed that "no one Federal judge possesses sufficient information on the nation's security upon which he can base a decision" and that "there are some Federal judges to whom we would not desire to furnish confidential information from our files on security matters."[134] In 1953 a memo containing "derogatory data" was prepared on eight federal judges for possible off the record use with pro-bureau congressmen "in connection with proposed wire tapping legislation." This memo was intended to "illustrate the fact that it is not practicable or feasible to require sanction of a Federal judge before engaging in wire tapping."[135] In 1954 Hoover and the Justice Department lobbied Keating, a Republican from New York, to scuttle yet another proposed wiretap bill that would have allowed the FBI to introduce wiretap evidence in court after a judicial warrant had first been obtained.[136] Hoover reported to his chief assistants about his meeting with Keating:

> I then discussed with Congressman Keating the character of some of our Federal Judges; their lack of knowledge of the background of subversive activities, which is very necessary to have in deciding upon the authorization for a wiretap; the subversive affiliations of some of our Federal Judges; and the unfitness of character, such as overindulgence in liquor and the loquacity of some of our Federal Judges. I stated that all of this would certainly lead to a great danger as to the disclosure of this very necessarily confidential operation. I further pointed out that certainly the Attorney General of the United States is actually more accountable to Congress than approximately three hundred Federal Judges are and that by centering in one place and placing responsibility in one man Congress would be able to keep in more intimate touch with any abuse that might be indulged in this project than they would be if were spread through the country in the hands of approximately three hundred Federal Judges.[137]

After the full House of Representatives opted for a law requiring a judicial warrant, the Justice Department withdrew its support for legislation. No wiretap law was passed.[138] Hoover's view had won, and for fourteen more years no wiretapping legislation was enacted.[139]

Bugging and Burglary

In the 1954 case *Irvine v. California*[140] the Warren Court made known its outrage about bugging accomplished by trespass when it blasted the illegal practices of state police authorities. A bug had been planted in a defendant's home by burglary; the Court ruled that it was a violation of the Fourth and/or the Fifth Amendment. Unfortunately for the defendant, he was tried in state court, and five of the justices set aside their anger and ruled that principles of federalism prevented them from requiring the trial court to exclude the evidence.

The FBI, meanwhile, continued to engage in burglary to plant microphones.[141] Reacting to the *Irvine* decision, which made it clear that bugging accomplished by trespass was unconstitutional, Attorney General Brownell sent a memo to Hoover. Brownell argued that *Irvine* was a state gambling prosecution, not a national security case. Besides, it was necessary for the FBI to continue to use bugs to carry out its internal security and national safety functions as well as to develop evidence. Under Brownell, bugging would be "unrestricted" when necessary to the "national interest." The attorney general sidestepped the issue of "trespass" and the resulting violation of the Fourth Amendment, saying that it would be resolved on a case-by-case basis in light of practical circumstances.[142] The effect of Brownell's sweeping authorization for bugging, a policy for which he "cited no legal support," was that the highest ranking federal law enforcement official gave Hoover carte blanche to burglarize and bug.[143]

There was no question that installing bugs through the use of trespass was illegal. The narrower issue was whether microphone surveillance was a violation of the Fourth Amendment, even if it were accomplished without trespass. The 1960 term offered the justices a chance to overrule the 1942 bugging ruling in *Goldman v. U.S.*,[144] which held that the electronic "overhearing" of conversations within a home was not a violation of the Fourth Amendment unless the government conducted the surveillance by trespass. Prior to the oral argument in *Silverman v. U.S.*,[145] one of Justice Harlan's clerks, Howard Lesnich, wrote that "*Goldman* in particular is nearly on all fours [identical] with this [*Silverman*] case. The real invitation is to overrule those cases. The Court has always been deeply divided on that question, and I don't know if there is a present majority to do it or not. . . . Since to me the only question is whether there are five

Justices ready and willing to throw over these cases, I cannot make a recommendation."[146]

The Court turned down the invitation to overrule *Goldman* and held that shoving a "spike mike" through the baseboard of an adjoining row house until it struck a heating duct in the house next door—turning the duct into a giant microphone that allowed the police to listen to conversations on two floors of the house—violated the Fourth Amendment. Justice Stewart wrote the opinion and Justices Clark and Whittaker concurred only because the bug physically penetrated the defendant's house. Justice Douglas was the only member of the Court willing to overturn the trespass analysis in favor of privacy, an analysis first suggested by Justice Brandeis in his *Olmstead* dissent. Douglas argued that it did not matter whether there was trespass because the "invasion of privacy is as great in one case as in the other.... Was not the wrong in both cases done when the intimacies of the home were tapped, recorded or revealed? The depth of the penetration of the electronic device—even the degree of its remoteness from the inside of the house—is not the measure of the injury." Douglas wrote that such a search should only be made upon a warrant issued by a magistrate or judge.[147]

The Court stopped just short of overturning *Goldman*. It would be five more years before Hoover was called to task for his illegal bugging policy. A two-and-a-half page Supreme Court ruling in the 1966 case *Fred B. Black, Jr. v. U.S.* would give no clue that behind the scenes the case had been the Supreme Court's equivalent of the Watergate burglary and cover-up. The Court as an institution was a victim of the FBI's Supreme Court program, and a member of the Court was a co-conspirator.

CHAPTER 3

Gavelgate: G–Men in the Conference Room

Our government is the potent, the omnipresent, teacher. For good or for ill, it teaches the whole people by its example. Crime is contagious. If the government becomes a law-breaker, it breeds contempt for the law; it invites every man to become a law unto himself; it invites anarchy. To declare that in the administration of the criminal law the end justifies the means—to declare that the government may commit crimes in order to secure the conviction of a private criminal—would bring terrible retribution. Against that pernicious doctrine this court should resolutely set its face.[1]

—Justice Louis Brandeis, dissenting in *Olmstead v. U.S.* (1928)

On February 9, 1963, agents of the Federal Bureau of Investigation checked into the Sheraton-Carlton Hotel in Washington, D.C., under assumed names. They drilled a hole into the common wall of an adjoining room and inserted a "spike" microphone through which they listened to and tape-recorded conversations in the suite of Fred B. Black, Jr., next door. According to the FBI, the bug was installed to investigate whether Black had ties to racketeers. The FBI kept the microphone going for three and one-half months.[2]

Black was a soft-spoken lobbyist, who loved horseracing as much as J. Edgar Hoover did.[3] More important, he was a business associate of Lyndon B. Johnson's friend, Robert (Bobby) Baker. Baker had been secretary to the Senate Democrats and was nicknamed "the mole"[4] for his fast, hunched-over walk. He came to the Senate as a fourteen-year-old page from South Carolina, studied law at night, and rose in power and influence on the coattails of his patron, Johnson.[5] Baker's and Black's fortunes were intertwined. Both men fell from grace in political and business circles after they were sued in connection with the corrupt business practices of Serv-U Corporation, a vending-machine company that placed machines in the plants of defense and aerospace contractors.[6] The Senate investigated Baker for influence peddling in obtaining contracts for the company,[7] and later he was convicted of income tax evasion.[8] For a brief time Washington lawyer Abe Fortas of Arnold, Fortas & Porter represented Baker, but Fortas was replaced by another all-star attorney, Edward Bennett Williams, before the case went to trial.[9] Just as Baker's and Black's futures were joined, so were their conversations, recorded in an FBI frenzy of bugging. Both men were overheard in electronic surveillance (ELSUR) directed at their business associates, Benjamin Sigelbaum in Miami and Edward Levinson, a Las Vegas gambling operator.[10]

In 1964 Black was tried in federal court in Washington, D.C., for federal income tax violations during the years 1956 to 1958. The prosecution's case showed that Black had received a total of $140,078 in income that he did not report.[11] Black's defense was that his underlings had prepared his tax returns. In one instance he sent his accountant receipts for hotel expenses to be claimed as deductions, not realizing, he said, that one of his clients had already paid the hotel bill for him. The jury believed the government and convicted Black, who was sentenced to between fifteen months to four years in prison and fined $10,000. Black appealed his conviction to the D.C. Circuit Court of Appeals and lost. By then Robert Kennedy had become a U.S. Senator, and Nicholas Katzenbach had been appointed attorney general.

On February 16, 1966, Black's attorneys filed a petition for a writ of *certiorari* (cert for short), lawyer jargon for a request that the Supreme Court exercise its discretionary authority to accept a case for review. Black asked the justices to overturn his conviction because, among other things, he did not receive a fair trial due to prejudicial publicity caused by the Senate's investigation of Baker. One of the newspaper headlines read: "BAKER ASSOCIATE BLACK GOES ON TRIAL FOR EVADING 91,000 DOLLARS IN U.S. TAXES."[12] The articles called Black an "influence peddler," a description reinforced at his trial when the prosecutor, in his opening statement, argued that Black was "a man . . . [who] knows his way around Washington and can get things done there for his clients."[13] Black also claimed that his constitutional rights against self-incrimination and assistance of counsel were violated when the government threatened to prosecute his former attorney, friend, and business partner to secure the latter's testimony against Black. His appellate attorneys wrote: "It goes without saying that the use of [Black's] *attorney* as a coerced 'Judas,' informer, and star prosecution witness not only violates [Black's] rights under the Fifth and Sixth Amendments, but shocks the conscience and all concepts of fairness."[14] To support this claim, Black's new lawyers cited *Coplon v. U.S.*, in which the D.C. Court of Appeals "reversed the conviction of [Judith Coplon] for the heinous crime of espionage because of the use of wire-tapping of conferences between [Coplon] and her counsel." Black's lawyers cited the right case, not knowing that their seventh and then weakest argument would ultimately save their client. As in the *Coplon* case, Black's conversations with his trial lawyer had been electronically overheard by the FBI. The only problem was that Black and his lawyers did not know about the bugging—yet.

The government opposed Black's request for the Supreme Court to hear his case. Black's unreported income came from five clients who employed him for various purposes, including leading them to classified construction job opportunities, trying to get a titanium development contract with the Navy, and acting as consultant to an aerospace firm on future government policy. None of Black's clients knew how the unreported payments were spent because he gave them no accounting of his expenses. The jury found that Black had specifically intended to evade his tax liability, and, the government said, the Supreme Court should let the jury's verdict stand by denying the petition for a writ of *certiorari.*[15]

It takes the vote of four of the nine justices to issue a writ of *certiorari.* The Supreme Court was not impressed with Black or his lawyers' arguments. After Black petitioned the Supreme Court asking that *cert* be granted (and before the justices voted on whether to accept his case), Court law clerks prepared a summary (called a *cert* memo), with a recommendation to the justices about how to proceed. One of Justice Douglas's law clerks referred to Black as "some sort of influence peddler," dismissed Black's contentions, and recommended that *cert* be denied. Justice Harlan's clerk, Charles Lister, also recommended that *cert* be denied, writing that Black "asserts a variety of defects in the trial, including prosecutor's misconduct, threats to witnesses, and inadmissible evidence. . . . [A]ll are inappropriate for review here."[16] Michael Smith wrote to Earl Warren that the case was close on the facts but that he found it "hard to believe that a wheeler and dealer like [Black] did not know what was going on. I suspect that he failed to report some of his income because it might have embarrassed his public relations activities. Still this constitutes a violation of the tax laws."[17]

As with all *cert* petitions, after the law clerks make their recommendations to the justices, the Court meets secretly to vote on whether to accept the case. The conference room—the sanctuary of the judicial temple—is situated next to the chief justice's chambers. While the justices are in conference, an employee of the marshal's office stands guard outside.[18] No secretaries or law clerks—no one other than the nine justices—are allowed inside when they take their places around the conference table and confidentially discuss and vote on each case. As Pulitzer Prize–winning Court reporter Anthony Lewis described it,

"The conference has a record for secrecy probably unrivaled in official Washington."[19]

At conference on May 2, 1966, the justices voted to deny *cert* in the *Black* case. Black's lawyers began preparing a request for a rehearing, asking the Court to reconsider its decision, even though there was no reason to believe that the Court would change its collective mind.[20]

But Solicitor General Thurgood Marshall was getting ready to provide a compelling reason for the Supreme Court to hear the *Black* case.[21] The solicitor general, the number three man in the Justice Department, is the government's ranking appellate lawyer. Marshall had been instructed by his boss, Attorney General Katzenbach, to tell the Court about the FBI's bugging of Black because some conversations with Black's lawyer had been overheard. A copy of the Justice Department's proposed memorandum to the Supreme Court was sent to Hoover for his comments.

Angry and flabbergasted by the memo, Hoover wanted to know why the department, having won the case, would give a convicted tax cheat information that might allow him to attack his conviction. Hoover objected vehemently to informing the Court about the bugging, since it had nothing to do with the tax prosecution. If the Court was told anything, he argued, it should be as little as possible. He also considered a number of items in the Justice Department's proposed memo to the Court to be lies or deceptions.

The draft of the department's memorandum claimed that Justice Department lawyers had not known about the bugging during the trial; only the FBI had known. While it was true that department lawyers did not know about the bugging during Black's trial in late April and early May of 1964, on August 24, 1965, Hoover wrote to Katzenbach telling him that Baker had been picked up in a "microphone . . . installed at the office of Fred Black."[22] Later that fall, Justice Department attorneys in the Criminal Division learned that Black's lawyer had been heard talking to Black. It was not until April 21, 1966, that attorneys in the Justice Department's Tax Division—the attorneys responsible for prosecuting Black—received this information and passed it on to the attorney general. Hoover was also concerned that the solicitor general was planning to "volunteer [to the Court] that microphone devices were also installed in the offices of [Black's] business associates in two other cities."[23]

Hoover instructed an assistant to meet with Justice Department attorneys to make sure that "the Department [was not going] to look like a knight in shining armor to the court and dump this whole thing on the FBI."[24] James Gale, Hoover's emissary to the Justice Department, was successful in removing any reference to the bugs placed on Black's business associates. The department's memo to the Court was also changed to say that the department lawyers "only recently learned that a listening device had been used." Hoover still was not satisfied with these changes, believing the memorandum was still misleading.

Katzenbach wrote to Hoover explaining his reasons for making the bugging public. He and his principal advisers believed that as "officers of the court," they "were under a duty to disclose . . . the fact of the inadvertent invasion of the attorney-client privilege." According to Katzenbach, "Any information obtained as a result of microphone coverage installed through trespass . . . is inadmissible as evidence in court," and there was an "inescapable duty" to report the overhearing of an attorney talking to his client, even if they believed "that it in no way affected the fairness of the trial."[25]

Another possible explanation for the Justice Department's disclosure was the fear of political damage: one Senate committee was already investigating ELSUR abuses by the federal government.[26] The bureau's extensive wiretapping and bugging of the Reverend Martin Luther King, Jr., had not yet been publicly exposed, though Katzenbach had been aware of the surveillance,[27] which, he had been told, was for the stated purpose of determining the extent of Communist influence on King and on the Southern Christian Leadership Conference. On one occasion Katzenbach had warned Hoover that these "particularly delicate surveillances" required extreme caution.[28] And though Cartha DeLoach's FBI Crime Records Division had worked hard to leak to the press the fruits of the surveillance, particularly King's sexual infidelities, the media refused to publish it.[29] The last FBI microphone surveillance of King had been turned off during January 1966 after Hoover became afraid of what a congressional investigation might discover.[30]

For the time being though, due to DeLoach, who was also the bureau's very effective congressional liaison, Congress was under control. In July 1965 a subcommittee of the Senate Judiciary Committee, chaired by Missouri Democrat Edward V. Long, began investigating government ELSUR, starting with the Internal Revenue Service's eavesdropping practices. The committee subsequently expanded its probe to include the surveillance practices of all federal agencies, including the FBI. Feeling that Long could not be trusted, Hoover sent DeLoach to stop the inquiry into the bureau's practices. In January 1966 DeLoach and another high-level bureau official visited Long to explain the FBI's surveillance practices. The meeting lasted for an hour and a half, after which DeLoach suggested to Long that he issue a statement "reflecting that he had held lengthy conferences with top FBI officials and was now completely satisfied, after looking into FBI operations, that the FBI had never participated in uncontrolled usage of wiretaps or microphones and that FBI usage of such devices had been completely justified in all instances."[31] DeLoach offered to prepare such a statement vindicating the FBI. According to DeLoach, Long reluctantly agreed. The press release the bureau prepared read in part:

> [M]y staff and I have not only conferred at length with top officials of the FBI, but we have conducted exhaustive research into the activities, procedures, and techniques of this agency.
>
> [I] am at the present time prepared to state, based upon careful study, that we are fully satisfied that the FBI has not participated in high-handed or uncontrolled usage of wiretaps, microphones, or other electronic equipment.
>
> The FBI's operations have been under strict Justice Department control at all times. In keeping with a rigid system of checks and balances, FBI installation of wiretaps and microphones has been strictly limited, and such electronic devices have been used only in the most important and serious of crimes either affecting the national security of our Nation or involving heinous threats to human life. Included among these are major cases of murder, kidnapping, and sadism perpetrated at the specific instruction of leaders of La Cosa Nostra or other top echelons of the extralegal empire of organized crime.
>
> Investigation made by my staff has reflected no independent or unauthorized installation of electronic devices by individual FBI Agents or FBI offices in the field. We have carefully examined Mr. J. Edgar Hoover's rules in this regard and have found no instances of violation.[32]

But the subcommittee had not investigated bureau ELSUR policies and had heard no testimony—Long had only talked to DeLoach for ninety minutes. As the Senate's Church Committee noted eleven years later: the Long Committee "did not learn of the bugging of a Congressman's hotel room, the bugging and wiretapping of Martin Luther King, Jr., or the wiretapping of a Congressional staff member, two newsmen, an editor of a political newsletter, and a former Bureau agent—all of which had occurred within the previous five years."[33]

Ten days after receiving the prepared release, Long had not issued it, so DeLoach visited him and "asked him point blank whether or not he intended to hold hearings concerning the FBI." Long said that he had no plans to hold hearings concerning the bureau. Upon his return to headquarters, DeLoach crowed to his second-in-command, Clyde Tolson, that "we have neutralized the threat of being embarrassed by the Long Subcommittee." DeLoach cautioned that the bureau had to "keep on top of this situation at all times" because newspaper pressure on Long might make him change his mind.[34]

Congress was on the verge of passing the Freedom of Information Act, which would give citizens the right to see records that the government collected. And, though DeLoach successfully blocked the Long Committee's investigation into FBI ELSUR practices, the Justice Department could not be sure that another Senate investigation would not unearth the bugging of Black and threaten the integrity of the department, not only in the public eye, but also before the Senate and the Supreme Court.

A year earlier, Attorney General Katzenbach had tightened Justice Department surveillance policies, which had formerly allowed Hoover free reign to bug and tap.[35] The new policies required departmental authorization for electronic eavesdropping, and a specific authorization had to be renewed every six months.[36] Katzenbach was arguably the first attorney general in decades to take concrete steps to reclaim from Hoover the authority to place electronic surveillances, authority that had been de facto surrendered to the powerful director, theoretically subordinate to the attorney general.

The microphone surveillance of Black had been personally ordered by Hoover without then Attorney General Robert Kennedy's specific written or oral authorization. But Kennedy, like his predecessor attorneys general, had known that the FBI employed bugging in national security and organized crime cases and had failed to intervene because he appreciated the information obtained.[37] Black's bugging was unrelated to Black's tax case.[38] Hoover needed extraordinary help to escape from his predicament of being blamed for conduct that a succession of attorneys general had tacitly approved with a wink and a smile. The Long Committee investigations had publicized the issue of government ELSUR. Through backroom dealing, Hoover narrowly escaped congressional inquiry into the bureau's surveillance practices.

Despite Hoover's objections, on May 24, 1966,[39] Solicitor General Marshall surprised the Court when he filed an unprecedented memorandum advising the justices that:

> [A]gents of the [FBI] installed a listening device in petitioner's hotel suite in Washington, D.C. The device (not a telephone wiretap) . . . was in operation from approximately two months before until approximately one month after the evidence was presented to the grand jury and the indictment was returned. . . . During that time the monitoring agents overheard, among other conversations, exchanges between [Black] and the attorney who was then representing him in connection with the tax-evasion charges on which he was convicted.[40]

The battle had already begun within the Executive Branch over who would assume responsibility for illegal bugging. The Black bugging had the potential of ending Hoover's career, and he knew it. He needed to convince the Court that former Attorney General Kennedy had authorized the bug and that he was simply following orders. The director despised Kennedy as did then President Lyndon Johnson. Likewise, Hoover did not trust Katzenbach, whom Hoover considered to be a "Kennedy man." And so DeLoach recruited a Supreme Court justice, a close personal friend and adviser to Johnson, to be his eyes and ears in the Supreme Court conference room as well as his advocate with the other justices and with the president. This justice could walk into the conference room of the U.S. Supreme Court and blame Kennedy for the bugging, thereby helping Johnson by damaging the reputation of his primary rival in the Democratic party. The selection of the FBI informer-justice makes perfect sense when one considers Hoover's own experiences with each one of the justices.

CHAPTER 4

A "Sniveling Liberal" Justice Makes the Best FBI Informer

Infiltration is the method whereby Party members move into non-communist organizations for the purpose of exercising influence for communism. If control is secured, the organization becomes a communist front. . . . The Trojan horse [of infiltration] has enabled the Party to wield an influence far in excess of its actual numbers.[1]

—J. Edgar Hoover, *Masters of Deceit* (1958)

In May 1966 J. Edgar Hoover needed a Supreme Court justice to be his informer and provocateur inside the Court's oak-paneled conference room. He had tried to cultivate most of the justices, liberals and conservatives alike, but based on Supreme Court voting records alone, Hoover had no reason to try to approach any member of the liberal faction, comprised of Chief Justice Earl Warren and Associate Justices Hugo Black, William O. Douglas, William Brennan, and Abe Fortas. But Hoover had access to far more than the public record on which to base his decisions. Let's consider each justice.

Mr. Justice Hugo Black

In 1966 Hoover did not have a relationship with Justice Hugo Black that would allow him to ask the justice for a favor. Black, then eighty years old, had been appointed by Franklin D. Roosevelt in 1937. Roosevelt had not asked the FBI to investigate the New Deal Senator from Clay County, Alabama, but this fact did not stop the press from criticizing the bureau when Black's former membership in the Alabama Ku Klux Klan was made public. Although the bureau had not had much personal contact with Black, the FBI had, in the summer of 1965, laid out the red carpet and "spoiled" Justice Black's second wife, Elizabeth, and the justice's two grandsons during their "very special tour" of the bureau. During the highlight of the visit, Hoover personally showed Mrs. Black and the children around his office, explaining the mementos and statuary that graced his office and then gave the children a Gemini and a Thor model missiles from his own model collection, which he kept in his outer office. Mrs. Black wrote thanking Hoover: "Dean,

Jimmy, and I are at a loss for words to thank you for our fabulous day at the F.B.I. The crowning thrill in a day of treats, surprises, and learning came a few minutes ago when the three autographed pictures arrived by special messenger."[2]

Unfortunately for Hoover, Mrs. Black and boys were not voting on the *Black* case.

Mr. Justice William J. Brennan, Jr.

Like Justice Black, William J. Brennan, Jr., President Dwight Eisenhower's 1956 nominee to the High Court, had no personal relationship with Hoover or any of his assistants. Brennan had been a justice on the New Jersey Supreme Court before his appointment. Roman Catholic, Irish, and a Democrat, Brennan was nominated by a Republican, whose selection was influenced by religion, nationality and political considerations. Brennan's appointment was supported by New Jersey Supreme Court Chief Justice Arthur T. Vanderbilt, Attorney General Herbert Brownell, and White House Appointments Secretary Bernard Shanley (an old friend of Brennan's). Although no Catholic had been on the Supreme Court since Justice Frank Murphy had died in 1949,[3] Brennan was subjected to an impotent tirade by fellow Catholic Senator Joseph McCarthy during the confirmation proceedings. Unlike his predecessor, Justice Sherman Minton, who generally could be counted on to support governmental actions in criminal prosecutions and loyalty/security matters, Brennan voted the opposite way. As late as 1958, Attorney General William Rogers still hoped that Brennan would pull away from the left wing of the Court—Douglas, Black, and Warren. Rogers told Hoover that he "believed . . . there was a possibility . . . Justice Brennan might eventually break away from the minority which holds the more extreme views." The attorney general told Hoover that greater care needed to be used in the selection of cases to take to the Supreme Court, so that Black and Douglas could not make enough of an issue of the facts of the case to turn it against the government's position.[4] The attorney general's wishful thinking about Justice Brennan did not come to pass. Instead of moving away from Warren, Black, and Douglas, the congenial Brennan became the liberal magnet on the Court who weaved consensus out of discord.

Mr. Justice William O. Douglas

From 1937 to the late 1940s, William O. Douglas corresponded regularly with Hoover and socialized with FBI agents. In 1944 the young Justice

Douglas was in such favor with Hoover that he gave the commencement speech at the FBI National Academy. A year later, Hoover trusted Douglas enough to send him confidential information regarding the bureau's espionage and counterespionage operations directed against Axis agents in Latin America.[5] On the more personal side, after Douglas suffered a near-fatal horseback riding accident in 1949, Hoover sent Douglas a get-well message, joining Douglas's "host of friends in wishing [him] a speedy and complete recovery." Hoover closed by saying, "If there is anything I can do, please let me know." There were things to do, and while Douglas was recovering, the bureau assisted him with his personal affairs. Plans were made for Justice Douglas to go hunting with two FBI special agents in the Arizona mountains after he recuperated from his injuries.[6]

By the early 1950s, some high-level FBI officials began to question Justice Douglas's patriotism because of his Supreme Court decisions.[7] Starting with his dissent in the 1951 *Dennis v. U.S.* [8] case, in which the convictions of the national officers of the Communist party for conspiracy to advocate the overthrow of the government were affirmed by the Court, Douglas's decisions began to be viewed with suspicion. Another "suspect" ruling was Douglas's temporary, last-minute stay of execution in the Rosenberg case.[9]

Although Douglas had an open mind when it came to the political philosophy of others, there was no doubt that he was a liberal who had no love for the ideology of Communism. Douglas was a strong anti-Communist, and his sentiments varied little from Hoover's. In a 1945 speech cited in a House Committee on Un-American Activities report on the Communist Party USA, Douglas stated that "Communism places state power in the hands of a small clique, who enforces that power by secret police with the weapons of murder and terror, and sees to it that the people are deprived of the means of replacement and change." In 1948 Douglas gave a speech at the University of Florida, where he denounced Communism as a force that planned world domination.[10]

In 1955 Justice Douglas had relied upon the FBI to choose a "trust-worthy" interpreter (from a list of applicants he provided) for his trip to Russia with Robert Kennedy. FBI Assistant Director Louis B. Nichols saw this as an opportunity to explain to Douglas, by then a critic of the government's loyalty programs, the FBI's internal security concerns. "Quite frankly," Nichols said to Clyde Tolson, "I saw in this an opportunity to get across to Douglas some of our problems with reference to internal security, particularly the problem of informants and the like, wherein he needs to have some education."[11] Nichols also said that the FBI had a moral and legal responsibility to stop a Supreme Court justice from getting "mixed up with the wrong type of people if this can be avoided."[12] To accomplish this lesson, two applicants with Communist connections were used to demonstrate the use of confidential sources of information in exposing subversives, so that the "value of informants could be forcibly brought to Justice Douglas' attention." Confidential sources were identified for Douglas, who was also given the information that they provided about the two applicants. According to the bureau's sources, the two applicants were said to be members of the International Workers Order (IWO) organization, subscribers to the *Daily Worker*, and contributors to the Joint Anti-Fascist Refugee Committee, among other associations that the bureau considered suspect or outright subversive. The names of both applicants were also found in the FBI's Security Index, which listed persons believed to be potentially dangerous to internal security. Douglas did not choose either of these applicants, but it is not clear that his decision was influenced by the FBI's presentation.

The FBI saw another opportunity in aiding Douglas's search for a loyal interpreter: "[I]t would be to the interest of [the] CIA, for example, or the State Department to have a translator with Douglas."[13] It is not clear whether either agency followed up on this suggestion.

It was about this time that the formerly close relations between the bureau and Douglas became an embarrassment to Hoover, who sought to keep it secret. Hoover's assistant, D. M. Ladd, noted several instances where "Justice Douglas rendered dissenting opinions, indicating his stand favorable to [Communist supported] issues." When the Justice Department requested information about Douglas in 1954, a notation on the FBI documents made clear that even the attorney general was not to learn of the close relations. "Information Not Being Disseminated: "Cordial relations have existed between Justice Douglas and the Bureau since 1937."[14]

The FBI dossier on Justice Douglas grew for another twelve years as agents collected hundreds of pages of information about Douglas's political views, his friends, and his sexual peccadillos.[15] Justice Douglas's Court rulings and beliefs eventually ended his cordial relationship with the FBI and its director.

Mr. Chief Justice Earl Warren

Earl Warren, another former supporter of Hoover, had traded information and favors with the FBI before he arrived at the Court. In 1933, when Warren as district attorney was setting up the Anti-Racket Council of Alameda County, California, he enlisted Hoover's help (an FBI agent ended up on the council's board of directors). Warren's office maintained its own files on subversive activities and offered them to the FBI.[16] By 1937 Tolson had noted that Warren was "quite friendly" with the bureau, friendly enough that an FBI car and chauffeur were offered to him during his stay in Washington. Warren wrote to Hoover to thank him for the courtesies shown him and to praise the FBI. "I still marvel at the progress you have made in the development of your great Bureau."[17] Agents kept Hoover apprised of Warren's bright political future and his bid for the post of attorney general, a steppingstone to the governorship of California. The Warren-Hoover alliance burgeoned during Warren's tenure as attorney general and reached its peak during his governorship of California, with the development of a secret bureau program—entitled "Cooperation with Governor Earl Warren"[18]—that provided Warren with information from its files.[19] From 1948 to 1953 Hoover authorized agents to furnish confidential information from the FBI's files directly to Warren. For example, Hoover instructed agents in charge of the FBI office in San Francisco: "Advise Governor Warren that [the] information is furnished in strictest confidence, and none of the information can be attributed to the FBI."[20] Warren was not the only beneficiary. A nationwide FBI "Responsibilities Program" began in 1951 to provide information "regarding subjects of Security Index cards to a large number of state and local officials," such as friendly governors and other anti-Communist government officials.

Requests for information made by Governor Warren illustrate the methods he used to combat the subversive threat during the Cold War years, tactics that are inconsistent with his judicial legacy as the champion of civil liberties. Warren requested FBI information about his political opponents, labor union members, and state university employees, using the FBI program primarily to check for derogatory information about prospective political appointees or employees. Subversive references about a subject invariably led to dismissal or nonappointment.[21] Warren often asked for FBI recommendations on whom he should appoint to state boards, including the State Crime Commission and the State Athletic Commission.[22] FBI officials were impressed that Warren never betrayed their confidence about his source of information.[23] Early in his career, Warren may have benefited at the polls due to the FBI's surveillance and disruption of leftist and Communist party groups that were actively opposing him.[24]

Governor Warren was then a fervent advocate of law-and-order policies. He supported the internment of the Japanese during World War II. He also was a committed anti-Communist. He had grown up poor and was a liberal on social issues, such as state-funded medical insurance.

Despite his progressive streak, which set him apart from many other Republicans, President Eisenhower believed Warren was a solid moderate, who would offer no surprises while on the Court. Eisenhower could not have been more wrong, and neither could Hoover.

By 1966 the tall, white-haired man had been chief justice for twelve years, and the FBI favors had stopped. In 1964 Warren had been removed from the Hoover's "Special Correspondents List;" the relationship had soured as a result of Warren Court rulings and the Warren Commission report on the assassination of John Kennedy, which was mildly critical of the FBI.

Mr. Justice Tom C. Clark

From all appearances, Hoover's best candidate to influence the Court in the *Black* case was the then sixty-seven-year-old Tom C. Clark. The FBI director had more than a good friend in the former attorney general, who favored bow ties and hailed from the Lone Star state. In 1948 Hoover had helped Clark's Supreme Court confirmation battle by providing him with ammunition about his opponents.[25] Clark and the director saw eye-to-eye on law enforcement issues generally, and the justice had sought Hoover's off-the-record help on at least one opinion he had written.

On June 5, 1958, Justice Clark was working on his dissent in *Kent v. Dulles,* in which the authority of the secretary of state to ban the issuance of passports to American Communists was at issue. Clark phoned Hoover and said that he could not find anything in Hoover's *Masters of Deceit* "concerning passport control." Clark asked "if he could get a [public] statement . . . [by Hoover] . . . regarding the use of passports, particularly in the communist setup and their activities." Clark said he needed "a short paragraph, of three or four sentences, concerning the importance of passport control and would like to be able to attribute these remarks to some specific statement . . . [by Hoover]." The director replied that he would be glad to help.[26] Four days later, Hoover sent a letter by special messenger to Justice Clark at his chambers. The letter directed Clark to a passage in *Masters of Deceit* concerning Communist assistance to Soviet espionage agents, including the provision of false passports.

On June 16, 1958, Justice Douglas, writing for the 5-4 majority in *Kent v. Dulles,*[27] struck down the secretary of state's passport policy. Justice Clark wrote for the dissent and cited Hoover, as he had on many other occasions, this time referring to *Masters of Deceit* "[f]or a comprehensive story of Communism in America indicating the necessity for passport control."[28]

There was no doubt that Clark revered Hoover. Justice Clark was not content to let his pro-government rulings speak for themselves. He reaffirmed his antiradical and pro–law-and-order credentials in his steady correspondence with Hoover. Clark even aided the FBI's public relations and propaganda programs by working directly with Hoover to educate other judges about the bureau's position on criminal law and national security matters.[29] And Clark kept Hoover apprised of how best to stay in the good graces of the largest organization of attorneys, the American Bar Association.[30] (One of Clark's law clerks in the early 1960s made his own contact with the bureau at about the same time he received his job offer to work at the Court.[31] The bureau was eager to develop friends among Court employees.)

Hoover rewarded Justice Clark by putting him on his "Special Correspondents List."[32] Of course, Clark's opinions favoring the FBI and law enforcement in general were noted by the bureau.[33] In his letters, Clark praised Hoover's public critiques of the justice system and wrote to Hoover with some of his own criticism about the "foggy" area of search-and-seizure law that the Supreme Court had created.[34] In 1966 Clark was still friendly with FBI agents, and he continued to receive personal favors from them.

Perhaps the greatest apparent benefit to the FBI in approaching Justice Clark about the *Black* case was that Clark's son, Ramsey, was deputy attorney general in the Justice Department and a friend of Cartha DeLoach.[35] The younger Clark became Attorney General Nicholas Katzenbach's liaison to the FBI about the *Black* case.[36]

Another asset for the FBI in approaching Clark was that he was "totally devoted" to President Lyndon Johnson.[37] In 1943, then Congressman Johnson had interceded with the Roosevelt administration to have Clark appointed an assistant attorney general. Almost twenty years later, on Tom Clark's request, Johnson helped Ramsey Clark get his first job at the Justice Department during the Kennedy administration.[38] The elder Clark was a member of LBJ's dominos club—an informal group that included the president's friends, Justice Abe Fortas, Jack Brooks, Bill Deason, and Congressman J.J. Pickle—all of whom played dominos occasionally on Saturday afternoons when the president was ill.[39]

And Johnson sometimes sought Justice Clark's advice.[40] So the Clarks, father and son, were friendly and beholden to President Johnson, who would benefit from Robert Kennedy being held responsible for the *Black* bugging. Though Justice Clark appeared to be the perfect candidate for Hoover to approach, Clark claimed that he had never talked to Johnson or any other president about a pending case.[41] And while Tom Clark had on at least one occasion been too free with information to a friend about the outcome of an upcoming ruling,[42] his son, Ramsey, said that the justice had never talked to him about court cases.[43]

Mr. Justice Potter Stewart

Potter Stewart, another "get-tough-on-crime" justice, respected the FBI, even though Hoover turned him down for a job with the bureau after Stewart graduated from Yale Law School. Stewart's wealthy Republican mother was in a group that opposed U.S. entry into World War II prior to Pearl Harbor. That was enough to keep the young Stewart from carrying an FBI badge. Hoover changed his opinion after Judge Stewart had proven himself on the federal appellate bench—to Hoover's liking. The director liked what he saw so well that Hoover helped Stewart get the nomination for the Supreme Court.[44]

But since Stewart did not know that Hoover had recommended him to the attorney general before his nomination, his support would not have seemed sure, and, even if Stewart had known, there was no reason to believe that he would have violated his judicial oath.

Mr. Justice John M. Harlan

Former Wall Street lawyer and law enforcement advocate, Justice John M. Harlan was not likely to speak to the FBI about Court business. President Eisenhower had nominated him on November 8, 1954, from the federal bench to fill the vacancy left by the death of Justice Robert Jackson. A lifelong Republican, Harlan had been chief counsel from 1951 to 1953 for the New York State Crime Commission, which investigated the relationship between organized crime and state government.[45] His nomination had the hearty support of the American Bar Association Committee on Judiciary and the recommendation of the president's advisers, Thomas Dewey and Herbert Brownell.[46]

The FBI had provided minor favors to Harlan over the years. And when Hoover courted the powerful, he expected favors in return.[47] But not even the director expected that a few small gratuities were enough to make Harlan receptive to judicial misconduct.

Mr. Justice Byron White

Justice Byron "Whizzer" White had been the "Paul Hornung of his day, a slashing, driving [football] halfback of matchless skills."[48] Whizzer played professional football to pay his way through Yale Law School. A

Rhodes scholar, White became the law-and-order Kennedy appointee to the Court.[49] Since he had served directly under Attorney General Kennedy and was a colleague of Katzenbach, White was considered a Hoover enemy on the *Black* case because of his perceived pro-Kennedy bias. But Hoover thought he could dig up something to force White off the case: there were FBI memos sent to then Deputy Attorney General White about eavesdropping that would force him to disqualify himself.

Mr. Justice Abe Fortas

Liberal Justice Abe Fortas was the most pro-Johnson man on the Court or probably anywhere else, for that matter. Their friendship began in the late 1930s when they were brought together by New Dealers William Douglas and Tommy Corcoran.[50] One justice who served with Fortas described Abe as "sitting in Lyndon Johnson's lap."[51] Justice Fortas sometimes behaved like a loving son, trying to please his father, even though Fortas, possibly one of the most brilliant legal minds to serve on the Court, was clearly intellectually superior. Other times the tall, boisterous president and the slightly built, softer-spoken lawyer acted like brothers.

Fortas was the most recent addition to the Court, and he had worked with the FBI before at the behest of Johnson. Hoover considered Fortas to be "screwball" and a "sniveling liberal,"[52] for Fortas was the attorney who had successfully argued the *Gideon* case in the Supreme Court, establishing the right of indigent criminal defendants to lawyers paid by the state. And the FBI had compiled thousands of pages of records over the years, describing Fortas's left-leaning friends, clients, and former membership in groups such as the National Lawyers Guild.[53] During Fortas's days at Yale Law School, the FBI had recorded his "acquaintances" as considering him "a liberal but not a communist."[54] In the 1940s and 1950s, Fortas's legal advice had been picked up in FBI wiretaps and bugs directed at the allegedly subversive clients of his law firm, Arnold, Fortas & Porter.[55] But DeLoach was friendly with Fortas, and Hoover trusted DeLoach's judgment, for Fortas was the only justice whom the FBI would consider approaching. Even Justice Brennan remembered that Fortas was "very close to Lyndon Johnson, and also close to J. Edgar Hoover. They used Fortas for a lot of things."[56]

Bizarre as it seems, FBI officials believed they had no choice but to attempt to convince the "screwball" liberal Justice Fortas to violate his judicial oath, betray the confidentiality of discussions in the Supreme

Court conference room, and blame Robert Kennedy for the FBI-ordered bugging.[57]

Hoover knew that Fortas, Memphis-born and Yale Law School–educated, was President Johnson's long-time friend and most trusted adviser. Johnson had, in fact, introduced Fortas to DeLoach, the FBI liaison with the White House.[58] In large part, Johnson owed his 1948 Senate election to Fortas's legal efforts, which ensured that his name was placed on the general election ballot after his contested victory in the runoff.[59] The rough-talking, arm-twisting Texan usually got what he wanted, and he succeeded in alternately enticing and pressuring Kennedy appointee Arthur Goldberg off the Court in 1965 to make way for Fortas, who required similar cajoling to accept the nomination to the Court's so-called Jewish seat.

Concerned that Fortas might be attacked for political reasons, Johnson had asked the FBI to discover any opposition to a Fortas nomination to the Court. On July 18, 1965, President Johnson phoned DeLoach and told him that he was thinking about appointing Fortas to an "important departmental position." Johnson wanted the FBI to find out "what opposition he would encounter after he named Fortas" to this unspecified position. Johnson told DeLoach to have agents interview Senators Eugene McCarthy and Robert and Edward Kennedy as well as some conservative senators in order to get them on record so they could not later issue negative press statements. Johnson told DeLoach that he did not care that Fortas belonged to "communist front organizations" in the early 1940s. Fortas "had matured" and was now well trusted and loyal. In what might be an understatement, Johnson said "he trusted Fortas as much as he did Lady Bird."[60]

DeLoach, a southerner[61] like Johnson and Fortas, was the perfect man for the president's job, for he was almost as close to Johnson as Fortas was.[62] Johnson had even installed a direct line to the White House in DeLoach's bedroom—not even Hoover was so privileged![63] By the mid-1960s, Johnson was not entirely trusting of the cranky septuagenarian Hoover, and he bypassed the director in favor of DeLoach.[64] DeLoach, a former college football player, was the administration's informant in the American Legion while serving as the head of the FBI Crime Records Division, which often acted as the bureau's publicity and propaganda section.[65] He was responsible for publicizing the bureau's achievements, mobilizing friends in the media to attack FBI enemies, and keeping the issues of crime and the Communist menace in the public eye.

After Johnson introduced Fortas to DeLoach the two men were soon working together on very sensitive matters at Johnson's behest.[66] When Johnson aide Walter Jenkins was arrested in 1964 for allegedly making homosexual advances to a man in the basement of a YMCA, it was DeLoach and Fortas who were called in for damage control.[67] During the U.S. intervention in the civil war in the Dominican Republic in 1965, it was Fortas who called Hoover and DeLoach to convey the president's orders about bureau actions there.[68] Fortas cooperated with the bureau on other ventures as well.[69]

DeLoach's interviews with eleven senators turned up no opposition to Fortas, and so President Johnson asked the FBI to do a rush background investigation of Fortas. The investigation covered all of the usual subjects, character, loyalty, reputation, and legal ability. There was no investigation of Fortas's sources of income.[70] Other than a laundry list of subversive references and classified reports about Fortas's advice to the president on foreign policy matters, the investigation was unremarkable.

On July 28, 1965, Johnson nominated Fortas to the Supreme Court. Fortas had initially rejected the offer to nominate him to the Court, writing, "I want a few more years to try to be of service to you and the Johnson family . . . and to stabilize the law firm."[71] But under pressure from the president, Fortas accepted the appointment. He wrote to Johnson, pleading that he did not want his presence on the Court to change their relationship: "I can only hope that you will continue to see me and to call upon me for anything that I can do to help." Johnson was happy to oblige.

At his Senate confirmation hearing, Fortas testified under oath that his friendship with Johnson would not interfere with his work on the Court. He also countered the time-worn charges that he had agreed with Communists in addition to representing them.[72] Even Senate Judiciary Committee chairman, Dixiecrat James O. Eastland (who was also the head of the Senate Internal Security subcommittee), took no interest in allegations about Fortas's ties to Communists. After twenty minutes of debate on the floor of the Senate, Fortas was confirmed as an associate justice on August 11, 1965. The Senate, the same day, confirmed Thurgood Marshall as the first black solicitor general of the United States.[73]

After Fortas moved into the Supreme Court building, it was not long before he called his "boss" to give the president the number of the private line into his chambers.[74] The other justices were aware of this direct line to the White House, and it made some of them uncomfortable.[75] Nevertheless, Fortas continued to have regular telephone contact with the president and frequent written correspondence. While Fortas sat on the Supreme Court, he continued to act as the president's informal legal counsel. He suggested judicial appointments, passed on legislation, and attended White House meetings. Fortas continued to advise Johnson about everything from Vietnam war policy to urban riots.[76]

In January 1966 Jack Valenti, Johnson's special assistant, sent a light-hearted letter to Justice Fortas praising a recent speech Fortas had made. "If you keep up with this speech making, I am going to suggest to the President that we get in the Supreme Court business—you are poaching on our preserve."[77] Joking or not, Valenti was right. Fortas was acting like a presidential adviser, not a justice of the Supreme Court. And soon the White House and the FBI would be getting into the Supreme Court business. The separation of powers square dance that Hoover had choreographed was about to begin. The Executive Branch would be leading, swinging its Judicial partner.

Fred B. Black, Jr., v. United States

When the Supreme Court denied *cert* in the *Black* case, both Justices Fortas and White participated in the Court's decision to let the conviction stand.

After the solicitor general's May 24th disclosure that federal agents had eavesdropped on Black and his lawyer, Fortas formally disqualified himself from participation in the case. He sent a short note to Chief Justice Warren on June 10, before the conference was held that same day.[78] White also disqualified himself, but not until Saturday, June 11, the day after the conference. In a letter to the chief justice, White explained that Marshall had personally advised him that a May 1961 memo from Hoover to White (when he was deputy attorney general) had been brought to his attention. Hoover had sent copies of the memo to Katzenbach and to Marshall on June 3, to prove that Robert Kennedy had approved the bugging. The 1961 memo to White said that "in the interest of national safety, microphone surveillances are also utilized [by the FBI] on a restricted basis, even though trespass is necessary, in uncovering major criminal activities."[79] "Trespass" was a legal euphemism for saying the bug was illegally installed, either after a burglary or after a hole was drilled through the wall.

To make sure the White House knew the "truth," Hoover also sent a copy of his memo to Johnson's special assistant, Marvin Watson, and he continued to keep Watson up to date about his battle with the attorney general over *Black v. U.S.* (On the morning of June 7, DeLoach and Ramsey Clark met in Watson's office at the White House.)

Marshall probably had good intentions when he notified White of the FBI memo. However, this contact, made in the absence of Black's lawyers, was an *ex parte* contact (as lawyers refer to it), which gives the appearance of favoritism and unfair advantage. It is an ethical violation for an attorney involved in litigation to contact a judge or justice about the merits of the case without his opponent's knowledge. Yet the Justice Department made it a policy to contact Justice White when they ran "across [his] tracks" in a case.[80]

At its June 1 conference the Court had already discussed the *Black* case. By the Friday, June 10, conference, the decision to issue the order in *Black* had already been discussed and voted upon.[81] The justices decided that Warren would prepare an order requiring the government to provide the details about the surveillance of Black.[82] Warren's proposed order noted at the bottom that "Mr. Justice Fortas took no part in the consideration or decision of this order."

Despite Justice White's participation at conference, White, in his June 11 letter, asked Warren to add an addendum to the *Black* order before it was issued that Monday. "In view of these matters [about the Hoover memo to me concerning the FBI's use of bugging]," White wrote, the upcoming order should indicate "that I took no part in the issuance of the order." But White had taken part in the issuance of the order the day before. Hoover had won a substantial victory: a likely pro-Kennedy vote would not be forthcoming.

On June 13, the High Court directed a most unusual order to the government in the *Black* case:

> The Court desires a response from the Government in this case, not limited to, but directed in particular toward the kind of apparatus used by the Government; the person or persons who authorized its installation; the statute or Executive Order relied upon; the date or dates of installation; whether there is in existence a recording of conversations heard; when the information concerning petitioner came into the hands of any attorney for the Government and to which ones, as well as what use was made of the information in the case against petitioner.

Chief Justice Warren followed White's instruction.

Mr. Justice White and Mr. Justice Fortas took no part in the consideration or decision of this order.[83]

That same day Hoover had DeLoach phone Justice Fortas privately to provide the "true facts."[84] Fortas returned DeLoach's call late the same night. DeLoach said that he wanted to see him about the *Black* case in confidence but that he recognized Fortas might view this as a "violation of judicial ethics."[85] Fortas said that he would meet with DeLoach about the *Black* case or "any other matter" in confidence. The two men agreed to meet at Fortas's home the next morning.[86] Looking back twenty-four years later, DeLoach said his "primary purpose [in] seeing Justice Fortas was to prevent [former] Attorney General Kennedy [from] causing Fortas to believe that the FBI had acted without authority in the Black case."[87]

DeLoach, who had studied law at Stetson University, and Hoover, who had a bachelor's and a master's of law degree from George Washington University, knew it was grossly improper to approach a justice about a pending case, especially a case in which he was involved.[88] DeLoach, described by one Washington newsperson as a "rattlesnake" and Hoover's "hatchet-man," was very good at his job;[89] the meeting with Fortas was DeLoach's most important mission.

At breakfast DeLoach talked to Fortas about the *Black* case. He said that Attorney General Katzenbach planned to present a "slanted version to the Supreme Court" in an effort to protect Kennedy who, DeLoach maintained, had authorized the installation of the bugs in Black's hotel suite. It was a fight for the presidency, Fortas chimed in: LBJ versus Kennedy. Senator Kennedy was trying to capture Vice-President Hubert Humphrey's liberals. If Kennedy's approval of this bugging were made public, Fortas said, Kennedy would be completely destroyed.[90] Hoover, Johnson, and Fortas shared their hatred for Robert Kennedy,[91] and John Kennedy was no better, as far as Johnson and Hoover were concerned. President Kennedy had reportedly said that the three most overrated things in the world were "the State of Texas, the FBI and the political wizardry of LBJ."[92]

Fortas told DeLoach that the "dumb" solicitor general had "ineptly and inadequately" presented the matter of the bugging to the Court. Fortas said that although he and Justice White had disqualified themselves, they had both attended the conference meeting and discussed the case.[93] The other justices, with the exception of White, who had worked in the Justice Department with Kennedy and Katzenbach, believed that the Court needed to order the government to provide it with information about the surveillance to prevent Katzenbach from hand-picking a federal district court judge favorable to Kennedy who might blast the FBI. Douglas and Black were especially eager to get more information about who had authorized the eavesdropping. Fortas told DeLoach that the Supreme Court had only two options: it could send the case back to the district court, or it could completely overturn the conviction. Fortas believed the Court would send the case back to the district court for another trial.

DeLoach gave Fortas several memos about specific microphone surveillances, including one memo Kennedy had signed. (There were no memos from Kennedy granting Hoover general authority to employ non-national security microphone surveillances after trespassing on the target's property. But orally and in writing, Kennedy had been put on notice that the FBI had illegally installed bugs in organized crime cases.)[94] Fortas agreed with DeLoach that Katzenbach would slant his reply to the questions posed by the Court. The best thing for him to do was "slip in the back door and see the president" at the White House and tell him what was going on.

Fortas and DeLoach also discussed the possibility of setting up a confidential arbiter to compose the government's response to the Court, to take the decision out of Katzenbach's hands. Fortas suggested Kenneth Royall, former secretary of the Army, or Lewis Powell, former president of the American Bar Association, to head up the commission. DeLoach said that Powell had generally supported Hoover's view on criminal matters, but on occasion he had been "somewhat naive and a little weak."

Fortas said that he had already taken steps to disqualify himself in the Jimmy Hoffa case and wanted to know if Kennedy had been involved in any irregularities regarding that case. DeLoach said that Kennedy had specifically asked the FBI to bug one of Hoffa's attorneys—a man named James Haggerty.[95] DeLoach claimed that the microphone was installed, even though the bureau was against it. Fortas said that he would sit with the rest of the Supreme Court on the *Hoffa* case and that he "would make certain that Kennedy was exposed."[96] He believed that the Supreme Court would affirm the decision of the lower court in the *Hoffa* case based on his conversations with the other justices.[97]

At the meeting Fortas also reminded DeLoach that he had secured the favorable reference to the FBI in the *Miranda v. Arizona* decision, a ruling written by Chief Justice Warren, which had been handed down the day before.[98] The case established the *Miranda* warnings (the right to hire counsel [or if indigent, to appointed counsel] and the right to remain silent) that police officers must read to criminal defendants prior to custodial interrogations. Fortas had phoned DeLoach before oral arguments in *Miranda* and then "advised other members of the Court that the Federal Bureau of Investigation had for many years advised subjects of their rights."[99] As a result of Fortas's *ex parte* conversation with DeLoach, the *Miranda* decision praised the FBI for its policy of reading suspects their rights prior to interrogating them.[100]

The breakfast meeting ended with Fortas saying that Johnson supported the FBI's use of eavesdropping in the security and criminal fields, but not for political matters. Fortas said that he knew the FBI was not guilty of such things but that it was Kennedy's "brash practices" that led to the "hysteria" about wiretapping and bugging currently underway. Fortas said that he would call the president before he left for Jacksonville, Florida, that morning.

Fortas phoned Johnson[101] before catching a mid-morning flight to Florida to meet with his benefactor, financier Louis Wolfson, and DeLoach left Fortas's home to brief Hoover. The director was amazed that Fortas had not "weasel[ed] out" by refusing to meet with DeLoach about a pending Court case. The director had doubts about setting up a pro-Johnson arbitrator to investigate the authorization of the Black bugging because it might turn into another "Warren Commission and end in a fiasco." The *Black* case was "the greatest crisis" the FBI had ever faced, Hoover said. "We have got to fight to save our lives," DeLoach agreed.[102] Hoover instructed DeLoach to brief Watson, the president's special assistant, about pro-Kennedy people working with Katzenbach. Although DeLoach and Hoover agreed that Deputy Attorney General Ramsey Clark was a Johnson man—and was honest—he tended to be too much of an idealist, and he was also loyal to Katzenbach.

Hoover told DeLoach that Fortas was not the only justice to speak to the government about a case secretly.[103] According to Hoover, a Justice Department official "went to see two Justices of the Supreme Court . . . [about the] Giancana case in Chicago and he was advised that if it came before the Supreme Court it would be reversed." Hoover said the Justice Department dropped the case as a result of this conversation.[104] Giancana was apparently Sam Giancana, the Chicago mobster whom the CIA allegedly recruited to assassinate Fidel Castro in 1960 and who reportedly had a mistress in common with President Kennedy.[105]

On Tuesday, June 21,[106] Fortas called DeLoach to tell him that the president had decided to set up a three person, pro-Johnson commission on electronic surveillance, not a single arbiter.[107] That afternoon Fortas spent two and a half hours with the president at the White House,[108] the last hour in the presidential living quarters on the second floor.[109] DeLoach also dropped in at the White House that afternoon to visit Marvin Watson.[110] From Watson's office DeLoach called LBJ,[111] who was in the presidential living quarters,[112] to discuss the press release that Fortas had ghostwritten about the creation of the wiretapping commission.[113] The president put Fortas on the phone, and the justice agreed to remove language in the press release to which DeLoach objected.[114] Fortas had collected so many documents from the FBI and the White House about the *Black* case that he opened two secret file folders apart from his official court records on the case.[115]

Hoover employed many avenues to Johnson. Even before DeLoach saw Watson on June 21, Hoover had already spoken on the phone that day with Watson about the *Black* case. Hoover reiterated his view that

Katzenbach was trying to protect Kennedy from the fallout of authorizing illegal surveillances.[116] At the end of the day Watson briefed the president about his talks with DeLoach and Hoover.[117]

The next day, Wednesday, June 22, Attorney General Katzenbach held an afternoon staff meeting in his office about the *Black* case; it was attended by Ramsey Clark, among others. On Thursday, June 23, Fortas and Johnson decided to scrap the wiretapping commission.[118] That afternoon Fortas called Watson, who had spoken with DeLoach that morning.[119] Less than ten minutes after Fortas got off the phone with Watson, Ramsey Clark also called Watson.[120]

While DeLoach had Fortas working within the Court and with the president, DeLoach himself was working with Ramsey Clark to change the wording of the Justice Department's supplemental memorandum, the government's response to the Court's questions about who had authorized the bugging and under what legal authority. Except in written communications, Hoover never tried to discuss the *Black* case directly with Katzenbach, though DeLoach did.[121] According to Katzenbach, even when he met with Hoover and the president in the Oval Office on Saturday morning, June 25 (to discuss FBI agents in the Dominican Republic—see above), the *Black* case was not mentioned.[122] And Katzenbach never discussed the *Black* case with the president at cabinet meetings or elsewhere,[123] believing it was better for Johnson not to be involved in the case. The attorney general had no idea that Hoover was going directly to the White House, attempting to influence the government's response behind his back.[124]

On June 28 Watson asked DeLoach to come to the White House. Watson said that Johnson had suggested that the FBI check with the commissioner of the Internal Revenue Service (IRS) about Kennedy's approval of ELSUR in tax cases.[125] Before becoming commissioner of the IRS in 1965, Sheldon Cohen had been the IRS's chief legal counsel for two years.[126] Cohen was a Johnson appointee and a former law partner at Arnold, Fortas & Porter. Cohen would probably be very helpful, DeLoach said, remembering that Fortas and he had worked together when the FBI was preparing its background report on Cohen after he was nominated to be director of the IRS.[127] Watson emphasized that the president was not issuing instructions to the FBI—he was simply suggesting. Earlier in the year LBJ had blasted Cohen for the IRS's ELSUR practices. "Sheldon—Stop it all at once—and this is final—no more microphone taps or any other hidden devices, legal or illegal if you're going to work for me."[128]

That same day DeLoach also met with Ramsey Clark to raise objections to the department's proposed supplemental memorandum. That memo, to be issued by the solicitor general's office, had to be approved by Katzenbach. As proposed, the memo was going to say that "the Director of the FBI authorized the listening device" or that "permission to place a listening device was given by a duly constituted authority." The FBI objected to either formulation, DeLoach told Clark, because it was Robert Kennedy who had authorized the bugging. DeLoach said that he did not want to "request an audience before the Supreme Court or to . . . put the absolute truth in a formal press release," but he would do that if he was forced.[129] This was another in a line of threats. (Earlier the bureau had warned Ramsey Clark that if the supplemental memo was not the "truth," the FBI was "perfectly willing to lay the evidence before Senator Long's Committee." And Long had already communicated to the Justice Department that he was willing to hold hearings on the *Black* case.[130]) Clark passed on DeLoach's warning to Katzenbach.

While the battle over the wording of the supplemental memorandum continued, DeLoach kept working on Watson, repeating the admonition that the attorney general was a Kennedy man and not to be trusted. On July 11 DeLoach asked Watson to remind Ramsey Clark that Johnson supported Hoover's position that Kennedy had authorized the bugging. DeLoach said that Ramsey Clark had evidently forgotten the earlier talk they had had at the White House. Watson equivocated; he and the president were in a precarious position on the *Black* case because they did not want to be seen as undermining their attorney general. Watson said that he would have talk with Ramsey Clark if the opportunity presented itself.[131]

That same day Ramsey Clark called Justice Brennan's chambers. Brennan's law clerk, Owen Fiss, returned the call. His message was recorded as: "Will be glad to help you [Clark] if he can or will have Justice Brennan call you [Clark] himself when he returns." On July 11 and 12, before the Justice Department filed its brief in the *Black* case, Justice Brennan and Ramsey Clark apparently spoke on the phone. Ramsey Clark's telephone logs at the Johnson Library do not reflect the content of this conversation.[132]

On July 13, despite the machinations of Hoover, Watson, and Fortas, Katzenbach's position on the *Black* case prevailed. The Justice Department's supplemental memorandum to the Supreme Court blamed Hoover for the bugging.

No specific statute or executive order was relied upon in the installation of the listening device in question. . . . Attorneys General have delegated to the Director of the Federal Bureau of Investigation the duty to gather intelligence to investigate violation of federal laws, and to collect evidence in cases in which the United States is or may be a party. . . . Under Departmental practice in effect for a period of years prior to 1963, and continuing into 1965, the Director of the Federal Bureau of Investigation was given authority to approve the installation of devices such as that in question for intelligence (and not evidentiary) purposes when required in the interest of internal security or national safety, including organized crime, kidnappings and matters wherein human life might be at stake. Acting on the basis of the aforementioned Departmental authorization, *the Director approved installation of the device involved in the instant case* (emphasis added).[133]

The government's supplemental memorandum stated that Hoover had been granted broad authority to conduct microphone surveillance. In addition to the threat of an FBI press release or a congressional investigation, Hoover's agents had enlisted the help of the last Republican attorney general, William Rogers, to support the director's contention that he had been granted general authority to bug in organized crime cases, despite the fact that this arguable grant of authority was not committed to paper by Rogers.[134] Every attorney general, including Kennedy, had used information the FBI provided, and they did not want to know how it was obtained.

The Justice Department's memo in the *Black* case confirmed what many had suspected about FBI eavesdropping. *Newsweek* reported that the FBI was "effectively exposed by its parent agency, the Justice Department, as an opportunistic and occasionally illegal user of eavesdropping devices." The revelations made July 13, 1966, "the most embarrassing day of [the FBI's] 58-year life. . . . Faced with this awkward revelation, the bureau officially held to its time-honored modus operandi— never apologize, never explain." The magazine said the "most startling admission" was that until 1965 "the FBI had standing authority to install eavesdropping devices in the homes and offices of any American citizen" when it decided internal security or the fight against organized crime required it.[135]

Hoover had nobody to blame but himself for the *Black* fiasco. He was finally caught exploiting the see-no-evil, hear-no-evil policies of his putative bosses. Hoover's only shred of hope to avoid being singled out by the Supreme Court as the one who authorized the Fourth Amendment violation (and the possibility of being forced out of his job a year after Johnson had exempted him from retirement at age seventy) rested with Justice Fortas or, possibly, with Justice Clark.

But Hoover was not going to wait for the Supreme Court to act. Katzenbach had stood his ground with Hoover, and an attorney general who was not an FBI patsy threatened all unauthorized or extralegal bureau activities. As a result, Hoover started to change bureau practices. Less than a week after the government filed its response in *Black*, a memo was circulated among ranking officials at FBI headquarters.

> We do not obtain authorization for "black bag" jobs [burglaries] from outside the Bureau. Such a technique involves trespass and is clearly illegal; therefore, it would be impossible to obtain any legal sanction for it. Despite this, "black bag" jobs have been used because they represent an invaluable technique in combatting subversive activities of a clandestine nature aimed directly at undermining and destroying our nation.[136]

The memo said that Assistant Director Clyde Tolson or Hoover himself had to approve each burglary and that the authorization was not to be filed with regular FBI records. Despite the implication that "black bag" jobs were to continue, a note at the end of the memo directed that these "surreptitious entries" would no longer be approved. Old bureau hands knew that if such jobs were going to be approved in the future, authorization would be given orally.

Left-Wing Supreme Court Law Clerks Revisited

During the summer of 1966, Fortas was also asked to help Hoover on another Court matter. Justice Brennan had already hired his law clerks for the upcoming term, and one was Michael Tigar, a graduate of the University of California Berkeley's Boalt Hall. A student activist there, Tigar had protested against the House Committee on Un-American Activities and participated in a youth gathering in Helsinki attended by Soviet citizens.[137] At least twenty-eight Congressmen blasted Brennan's selection and threatened to seek an investigation. Tolson prevailed upon Fortas to talk to Brennan. Fortas apparently told Brennan that an inquiry into Tigar's background might be embarrassing to the Court.[138] Brennan backed down, and Tigar was let go the week he came to work.[139] Justice Douglas was furious that Brennan caved in and told him so.[140] Douglas did not know that his good friend Fortas had been the FBI's mouthpiece. The political activities of Vern Countryman, one of Douglas's former law clerks, continued to be watched by the FBI and the CIA into the 1960s because of his "history of leftist affiliations" and membership in the National Lawyers Guild.[141] And Tigar was at least the second Brennan law clerk that the FBI had attacked.

For Supreme Court justices and clerks alike, the winds of the Cold War blew as chilly in 1966 as they had in 1957.[142] And again Justice Douglas was singled out for special treatment.

CHAPTER 5

Justice Douglas
and the Parvin Foundation

Douglas married his first wife, Mildred Riddle in 1923 and was divorced from her in 1953. The following year he married Mercedes Hester, 18 years his junior, and was divorced by this woman in 1963 on grounds of cruelty. Shortly after this divorce, he married Joan Martin, 23 years of age. She divorced him in June, 1965, on grounds of cruelty and personal indignities. Douglas married Cathleen Heffernan, a 23-year-old Los Angeles student on 7/15/66. Douglas's marital ventures have caused a great deal of criticism and during July, 1966, six resolutions were submitted in the House of Representative by various Congressmen seeking an investigation of his moral character.[1]

—A once secret FBI memo

While Hoover and his assistants were trying to deflect blame for the Fred Black debacle, Justice William O. Douglas was having problems of his own. In 1966 Douglas was sixty-eight years old and soon to marry his fourth wife, Cathy Heffernan, a petite, twenty-three-year-old blonde college student.[2] Within days of this marriage there were calls for the House Judiciary Committee to investigate Douglas's moral character.[3] Nothing came of this politically motivated attack, although Hoover, for one, had been receiving tidbits about Douglas's personal life for years. Even Justice John Harlan had a file of newspaper clippings on Douglas, which included articles like "Justice Douglas Takes 4th Bride, 23," complete with a photograph of Douglas and Cathy kissing.[4]

Cartha DeLoach met with Deputy Attorney General Ramsey Clark on August 3 about the *Black* case and related microphone surveillances in Las Vegas.[5] Clark said that Attorney General Nicholas Katzenbach had received rumors that Justice Douglas had been involved in payoffs with Las Vegas hoodlums. Douglas had "so many albatrosses around his neck that one more derogatory allegation would certainly ruin him," Clark said. DeLoach confirmed that the FBI had received information that Douglas was friendly with Las Vegas hoodlums and had asked one of them to visit him in Washington. Clark "dropped the matter immediately."[6] He had evidently heard enough. Clark knew that when the bureau used illegal methods, it often passed the information on to the Justice Department without saying from where it came.[7] Douglas might have been mentioned or overheard speaking in a bug or wiretap targeting someone in Las Vegas. When asked about this twenty-two years later, Clark said that Douglas might have been picked up in a bug targeting a Las Vegas laundry operator during the summer of 1966.[8]

After DeLoach's meeting with Clark, Hoover ordered DeLoach's FBI Crime Records Division to prepare a memo on Douglas, showing any "tieups between Justice Douglas and the hoodlums in Las Vegas and elsewhere."[9] A six-page memo stamped "Secret" was prepared on Douglas, describing his once-cordial relationship with the bureau and a laundry list of pro-Communist decisions, subversive friends, and suspect writings. Part of the memo is still censored (under privacy and law enforcement exemptions), and this may include allegations about Douglas and mobsters or references to Douglas in wiretaps or bugs on suspected mob targets. This secret memo concludes with the statement that Douglas had been known to get drunk and paw women.[10]

While the FBI was telling Clark stories about Justice Douglas, Ramsey's father, Justice Tom Clark, was skeet shooting with agents at the FBI academy in Quantico, Virginia. During this excursion Clark told one of the agents that he was thinking of calling Hoover in the fall to have lunch at the Supreme Court with members of the Court.[11] The day after his outing, Clark phoned Hoover to tell him how much he enjoyed his trip to Quantico and how impressed he was with agent George Zeiss's trick shooting. Clark said he was glad to see that the academy was going to be getting more money from Congress and that, at a recent talk he gave at Bohemian Grove on the subject of law enforcement, he repeated Hoover's "feelings on the limitations placed on law enforcement as a result of the [Court's] new [criminal law] rulings." Clark, who had dissented in part from the *Miranda* ruling because it went "too far," told Hoover that he had received more than two hundred letters from people complaining about the new criminal law decisions and about Justice Douglas's recent marriage.[12]

On September 12, 1966, a "reliable source" at the Supreme Court told DeLoach that Justices Fortas and Clark were "leading the fight to get all aspects of the truth concerning [the Black bugging]" by working together with the other justices to force into the open Robert Kennedy's authorization of microphone surveillances during the time he was attorney general.[13] The informer also said that Justices White and Douglas seemed satisfied with the way the case was progressing. The Court was planning to schedule oral arguments in the case and question Solicitor General Thurgood Marshall about his evasive brief. The Court was said to be leaning toward issuing a "sweeping statement" against the usage of bugging, except in an attempt to save human life, which would endanger all pending cases where electronic eavesdropping was used. The informer said all of the justices except Douglas and White were very angry about Katzenbach's handling of the case.[14]

Was the informer Fortas or another justice? It seems odd that DeLoach or Tolson would use the phrase "reliable source" if they were speaking of Justice Fortas when Fortas's name had been written in numerous other memos that were kept in Hoover's secret Black folder and in their own office files. But because Fortas continued to talk to DeLoach about the *Black* case, it is likely that the "reliable source" was, in fact, Fortas and that he was the FBI's only justice-informer on this case. Whoever the source, it was clear that there were diverse opinions at the Court about what should be done.

One of the chief justice's law clerks, Michael Smith, was clearly disgusted by the Black bugging. Early in the case, prior to the Court breaking for the summer, he wrote a memo to Earl Warren arguing that "to allow a retrial would be to encourage law enforcement officers to violate constitutional rights. . . . The Court should reverse outright and thus underscore the heinousness of the [government's] conduct."[15] Justice Clark's clerk, Charles Reed, was more restrained, writing to his boss that the conviction should be vacated and the case sent back to the trial court for a further hearing.[16] On September 15 Benno C. Schmidt, another of the chief justice's law clerks, suggested to Warren that Black's conviction be vacated and that the district court, not the Supreme Court, determine whether a new trial was necessitated by the illegal bugging.[17] Harlan's clerk, Matthew Nimetz, advised him that Black's constitutional right to counsel had been interfered with and "eavesdropping, police spies and the like—used after indictment and to intercept attorney-client communications—are reprehensible tactics." Like Smith, Nimetz noted in his bench memo that dismissing the case against Black would deter future illegal eavesdropping. But Nimetz said that "although there is considerable validity to the deterrence theory in the abstract, it is too high a price to pay in most cases." If the government were right, he said, and the bugging was unrelated to the tax case, "Black obtains virtual immunity from prosecution as to any crime he committed during that period."[18] Everything considered, Nimetz recommended that Black's conviction be vacated and that the trial court should hold a hearing to determine if any evidence was obtained through the unlawful surveillance.

On September 21 the major players in the *Black* case were in close contact, although it is not known what they were discussing. Lyndon Johnson phoned Fortas twice and DeLoach called Marvin Watson twice at the White House.[19] On September 22 Deputy Attorney General Clark, the Justice Department's liaison with the FBI on the *Black* case, phoned Fortas, the attorney general, the solicitor general, Watson, and DeLoach.[20]

On October 3, before the Supreme Court's first conference of the new term, Fortas phoned Ramsey Clark.[21] Later that day Katzenbach left the Justice Department: no longer able to do his job because of the increasing difficulties between himself and the FBI, Katzenbach took a new job as undersecretary of state at the State Department. Ramsey Clark became acting attorney general.

The FBI had no kind words for Justice Douglas; neither had the press. The climate grew worse for Douglas on October 16, 1966, when the Los Angeles *Times,* in an article by reporter Ronald J. Ostrow, disclosed that Douglas had for four years been receiving $12,000 a year in expense money from the tax-exempt Albert Parvin Foundation, of which he was president. The foundation, established to educate leaders in emerging foreign nations, was funded primarily by mortgage income from the Las Vegas Flamingo Hotel and Gambling Casino,[22] and Albert B. Parvin, the foundation's largest supporter, had an interest in three other Las Vegas casinos. The foundation also had income from stock in Parvin-Dohrmann Company, which had been donated by Parvin and others. That summer the corporation had acquired the Fremont Hotel and Gambling Casino in Las Vegas. One of the Fremont's employees, Edward Levinson, had taken the Fifth Amendment during a Senate investigation of Bobby Baker's business dealings. Levinson also had a lawsuit pending against the FBI for illegally bugging his office,[23] bugs that had snagged some of Black's conversations.

After the *Times* article, Douglas lashed out, believing not only that the FBI had leaked information for the article but also that the Supreme Court "Conference Room was bugged."[24] He circulated an emotional draft opinion in the *Black* case.

> There has been a studied effort made to drive me out of this case. Vicious articles have been printed . . . carrying libelous innuendos that link me with this petitioner, with the underworld, and with others associated with him. I have no acquaintance with petitioner [Black] and no connection whatsoever with him, with his associates, or with the underworld. I file this separate opinion because this is not the first time that powerful forces have tried to drive a Justice out of a particular case.[25]

Fortas was given a copy of Douglas's proposed opinion. He scrawled a handwritten note to Douglas, his former Yale Law School professor and mentor.

Bill,

I hope you don't file that. I hope you don't say anything, but go along routinely. Anything you say will just add fuel to the smoke-fire. This statement may force the FBI to hop on Parvin with all its resources. I don't know the origin of all this. Here is S[olicitor] G[eneral Thurgood Marshall]'s volunteered statement to C.E.A. [Carolyn E. Agger, Fortas's wife]: That a LA Times newspaper man looked at the file of the Parvin Foundation in the LA IRS office and went on from there. This may or may not be all of it—but I wouldn't honor the effort if it has been made—by a statement—and I wouldn't start a fight which you—by reason of your position—can't carry through.

Abe[26]

The Internal Revenue Service or the FBI could have leaked information for the story, but was Fortas's warning to Douglas coming from a concerned friend or an FBI snitch? Douglas had no way to know that the bug in the conference room was Fortas. Douglas suspected that "only one who had access to the privacy of the Conference Room would have known that I was the key person in the case" and that at the October 14 conference the Court was split four justices (Brennan, Clark, Douglas, and Warren) to three (Black, Harlan, and Stewart) to grant rehearing in *Black.* [27] "If I was out of the case, a Court of six would probably end up equally divided," Douglas wrote.[28]

Regardless of Fortas's motives in advising Douglas to not publicly attack the FBI, it was sound counsel. Justice William Brennan, who had no ulterior motive, begged Douglas not to file his separate opinion. "I say this for all the reasons that Abe gives but I add that anything you say will be distorted as an admission of impropriety. . . . To say nothing is to treat it for what it is—just nothing."[29] Douglas followed the advice of his two closest friends on the Court and withdrew his opinion.[30]

Douglas was convinced that the FBI was determined to ruin him. He wrote to Parvin that the "FBI is at present the main force in the drive" to get him off the *Black* case—and off the Court completely.[31] Douglas's concern that the FBI might have bugged the conference room could be dismissed by some as the paranoia of an old man. But Douglas had good reason to be worried. In 1946 the FBI had listened in on Court business and may have inadvertently eliminated Douglas for the position of chief justice. During the spring of 1966 the Central Intelligence Agency had opened his mail and passed it on to the FBI.[32] The FBI was still listening in on some of his phone calls. And—as the cliché goes—just because you're paranoid, doesn't mean that they're not out to get you.

President Lyndon B. Johnson leaned on his friend and advisor, Abe Fortas, before and after he nominated Fortas to the High Court. July 30, 1965 (courtesy of the Lyndon B. Johnson Library).

FBI Director J. Edgar Hoover. July 24, 1967 (courtesy of the Lyndon B. Johnson Library).

Associate Justice Byron White (left) swears in former Attorney General Nicholas Katzenbach as Under Secretary of State on October 3, 1966. President Lyndon B. Johnson looks on (courtesy of the Lyndon B. Johnson Library).

FBI Assistant Director Cartha DeLoach (center) and President Lyndon B. Johnson meet with Eldon James, the national commander of the American Legion. March 3, 1966 (courtesy of the Lyndon B. Johnson Library).

Cartha DeLoach (left) was almost as close to President Lyndon B. Johnson as was Justice Abe Fortas. March 3, 1966 (courtesy of the Lyndon B. Johnson Library).

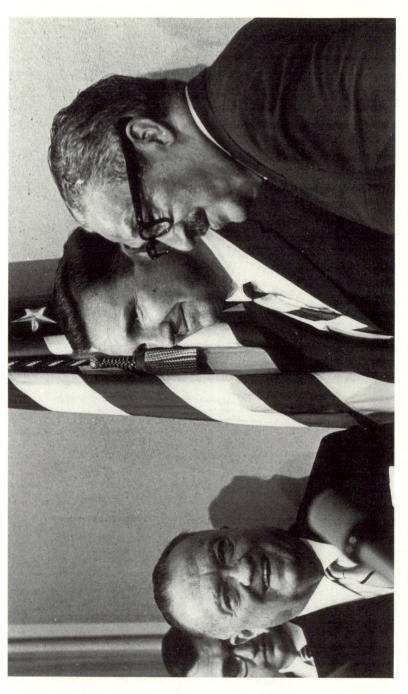

A light moment between FBI Director J. Edgar Hoover and his antagonists, Attorney General Ramsey Clark (center) and Solicitor General Thurgood Marshall. June 21, 1967 (courtesy of the Lyndon B. Johnson Library).

Associate Justice Tom Clark maintained his friendship and loyalty to President Lyndon B. Johnson while he was on the Supreme Court. November 16, 1967 (courtesy of the Lyndon B. Johnson Library).

Marvin Watson, special assistant to President Lyndon B. Johnson, works the phones. March 9, 1965 (courtesy of the Lyndon B. Johnson Library).

Marvin Watson, President Lyndon B. Johnson, and J. Edgar Hoover walking together on September 22, 1966 (courtesy of the Lyndon B. Johnson Library).

President Lyndon Johnson and the Clark family, February 15, 1965. Just over a year later, Ramsey Clark was the Justice Department's liaison with the FBI on the *Fred Black* case, and his father wrote the opinion for the Court. From left to right: Mary Clark (Mrs. Tom); President Johnson; unidentified boy; Georgia Clark (Mrs. Ramsey); Ramsey Clark; Tom Clark (photograph by Abbie Rowe of the National Park Service, courtesy of the National Archives, 79-AR-9034-A).

CHAPTER 6

Return of *Fred B. Black, Jr.,* *v. United States*

My dear Congressman:
[Y]our impression that the FBI engaged in the usage of wiretaps and microphones only upon the authority of the Attorney General of the United States is absolutely correct. . . . [1]
—J. Edgar Hoover to Representative H.R. Gross, December 7, 1966

In contrast to the situation in the 1940s and 1950s, longtime friends Abe Fortas and William Douglas viewed the FBI from opposite sides in 1966. On October 26, the FBI threat against Douglas materialized. Hoover sent a letter to Acting Attorney General Ramsey Clark and to Marvin Watson, detailing Douglas's connections to Albert Parvin.[2] What Hoover evidently did not know was that two years earlier Douglas, with the help of Abe Fortas, had tried to talk Lyndon Johnson into getting involved in a Parvin-sponsored symposium about the Vietnam War.[3]

A week before Hoover sent his memo to the White House, the Los Angeles *Times* had editorialized that the "acceptance of outside income by a member of the highest court in the land . . . raises grave ethical questions."[4] Even if Justice Douglas was not actively engaging in improper behavior, judges are required to avoid the appearance of impropriety. In spite of the controversy, Douglas remained as president of the Parvin Foundation, and at the next board meeting he even suggested that they retain tax attorney Carolyn E. Agger (Fortas's wife) of the law firm Arnold & Porter. Douglas had been visited by agents of the Internal Revenue Service, who asked to look at Parvin Foundation records to see if there were any violations of the tax-exempt status.[5]

Douglas was not going to stop his work with Parvin, and he was not going to apologize. In a letter to Chief Justice Earl Warren, Douglas practically bragged about his efforts on behalf of the Parvin Foundation, saying that it did not interfere with his work on the Court. Douglas pointed out that many justices were involved in extrajudicial pursuits and his was no different. (Douglas did not mention Fortas's relationship with the Wolfson Foundation to support his position.) He did recount how the idea for a non-profit foundation to "combat the forces of communism at the world level" was inspired when Parvin read his book

America Challenged in 1960. Douglas wrote that the foundation's work was helping to turn back the "tides of communism" by contributing to democratic leadership in Latin America and elsewhere.[6]

Douglas may have overemphasized the anti-Communist motivation behind the foundation's work, knowing that the FBI viewed some of its beneficiaries, such as the Center for the Study of Democratic Institutions, as subversive. The FBI had already noted Douglas's ties to the Fund for the Republic and the center. The chief justice passed Douglas's letter to the other justices and to Senator John J. Williams (R–Delaware), who had written to Warren criticizing Douglas about the Parvin matter.

Although Justices Abe Fortas and Byron White had formally disqualified themselves from participating in the *Black* case, both men continued to receive copies of proposed opinions circulated by the other justices.[7] Fortas and White did not vote in *Black*, but they were present in the conference room when the case was debated,[8] and Fortas continued to lobby informally and covertly.[9]

The memos that Hoover sent to Watson had been passed to Fortas, who had placed them in a secret file about the *Black* case. In fact, Justice Fortas maintained four files on the *Black* case—two official court files and two secret files. The first file was the official *Black* court folder, which contained copies of the opinions and memos circulated by the other justices. Other internal court documents relating to *Black* were filed in the *Davis* case folder, an eavesdropping case that would be decided at the same time by the Court. This folder was Fortas's second official file about *Black*-related matters. The third *Black* folder was a secret file on the case; it contained FBI documents given to Fortas by Watson, some of which contained the original White House stamp recording the date and time at which they were received. In addition to five FBI memos, this file contained a two-page blind memo, unsigned and undated, entitled simply "BLACK." The fourth file was entitled "Technical and Microphone Surveillances." This file contained FBI documents that DeLoach gave Fortas at their June 14 breakfast meeting, including the 1961 Hoover to White memo and a memo showing that Robert Kennedy had signed an authorization for a leased telephone line microphone setup in New York that same year.[10]

The two-page blind memo ("BLACK") was apparently prepared by Fortas for his unrevealed clients—Johnson and DeLoach. The memo stated that the case should be "set for hearing on these questions: (1) Where the Government admits that, by the means of a microphone installed through the wall of Petitioner's hotel suite, it has monitored conversations between Petitioner and his counsel, have Petitioner's constitutional rights been violated regardless of the use or non-use of the fruits of the monitoring?" (2) Did it make any difference that the tape-recordings of the bug had been erased? (3) "When and how" were Justice Department officials "made aware of the installation of the listening device?"[11]

This last question echoed one of Hoover's on-going concerns in his battle with Katzenbach over the wording of the government's two memoranda sent to the Court. Hoover had written an angry letter to Katzenbach on May 26, pointing out that the solicitor general's first memorandum to the Court, which said that "long after the trial, in the fall of 1965, attorneys in the Criminal Division of the Department learned that a listening device had been installed in [Black's] suite" was false. Hoover reminded Katzenbach that he had personally sent him a memo on August 24, 1965, advising that a microphone was used against Black and had picked up conversations with Bobby Baker (but not mentioning that Black's lawyer had been picked up as well). The FBI had argued that the attorney general should have disclosed details of the bugging to the D.C. Court of Appeals as soon as he learned of them, before the Circuit Court of Appeals affirmed the conviction on November 10, 1965, and before the Supreme Court decided to consider the case.

Due to Hoover's prompting, the government's supplemental memorandum to the Court correctly stated that the FBI had initially told the Justice Department about the bugging of Black in August 1965, more than a year after Black's conviction for tax evasion. Justice Fortas suggested that the solicitor general be asked when the Justice Department first learned about the bugging, which would spread some of the blame to the Justice Department for withholding information. This third question had been raised *after* Fortas had received copies of the FBI memos from Watson and DeLoach that claimed that the Justice Department was not being truthful in its proposed response to the Court.

That Justice Fortas had prepared a memo on the *Black* case after the government had filed its supplemental memorandum in July is not important in and of itself. What is important is that Fortas framed the issues about the FBI's notification of the Justice Department in such a way as to divert attention away from the FBI by calling into question the Justice Department's assertions about when it learned of the interceptions. It is not clear how Fortas circulated this memo because, unlike the official correspondence between the justices clearly signaling the chambers from which it was issued and the date of issuance, Fortas's memo had neither a name nor a date. But the memo was circulated. One copy is in John Harlan's papers, stapled to a draft of Harlan's dissent in the case.[12] Not only had Fortas reported the justices' conference discussions to the White House and the FBI, but he had also worked to influence the conference debate.

Chief Justice Warren assigned the job of writing the *Black* opinion to Hoover's longtime ally, Tom Clark.[13] Clark was also to write the opinion concerning the John W. Davis case, which dealt with a related eavesdropping issue. A federal prisoner, Davis had been held temporarily in a Florida state jail, where jailers had installed tape-recorders in the walls of the cells in which prisoners met their visitors. Davis claimed that conversations with his attorney might have been taped. The Court was divided over the issue of whether the Court should require the solicitor general to provide information about whether Davis's conversations were actually recorded.

The *Davis* and *Black* cases had both been set for conference on October 3, but Justice Potter Stewart wanted more time to think about *Davis*, and the cases were put over to October 14. At that conference, Clark, Douglas, Fortas, and Warren wanted the government to tell the Court whether Davis's cell at the Florida jail had been bugged. The rest of the justices wanted to have the district court determine the issue by sending the case down for a new trial. Justice Black was adamant that it was "wholly and completely inappropriate" to make the government respond. "I can think of no possible circumstance under which a mere monitoring of the conversation between a defendant . . . and his lawyer would justify a dismissal of his case."[14]

The *Black* case was even more problematic. Justice White had been indirectly implicated in the illegality, due to his receipt of the Hoover memo about microphones installed by trespass. In the average case accepted by the Supreme Court for review, oral argument is scheduled after both parties to a controversy[15] have sent their legal briefs to the Court. The opposing attorneys argue their case and are interrogated by the nine justices in the courtroom. On the Friday after oral argument, at 10:00 A.M., the justices retire to the conference room to vote. But the *Black* case was no ordinary case.

At a later conference discussion of the *Black* case, at least four of the justices had voted to hold oral argument and ask the solicitor general a number of questions. It looked like the FBI's source from September 12 (who had predicted that the Court would put Solicitor General Marshall on "the griddle" at oral argument) was indeed "reliable." Justice Harlan strongly disapproved the unprecedented procedure of asking factual questions of the government at oral argument. Had Justice Fortas, during conference, convinced the rest of the Court to interrogate Marshall during oral argument in an attempt to "expose" Kennedy's role in authorizing the bugging?

Justice Harlan had not bought any of it: he wrote to his brethren: "I wish to record my disagreement with the step taken today in the unusual situation that this case presents.... Without anything more before it than the representations made by both sides, the Court has set Black's petition for reconsideration of the denial of certiorari for oral argument on three questions propounded in its order. I think this unusual procedure is precipitous, ill-advised, and out of keeping with orderly judicial process." Harlan believed that the facts of the case had yet to be determined. "Such an inquiry should be conducted in the customary manner through adversary proceedings at the trial level and not by means of colloquy with the Solicitor General in our courtroom. The orderly procedure is to remand this case to the District Court for a hearing and findings on the occurrences in question."[16]

On October 20, Justice Clark circulated a memo to his brethren suggesting that *Davis* and *Black* be handled jointly because of "the close relationship of the single issue in each case."[17] Clark proposed that *cert* be denied in *Davis*, which would leave the bugging issue to be decided by the district court. Clark had given in to Black and the others who did not want to deal with *Davis*. As for the *Black* case, Clark, despite his pro-Hoover bias, knew that Black's constitutional right to counsel had been violated by the FBI bug. Clark proposed that Black's conviction be vacated and the case be sent back for a new trial. He wrote that this "will also remove any doubt as to Black receiving a fair trial free from tainted evidence. The appearance of justice, like Caesar's wife, must be beyond reproach."[18] Justice Black's absolutist position on the Fourth Amendment was that the invasion of privacy issue itself was irrelevant because the Fourth Amendment protects citizens against unreasonable searches and seizures of "persons, houses, and effects," not seizures of words. So, despite the intrusiveness of the bugging, Justice Black prevailed upon Clark to remove the references to the Constitution, arguing that this "would indicate that we are passing on the constitutionality now—I do not want to do that."[19] Black also objected to the reference to Caesar's wife, for reasons that he did not articulate.

On October 25 at 10:30 A.M., Fortas called DeLoach at FBI headquarters and "expressed appreciation for the information the Director" had passed along to him about a confidential matter.[20] DeLoach said that the FBI was "concerned about the Black case" and asked Fortas "if he knew when a decision would be handed down." Fortas replied that there would be a decision on Monday, November 7. DeLoach asked if the FBI should "prepare for the worst"—a "sweeping proclamation denouncing the use of electronic devices." Fortas said that "the court's thinking had changed somewhat concerning this matter" since they last talked. According to Fortas, "the court actually felt that the Black case and its various problems [meaning the microphone] should not be handled at [the] Supreme Court level." By this, DeLoach understood Fortas to be saying that "the Black case was to be remanded to the lower court." DeLoach reported his conversation to Hoover and Tolson. Hoover ordered DeLoach to "find out the identity of the judge who handled the matter in the lower court."[21] Fortas's unethical contact with the FBI once again gave the bureau a tactical advantage.

At the next Supreme Court conference, Clark's proposal to handle *Black* and *Davis* together was accepted with minor revisions by Warren, Douglas, Black, and Brennan.[22] (Fortas and White had agreed to the joint handling of *Davis* and *Black* and had participated in the *Davis* ruling. Douglas was apparently so confused by White's and Fortas's participation in only part of the joint *Davis* and *Black* ruling that his conference notes show that White voted with the majority to vacate and remand the *Black* case while Fortas did not participate in *Black*.)[23] It was decided that the majority's joint opinion in *Davis* and *Black* would not be signed by Justice Clark, its primary author. An unsigned opinion, called a *per curiam* ruling, is often used for relatively unimportant rulings—or in the most important decisions, when the Court desires the appearance of speaking with one voice.

As Fortas had advised the FBI, on November 7 the Supreme Court issued a two-and-one-half page *per curiam* decision vacating Black's conviction and sending the case back to the district court for a new trial because the FBI's bugging of his suite had picked up conversations between Black and his attorney.[24] Justices Harlan and Stewart dissented, believing that the case should first be sent back to the trial court to resolve the issue about whether a new trial was necessary since the government claimed that it did not use any information from the microphone surveillance in his tax case. The ruling did not mention Hoover. Once again the FBI director's illegal conduct, while embarrassing, did not affect his position. Hoover was fortunate: he had Justice Fortas as an informer and public relations man and an old friend, Justice Clark, writing the opinion in *Black*. The director was also skillful enough to let the chief justice and Fortas know that Justice White, the second in command at the Justice Department a year before the Black bugging, had received at least one FBI memo about bureau eavesdropping practices.

The language of the *Black* opinion was clinical and without passion, offering no indication that the justices were outraged by the FBI's actions. The justices did not quote the words of Hoover, as Justice Felix

Frankfurter had done in the 1954 *Irvine v. California* case involving bugging accomplished by trespass: "[W]hen any person is intentionally deprived of his constitutional rights those responsible have committed no ordinary offense. A crime of this nature, if subtly encouraged by failure to condemn and punish, certainly leads down the road to totalitarianism."[25] Instead, the ruling ended with the assertion:[26] "Mr. Justice White and Mr. Justice Fortas took no part in the consideration or decision of this case."[27]

CHAPTER 7

Paint It *Black*

Berger v. New York
by Associate Justice Abe Fortas

A New York Judge permits a bug
that lands Ralph Berger in the jug
for bribing the liquor board.
A mike concealed on the wall of his room
was entirely effective to lower the boom
and bring Ralph Berger to his doom.

But Berger's case I would assume
will sweep the bugs with a pretty good broom.
Big Brother's day is not yet here.
I think we'll hold that this device
Is not legal nor is it nice. . . . [1]

During Justice Abe Fortas's second term on the Court, listening to the oral arguments of lawyers had become either extremely boring or greatly stimulating. In addition to his extrajudicial sidelines, which included freelancing for the FBI and the White House, playing the violin, and working on behalf of the arts, Fortas sometimes wrote poetry about the cases while they were being argued before the Court. For half a century the Supreme Court might as well have been writing rhyming couplets about eavesdroppers and wiretappers. Although the decision in *Black v. U.S.* was a slap on the FBI's wrist, it was the strongest warning to date. Not since *Coplon* had Hoover's world been so threatened. Even after the Justice Department took the unprecedented step of admitting in Court that the FBI had engaged in illegal bugging with the Justice Department's tacit approval, the bureau's target was sent back to the trial court for another trial. The lesson the FBI had learned from *Black* was that "illegal Government activity in a criminal case, such as a 'bug' or wiretap" does not "make prosecution and conviction impossible" because "the illegality is of no effect if there is no 'causal connection' between the illegal action and the Government's proof."[2] The FBI was concerned that "the group which now commands a majority on the Court" would in future cases involving illegal eavesdropping send cases back for a new trial rather than require that the trial court hold an evidentiary hearing to decide if the trial evidence was tainted by illegally obtained evidence.[3]

Fortunately for Fred Black—and unfortunately for the FBI—Black was acquitted at his retrial. Although Black and other FBI victims could sue the government for violating their rights, not everyone had Black's resources to undertake such a task. On another level, *Black* served as notice to Hoover that the Justice Department did not approve of his conduct: no more winking at illegal bugging while happily using the information. Attorney General Ramsey Clark was no Robert Kennedy. Now if the FBI broke the law, the Justice Department might reveal it to the Court,[4] and Hoover would have to take sole responsibility for any illegal acts. Even so, Hoover would have the help of Justice Fortas when the FBI needed a legal justification for wiretapping without a warrant in national security cases. Fortas was Lyndon Johnson's and, increasingly, the bureau's ace on the Court. For the prior thirty-eight years, the Supreme Court had provided Hoover with innumerable legal loopholes to justify the FBI's warrantless electronic surveillance. But the good old days of agents' tapping and bugging without warrants were coming to a close.[5]

Despite widespread warrantless FBI bugging and wiretapping, at least a part of which the Court had been aware or had suspected, the Warren Court at the end of 1966 was still allowing the government a great measure of latitude in collecting evidence against persons accused of crime. After *Black,* the Justice Department started disclosing electronic surveillances to the courts whenever the information thus secured was, in the Department's view, related to the prosecution. In fall of 1966, the Justice Department ordered the FBI to establish an ELSUR (electronic surveillance) "early warning" system, which required "the Bureau to set up and maintain appropriate indices with respect to electronic surveillance and the material derived therefrom."[6] The department finally had required its component agency to index its ELSUR records properly through a central ELSUR index at FBI headquarters, which contained the "names of all individuals overheard, even incidentally" on warrantless electronic surveillances and, after 1968, court-ordered surveillances.[7] The ELSUR index was to include the names of all persons overheard in wiretaps and bugs from January 1, 1960, forward. For a number of years, even the names of persons mentioned in the phone conversation were listed, but the index was not a complete record because some taps and bugs, like some of those targeting the Reverend Martin Luther King, Jr., and at least two other targets, were excluded under "June Mail" procedures.[8]

In December 1966 the fight over who had authorized illegal FBI buggings during the years 1961 to 1964—Hoover or Robert Kennedy— was splashed on the front pages of the nation's newspapers. To prepare his case for the media, Hoover declassified a number of documents pertaining to microphones and wiretaps that had been shown to Attorneys General Kennedy and Nicholas Katzenbach.[9] Hoover accused Kennedy, and Kennedy accused Hoover, of lying about his role.

Congressman H. R. Gross, a Republican from Iowa, had written to Hoover asking if Kennedy's denials were true. In his reply to Gross, Hoover sent copies of FBI documents as proof that Kennedy had authorized the use of microphone surveillance.[10] The letter and attachments were released to the press by Gross. The front-page headline in the New York *Times* read: "ROBERT KENNEDY AIDED BUGGINGS. F.B.I. Chief Says in a Letter That Ex-Attorney General Was Briefed Frequently."[11]

Hoover had already sent Johnson a "complete set of logs of the electronic coverage" of Black, which included conversations involving Bobby Baker. Hoover's letter questioned "whether the President's name appeared in these logs." The director reminded Johnson that these surveillances had been revealed over Hoover's "repeated objections" to Katzenbach and Thurgood Marshall, who had both insisted on "calling [them] to the attention of the Supreme Court" and thereby opening "Pandora's box."[12]

Despite the battle in the press and at the White House over electronic snooping, the Supreme Court still had not yet ruled that warrantless wiretapping or warrantless eavesdropping, accomplished without trespass, was a violation of the Fourth Amendment.

CHAPTER 8

The FBI versus the Supreme Court, Jimmy Hoffa, and Privacy

[I]n connection with surveillance of the telephone of Dr. Martin Luther King, Jr. [on September 4, 1964, in Atlanta]...[King] was invited to attend [Cassius Clay's] next championship fight. Clay also told MLK to take care of himself, that he is known world wide, and admonished him that he "should watch out for them whities...."[1]

— Wiretapped conversation of Dr. Martin Luther King, Jr., and Muhammad Ali

The Justice Department of Robert Kennedy had sanctioned questionable if not illegal methods in its well-publicized campaign to put Jimmy Hoffa, president of the International Brotherhood of Teamsters, behind bars. Seized with similar gusto, Justice Abe Fortas, to help Lyndon Johnson, violated his judicial oath to uphold the Constitution, revealed confidential Supreme Court conference matters to the FBI, and pledged to Cartha DeLoach that he would expose the lawless side of Robert Kennedy, even though Fortas probably agreed with Kennedy's sentiments about Hoffa: a thug corrupted by ties to the mob.

Hoffa was not an attractive petitioner to the other justices, either. Byron White was deputy attorney general while Kennedy's "Get Hoffa" squad benefited from the work of FBI agents who were bugging and placing informers on Hoffa's legal team. Consequently, White recused himself in every Hoffa case that was related to his tenure at the Justice Department.[2]

Unlike White, Fortas acted in a strange manner when it came to cases related to Hoffa. For instance, Fortas recused himself in a case in which the Teamster leader had been convicted of jury tampering, though he had no apparent reason for doing so. In the related case of Hoffa lawyer Z. T. Osborn, who had also been convicted of attempting to bribe a juror, Fortas initially disqualified himself but eleven months later participated in the Court's decision.

Fortas's dealings with the Johnson administration in his pre-Court days explain some of his behavior on the bench. In 1964, a year before

Fortas was nominated to the Supreme Court and four months after Hoffa was convicted in Chattanooga of jury tampering in the Nashville Test Fleet case,[3] a lengthy internal Justice Department memo about the government's prosecution of Hoffa was delivered to Fortas at his Arnold, Fortas & Porter office at the request of Deputy Attorney General Nicholas Katzenbach. As Johnson's personal legal adviser, Fortas often received government documents. The Hoffa memo was a response to charges that the government had engaged in bugging or other misconduct.[4] Fortas called the memo an "impressive rebuttal" to the charges. Two months earlier Fortas had joked about Hoffa's on-going legal troubles in a letter to Jacob E. Davis II of the Kroger Corporation and he asked Davis, a Johnson campaign contributor and client of his firm, if he had "some good word on [his] friend Hoffa?"[5] A young Jimmy Hoffa and the Teamsters Union had successfully struck Kroger in 1937, and evidently Hoffa was not on the supermarket chain's favorite person list.[6] Despite Fortas's communications about Hoffa's cases, Fortas disqualified himself in only one of the cases involving Hoffa that came before the Court.[7]

When Fortas had met with Cartha DeLoach about the *Black* case on the morning of June 14, 1966, Fortas told DeLoach that "he had already taken steps to disqualify himself in the Hoffa case." (Four and a half months earlier, on January 31, 1966, Fortas had disqualified himself in cases involving Hoffa and Osborn.) Fortas had told DeLoach that the Fred Black, Bobby Baker, and Jimmy Hoffa cases would continue for years. He wanted to know if there was any information he could use against Kennedy in connection with the Hoffa case. DeLoach said that as attorney general Kennedy had specifically asked the FBI to bug one of Hoffa's attorneys, James Haggerty. Justice Fortas said that he would sit with the rest of the Supreme Court on the Hoffa case and would make certain that Kennedy was exposed. Fortas revealed that, based on his discussions with the rest of the justices, he believed that the Supreme Court would definitely affirm the decision of the lower court in the Hoffa case.[8]

James E. Haggerty, Sr., was one of Hoffa's lawyers in the Test Fleet case, which, coincidently, had taken place during the Cuban missile crisis.[9] This case may not have been the only time that the government bugged Haggerty while he was representing Hoffa. In 1961 Hoffa's attorneys, Haggerty and William E. Bufalino, rented a room at the San Juan Hotel in Orlando, Florida, while they worked on Hoffa's defense in a case there. The men found "an electric wireless transmitter" under the shelf of the telephone table in their room.[10]

Osborn was another of Hoffa's Nashville lawyers during the Test Fleet trial. While Osborn was preparing for trial, he hired an investigator to check into the background of the people who would be in the pool of prospective jurors for Hoffa's case. The FBI had already entered into an agreement with this same investigator to serve as their informant. The man, a Nashville policeman named Robert Vick, under authority of a judicial warrant, was wired by the FBI with a recorder that picked up Osborn asking Vick to attempt to bribe one of the potential jurors in Hoffa's case.[11] The government claimed that Vick had agreed to report only the "illegal activities" he observed concerning jury tampering and that he was not sent to spy on defense preparations.

At the conference Chief Justice Earl Warren voted to affirm the conviction; he did not believe that Osborn had been entrapped.[12] Justice Hugo Black agreed—he would vote to affirm. Justice William Douglas believed that the government's use of informers in the Osborn and Hoffa cases violated the "constitutional right of privacy," and he would vote to reverse the conviction. It was "dangerous," Justice Tom Clark argued, "to allow a judge to give judicial sanction" to the FBI wiring up an informer and sending him in to record conversations with an attorney working on a pending case.[13] Justice John Harlan voted to uphold the conviction and was "astonished" to hear the normally pro-prosecution Clark make such a comment.[14] Justice William Brennan "denounced" the government practices in the case, but was still leaning toward affirming. Justice Potter Stewart voted to affirm. Justice Byron White had earlier disqualified himself. Justice Fortas voted to affirm.[15] Before the ruling was issued, Clark changed his position and joined the majority's opinion. Douglas was the only dissenter, citing the "penumbral rights" emanating from the Bill of Rights, which "create zones of privacy." Douglas warned that "we are rapidly entering the age of no privacy, where everyone is open to surveillance at all times; where there are no secrets from the government."[16]

Fortas privately questioned whether he should participate in Hoffa's related case. He had told DeLoach that he would expose Kennedy's authorization to bug one of Hoffa's attorneys, but there was no way to mention it in the context of this particular case. In response to Hoffa's *cert* petition in the jury tampering case, Fortas's clerk, Daniel Levitt, prepared a memorandum for his boss. Levitt recommended that Fortas vote to deny *cert.* "[M]any of the practices in this case are troubling," he wrote, "[but] this is . . . an alleged jury tamperer perfectly capable of tampering again and intimidating witnesses and jurors alike."[17] At the end of another memo on Hoffa, Levitt had written: "In any event, there is the question of your non-participation."[18] It would be dangerous for Fortas to vote on this case because at least two former Justice Department attorneys were aware that Fortas had received departmental memos about it. So, in *Hoffa*, Fortas did not back away from his original decision to recuse himself, as he had done in the *Osborn* case. Fortas did not vote in *Hoffa*.

The majority of the Court did not consider that the use of a government informer sent to befriend Hoffa, who was already facing criminal charges, was ground for reversal. The Court upheld Hoffa's conviction for attempting to bribe jurors.[19] This was the result that Fortas had predicted in his conversation with DeLoach during the summer.[20]

The chief justice dissented vigorously in *Hoffa*. Warren described informer Edward Partin as "a jailbird languishing in a Louisiana jail under indictments for such state and federal crimes as embezzlement, kidnapping and manslaughter (and soon to be charged with perjury and assault)."[21] It was Partin who had contacted federal authorities and told them he was willing to become an informer against Hoffa, who was about to be tried in the Test Fleet case. It was obvious, Warren said, that Partin's motive was to receive help with his state and federal criminal charges and that is why he traveled to Nashville and "manifested his 'friendship' " to Hoffa, "thereby worming his way into Hoffa's hotel suite and becoming part and parcel of Hoffa's entourage."[22] Warren intended his dissent to set guidelines for the permissible use of government informers and to register his disapproval of employing "unsavory" characters who had great incentive to lie.[23]

Harlan's law clerk, Matthew Nimetz, may have summed up the feelings of the Court about *Hoffa* when he wrote in his memo: "[T]he Government pushed . . . the limit[s] of propriety in its well-known campaign to 'get' Hoffa."[24]

Although Justice Fortas had once vowed that he would not leave behind a shred of paper for the vultures of the press to gnaw on after he was dead, he left a substantial paper trail in *Osborn*. Not only did Fortas keep the Justice memo he had received about Hoffa's lawyers, but he placed it in a private file folder entitled "White House—Problems at Dept. of Justice." He also recorded the conference discussions of the other justices about *Osborn*, and he left a public record of his disqualification and later requalification in the published Supreme Court reports. Fortas's flip-flop in the case would have been unusual, even if he had not engaged in grossly unethical backroom discussions with the FBI about *Hoffa*. The conflict that barred Fortas's participation in *Hoffa* did not disappear when the *Osborn* ruling was issued.

Having lost his 1966 jury tampering case in the Supreme Court, Hoffa offered a $200,000 reward to anyone who could prove that his phone had been tapped or his room had been bugged during his trial.[25]

The offer flushed out David Nichols, a man with a history of trouble with the law, who claimed to have snitched for the FBI for ten years and also tapped phones for them. According to Nichols, the FBI and the Justice Department's "get Hoffa" squad had provided him with bugging equipment to wire Hoffa's room during his trial in Chattanooga.[26] Armed with an affidavit from Nichols and four others who said Hoffa and Bufalino were the subjects of systematic electronic surveillance by the government, Hoffa filed a motion with the Supreme Court in January 1967, asking the Court to overturn his conviction and send the case back for a new trial.[27] (For an unknown reason, Hoffa's lawyers apparently believed that Fortas was likely to vote Hoffa's way. They had no way of knowing that Fortas had received government memos about the case when Fortas was in private practice. Hoffa's attorneys filed papers indicating that their client "waived" any objection to Fortas's participation in Hoffa's case. Fortas then "participated" in every subsequent Hoffa case that reached the Court during his tenure.)

The FBI was worried about Hoffa's motion to reopen his case.[28] An internal bureau memo noted that "some disgruntled employee might possibly leak the information with the . . . result of embarrassment to the Bureau and aid to Hoffa."[29] The FBI searched its electronic surveillance indices at fifty-seven field offices.[30] Eventually the solicitor general admitted to the Court that one of Hoffa's co-defendants, S. George Burris, had been overheard in an illegal bug installed by the FBI in the office of Benjamin Sigelbaum six months after indictments were issued.[31] Black's conversations had also been picked up in this bug.

Fortas now had the opportunity to bring up the issue of Kennedy's authorization for FBI bugging, but there appears to be no written documentation to prove that Fortas followed through on his vow to DeLoach. Fortas voted with the majority of the Court to vacate Hoffa's Chicago conviction for mail and wire fraud, and the Court sent the case back to the trial court for a hearing to determine whether any of the evidence was tainted by electronic snooping.[32]

The district court in Chicago held a hearing on the electronic surveillance issue and upheld Hoffa's conviction, finding that the evidence at trial was not tainted by the illegal eavesdropping by the FBI. Once again Hoffa appealed to the Seventh Circuit Court of Appeals. During the oral argument the U.S. attorney "disclosed for the first time . . . that eavesdropping of certain attorneys [in this case] had occurred." The Court of Appeals read the transcripts of the bugged conversations and ruled that they were irrelevant to the prosecution against Hoffa.[33] Although some of the recordings involved the conversations of defense attorneys, the district court ruled that this did not interfere with Hoffa's defense.

Hoffa's attorneys were not allowed to read the wiretap transcripts, which gave Hoffa another good *certiorari* issue.[34] Pointing to the court's failure to give Hoffa access to the transcripts, Hoffa's lawyers again asked the Supreme Court to review his case. Other electronic eavesdropping cases at the Supreme Court were also making headlines.

During the spring of 1967 the Supreme Court issued a ruling that appeared to threaten all government electronic surveillance not involving national security matters. The Court struck down New York's electronic surveillance law. Justice Clark, writing for the majority in *Berger v. New York*,[35] said that the wiretapping and microphone authority given by the statute was similar to the "general warrants" that gave British customs authorities blanket authority to conduct general searches for import tax violations and that were a motivating factor behind the Declaration of Independence. The Fourth Amendment required that a search warrant "particularly describ[e] the place to be searched, and the persons or things to be seized." The New York statute did not require prosecutors to describe particularly the conversations or information to be "seized" and therefore, Clark wrote, gave the police a "roving commission to 'seize' any and all conversations." The law allowed the police to get two-month extensions on wiretap warrants by showing that they were "in the public interest" and there was no provision for a termination date on the eavesdropping. The statute afforded no notice to subjects of the electronic search, as is required of conventional search warrants. In short, the "blanket grant of permission to eavesdrop is without adequate judicial supervision or protective procedures."[36] Justices Black, Harlan, and White dissented.

After *Berger v. New York,* law enforcement authorities were not sure a wiretapping statute could be written that would not violate the Fourth Amendment. As Justice Black asked: How can a search warrant be written that particularly describes conversations to be "seized" in the future?[37] He wrote that *Berger* "set up what appeared to be insuperable obstacles to the valid passage of [State] wiretapping laws."[38]

Legal advisers at FBI headquarters were unsure of *Berger's* effect. They believed that the decision permitted "electronic surveillance generally where no trespass [is] involved, but some doubt remains in this area."[39] Believing that *Berger* "in effect overruled *Olmstead v. U.S.,* which held 5–4 . . . that wiretapping is not a search and seizure," a bureau official recommended that the Section 605 of the Federal Communications Act be amended to "allow wiretapping under appropriate safeguards."[40] Legislation was needed because the Court's "new philosophy"—that the Fourth Amendment "protects the 'right of privacy' " rather than strictly protecting the person, "premises or tangible things"—suggests electronic surveillance might be further restricted by the Court.[41] The FBI saw the writing on the wall—Justice Louis Brandeis's famous dissent in the *Olmstead* case was threatening to become the law of the land.

Enter Justice Marshall—Exit Justice Clark

At the end of the 1966 term, in June 1967, Justice Tom Clark resigned. Johnson had elevated Clark's son, Ramsey, from acting attorney general to attorney general; the elder Clark chose to retire rather than disqualify himself from the many cases that the Justice Department would bring before the Court.[42] Johnson nominated his solicitor general, Thurgood Marshall, to fill Clark's position. Marshall was probably best known for his work as counsel for the Legal Defense and Education Fund of the National Association for the Advancement of Colored People. He had argued over thirty cases before the Supreme Court and won over 90 percent of them, including the historic *Brown v. Board of Education* case in 1954, which banned forced racial segregation in the nation's public schools. President John Kennedy had appointed Marshall to the Second Circuit Court of Appeals. In 1965 Johnson selected him as his solicitor general. The great-grandson of a slave became the first black justice on the Supreme Court.[43] A liberal civil rights advocate had replaced a moderate conservative on the High Court. Hoover was not pleased. Unable to influence Johnson, the bureau leaked anti-Marshall information to the press during the confirmation hearings.[44] The director was sure that Marshall would join Douglas, Warren, Brennan, and Fortas as they continued to expand the Bill of Rights to cover state criminal procedures by incorporating them into the due process clause of the Fourteenth Amendment. The rights of criminal defendants in federal courts would also be strengthened. First Amendment freedoms would be bolstered against federal and state encroachments; protection to members of "Communist-front organizations"[45] could even become possible. And, finally, thirty-nine years after the Supreme Court first ruled that warrantless wiretapping was not an illegal search or seizure under the Fourth Amendment, the Court would reconsider the constitutionality of warrantless eavesdropping, first taking up the issue of bugging, then wiretapping.

During the 1967 term, the Supreme Court overruled its 1942 *Goldman* decision.[46] Electronic technology had exponentially improved, and the Court, in *Katz v. U.S.,*[47] ruled that when the government eavesdropped on citizens without a judicial warrant, the Fourth Amendment was violated whether the surveillance was accomplished by trespass or not. The FBI had placed a microphone in a public telephone booth and had recorded Charles Katz's conversations without a warrant. Katz's conviction for transmitting wagering information by phone was overturned.

Justice Fortas teamed up with Justice White to offer the Johnson administration (and soon Richard Nixon's administration) the new justification for warrantless wiretapping used to "protect the security of the Nation." Inherent presidential authority flowing from the Constitution, White and Fortas argued, was unfettered by the Fourth Amendment's warrant requirement. Justice White put his views in a concurring opinion with which Fortas agreed.[48] Fortas, whether to protect his liberal reputation or to avoid the charge that he was acting once again as a Johnson crony, joined Justice Stewart's majority opinion without qualification.

Fortas had asked Stewart to limit the *Katz* opinion on its facts to non-national security surveillances. Fortas said that he agreed with White that they should "insert something reserving national security cases in which maybe the Constitution would permit electronic espionage on authorization by the President or the Attorney General."[49] Stewart inserted part of Fortas's suggestion into a footnote but left out the reference to presidential authority. The footnote made clear that the Court was not deciding whether safeguards, other than a judicial warrant, were constitutionally acceptable in a case involving national security.[50]

Fortas himself had been picked up in warrantless national security wiretaps and bugs before and after he was nominated to the Supreme Court in 1965. In the 1940s and 1950s Fortas's law firm of Arnold, Fortas & Porter represented over one hundred clients in loyalty cases.[51] These clients had been subpoenaed to testify before the House Committee on Un-American Activities (HUAC), before other congressional committees investigating communists, and before grand juries. A number of Fortas's clients were wiretapped and bugged by the FBI, and his legal advice to them was overheard.[52] Fortas represented Owen J. Lattimore, an expert on China and the director of the Page School of International Relations at Johns Hopkins University, whom Senator Joseph McCarthy falsely accused of being the "top Russian espionage agent in the United States." The 1954 FBI investigation of Justice Douglas was in part a result of Douglas's association with Lattimore. Fortas also represented Dr. Edward U. Condon, a nuclear scientist and director of the National Bureau of Standards, when he was hounded by HUAC and investigated by the FBI. A special subcommittee of HUAC labeled Condon "one of the weakest links in our atomic security," despite the fact that the Commerce Department loyalty board had cleared him.[53] Like other attorneys representing alleged subversives,[54] Fortas's legal strategy and public relations tactics were monitored through bugs the FBI placed in

Condon's home[55] and by informants who tailed Condon and kept track of Fortas.

While on the Supreme Court, Fortas had been discussed by others in conversations that were wiretapped or bugged by the FBI.[56] Despite this, in 1967 Justice Fortas agreed with *dictum* (non-binding language in court rulings) that might encourage warrantless electronic surveillance. Justice Fortas wrote to Stewart that the *Katz* ruling "will be a landmark in the Court's history."[57] Justices Douglas and Brennan disagreed. As if able to see the future, they argued that Justice White's concurrence was "a wholly unwarranted green light for the Executive Branch to resort to electronic eavesdropping without a warrant in cases which the Executive Branch itself labels 'national security' matters."[58] Douglas wrote that "spies and saboteurs are as entitled to the protection of the Fourth Amendment as suspected gamblers like [Katz]." The requirement of the Fourth Amendment for a warrant is not satisfied when the "President and Attorney General assume both the position of adversary-and-prosecutor and disinterested, neutral magistrate."[59] As Justices Douglas and Brennan predicted, the Justice Department and the FBI interpreted *Katz* as having "no effect on eavesdropping in national security cases."[60]

For thirty years Hoover had resisted legislation that would give judges specific authority to issues warrants for wiretaps and bugs. In the give and take of congressional battle, his almost unfettered discretion might have been limited. After *Katz*, it was the FBI, not the Justice Department, that pushed its friends in Congress for federal legislation to allow wiretapping in criminal cases.[61]

The Supreme Court was attacked for the *Katz* decision by law-and-order proponents such as William H. Duckworth, chief justice of the Georgia Supreme Court. He was so outraged about *Katz* that he wrote a bitter, two-page letter to Justice Harlan. Duckworth claimed that the ruling forced the public "to endure crime, solely because some individual officer personally violated rights of the criminal. . . . Concerned and thinking people throughout America are alarmed when our highest court constantly throws road blocks in the path of enforcing the law against criminals." Duckworth said that Supreme Court decisions have allowed the criminal to have "field day." Responsibility for the "floodtide of crime lies primarily at the feet of the majority of the Supreme Court," wrote Duckworth.[62] Presidential candidate Richard M. Nixon and Federal Judge Warren Burger would make similar statements about the Warren Court.

The FBI's electronic spying during the early and middle 1960s made it very difficult for the Justice Department in 1968 to get criminal convictions to stand on appeal against defendants who had been snagged in the illegal wiretaps or bugs. The Justice Department's policy under Attorney General Ramsey Clark required the government to disclose to the federal courts any electronic surveillance of a criminal defendant when a two-part test had been met: (1) The defendant was present or participated in a conversation overheard by unlawful electronic surveillance, and (2) the government obtained information from the surveillance that "is arguably relevant to the litigation involved."[63]

The Supreme Court, with Justice Black dissenting and Justice Marshall abstaining, ruled in *Kolod v. U.S.*[64] that the Department of Justice procedure was not good enough. "We cannot accept the Department's *ex parte* determination of relevancy in lieu of such determination in an adversary proceeding in the District Court."[65] After being convicted, the defendants in *Kolod* claimed that their Chicago office had been bugged. The government did not admit that the defendants had been picked up in ELSUR; it said only that "no overheard conversation in which any of the petitioners participated is arguably relevant to this prosecution." Seven justices took this to mean that Willie Israel Alderman, "Milwaukee Phil" Alderisio,[66] and Ruby Kolod, convicted of conspiracy to make murderous threats, had been wiretapped or bugged. The cases were sent back to the district court for further proceedings concerning whether electronic surveillance had tainted the trial.

In 1968 Hoffa once again asked the Supreme Court to review his Test Fleet jury tampering conviction because he claimed that the government had used evidence obtained through illegal electronic surveillances. Justice Fortas's law clerk, Martha Alschuler, only the third woman to have clerked at the Court until then,[67] forcefully wrote in her bench memorandum that the Justice Department had earlier lied to the Court. "[T]he Government has not even the sense of propriety to come up with some excuse for its failure to reveal the information [about bugging] before. At one point they say their lying is due to the fact that *Kolod* was decided last January and the announced government policy was to reveal that a defendant's conversations had been overheard only when [they were] 'arguably relevant' to the prosecution." Fortas scribbled a note on the memo: "I agree—this is very difficult—but I'd hold for [the] *Alderman* [case]."[68]

The pending *Alderman v. U.S.*[69] case pivoted on whether criminal defendants had a right to see the fruits—the transcripts—of illegal government electronic surveillances so that they could make arguments to the Court about whether the information had improperly crept into evidence or provided leads for prosecutors. The alternative, favored by the government, was for the Court to examine the documents *in camera*—in the privacy of its chambers—and make a determination without the defense ever seeing the materials. The high-visibility cases involving Jimmy Hoffa, Muhammad Ali, and tens of other people caught up in illegal FBI ELSUR would await the ruling in *Alderman*.

The war in Vietnam and domestic strife had destroyed Johnson's chances of reelection; in the spring of 1968 he announced his decision not to run for another term. Johnson's informal war adviser, Justice Fortas, had told him what he wanted to hear, encouraging him to continue the war's escalation.[70] Martin Luther King, Jr., and Robert Kennedy were dead, victims of assassins. And momentous changes were about to take place within the Supreme Court. With Johnson out of the race, Chief Justice Warren knew that Richard Nixon, his fellow Californian and longtime political nemesis, was likely to become the next president. Warren did not want Nixon to be able to choose his successor. At the end of the Court's term, Warren visited Johnson. To allow Johnson to make the nomination and to preserve his options if the nomination were defeated, Warren resigned, effective "upon the appointment and qualification of my successor." Next to Arthur Goldberg's resignation from the Court to make way for Fortas, Warren's conditional resignation had perhaps the most disastrous and unforeseen consequences for the Supreme Court as any retirement decision ever made by a justice.

CHAPTER 9

Death of
the Earl Warren Court

[I] cannot conceive of any President of the United States, and certainly
not this President, talking to a Supreme Court Justice, whether his own
nominee or not, about anything that might possibly come before the
Court. . . . Presidents of the United States do not do that: Justices of the
Supreme Court would not tolerate it. That is our country, Senator
[Ervin]. That is our country.[1]
—Justice Abe Fortas before the Senate Judiciary Committee, 1968

During the summer of 1968 the Warren Court had begun its painful last
throes. Champion boxer Muhammad Ali's admonition to the Reverend
Martin Luther King—"watch out for them whities"—might have been
sound advice for Abe Fortas, who, like Ali, had been picked up in
electronic eavesdropping devices directed at King.[2] During the turbu-
lent summer and fall of 1968, Fortas was Earl Warren's heir-apparent as
chief justice. Homer Thornberry, a federal judge and friend of Lyndon
Johnson, was in line to take Fortas's place as associate justice. But even
with help from the FBI, Fortas's nomination was on shaky ground.

Newspapers carried headlines about political assassinations—King,
then Robert Kennedy—inner cities in flame, Black Panthers, Students
for a Democratic Society, antiwar demonstrations, Hippies, and Yippies.
America was preoccupied with the issue of crime, which often coalesced
with the issues of the Vietnam War and race relations. And the Warren
Court was frequently blamed. Federal Judge Warren E. Burger, "close
friend of the [FBI] Director and a staunch supporter of the Bureau over
the years," rode the anticrime bandwagon, complaining that his colleagues on the bench "nit-picked" in criminal cases in an effort to
obtain "perfect" trials rather than "fair ones" and ended up producing a
"society incapable of defending itself" against the criminal.[3] Domestic
turmoil was so severe that Justice Fortas offered his own "alternative to
violence" in a small book called *Concerning Dissent and Civil Disobedience.* Fortas condemned lawbreaking, even when done in the name of
righteous, political causes, and argued for the rule of law in effecting
political change. "Protesters and change-seekers must adopt methods
within the law. . . . Any mass demonstration is dangerous, although it

may be the most effective constitutional tool of dissent. . . . The functions of mass demonstrations . . . do not include terror, riot, or pillage."[4]

Congressional action to fight crime culminated in the push for passage of the Omnibus Crime Control and Safe Streets Act of 1968.[5] Title III of the act regulated the interception of wire and oral communications, effectively amending the Section 605 of the Communications Act of 1934,[6] to allow the FBI to wiretap. The law also regulated nonconsensual microphone surveillance. "Much of Title III was drawn to meet the constitutional requirements for electronic surveillances enunciated by [the Supreme Court]" in *Berger v. New York* and *Katz v. U.S.*[7] After obtaining a judicial warrant, the FBI was allowed to wiretap and bug to obtain evidence of specified crimes. Warrants could be authorized for electronic surveillance directed at serious Atomic Energy Act offenses as well as offenses relating to espionage, sabotage, treason, riot, murder, kidnapping, robbery, extortion, presidential assassination, and a host of others.[8]

The FBI, believing that the Supreme Court would continue to restrict warrantless electronic surveillance, had secretly lobbied Congress to authorize wiretaps and bugs in criminal cases, a position that had been opposed by Ramsey Clark's Justice Department. President Johnson and his attorney general backed a bill that would allow electronic snooping only in national security cases.[9]

Prior to this, Hoover had always opposed legislation that would grant federal judges the authority to issue warrants for wiretapping and bugging.[10] But by 1968 the combined effects of the Long Committee investigation and the *Black, Berger,* and *Katz* rulings had forced Hoover to support legislation that would require him to ask a neutral and detached judicial official to do what Hoover had been doing on his own for decades.

The bureau had begun its behind the scenes lobbying for wiretapping legislation during the winter of 1966–67. Though the Johnson administration favored a law that allowed electronic surveillance only for national security, Hoover disagreed.[11] As a result, Cartha DeLoach worked with friendly senators to support Hoover's position. DeLoach received cooperation from several senators, including John McClellan, chairman of the Senate Subcommittee on Criminal Laws and Procedures, and James O. Eastland, chairman of the Senate Judiciary Committee, to ensure that any proposed wiretapping and bugging provisions would allow electronic devices to be used against non-national security targets—and let the FBI do what it had always done in the national security area—eavesdrop at will.[12] Senator Eastland had already sent his proposed wiretap legislation to the FBI for comment.[13] The former U.S.

attorneys of the Southern District of New York, backing the bureau's position, had sent a letter to Senator McClellan, urging him to amend the Federal Communications Act to allow wiretapping for federal and state crimes.[14] Other bureau allies, including New York Governor Nelson Rockefeller and sympathetic members of the press, also supported Hoover's efforts to get such legislation passed.[15]

Senator Edward Long had introduced his own wiretapping legislation, the Right of Privacy Act, which was cosponsored by twenty-two other senators and supported by the Johnson administration.[16] This act limited FBI technical and microphone surveillance authority to national security cases.[17] Hoover may have viewed the bill as a double-cross by Long. The FBI had compiled "dossiers on the personal lives of the senator [Long] and his committee colleagues (which undoubtedly contributed to silencing the Long committee's probe of government eavesdropping in the first place)."[18] FBI leaks were behind a *Life* magazine expose about Long receiving $48,000 in referral fees from a lawyer "for the Teamsters Union and its president, James R. Hoffa, as a concealed bribe to prevent or reverse Hoffa's conviction on criminal charges." This article appeared after Long's committee had begun hearings on a wiretap bill in the spring 1967.[19]

Despite effective lobbying by DeLoach, the FBI was not able to amend Title III to grant immunity to FBI agents in suits for damages brought by targets of the electronic spying, even though such agents were acting under presidential authority.[20] And though the bureau considered the statutory requirement of requesting a judicial warrant before authorizing electronic surveillance "cumbersome," it believed that Title III "would provide improved means of gathering top-level intelligence against La Cosa Nostra" and that that information "would be legally admissible" in court.[21] Title III specified that it was not limiting

the constitutional power of the President to take such measures as he deems necessary to protect the Nation against actual or potential attack or other hostile acts of a foreign power, to obtain foreign intelligence information deemed essential to the security of the United States, or to protect national security information against foreign intelligence activities . . . [or] to protect the United States against the overthrow of the Government by force or other unlawful means, or against any clear and present danger to the structure or existence of the Government.[22]

FBI electronic intercepts—placed by virtue of the *constitutional* power of the president—would be admissible as evidence in court. But where was the constitutional power of the president to wiretap and bug without a warrant? Opponents of Title III argued that this open-ended language invited abuses by the White House. Proponents claimed that the language simply affirmed the president's inherent powers.[23]

Although Hoover had realized that it would be the Supreme Court that would determine the extent of the president's electronic surveillance (ELSUR) authority consistent with the Fourth Amendment, the bureau had lobbied to expand the statutory language acknowledging inherent presidential authority. The FBI had argued that authority to place electronic intercepts "to protect the United States against the overthrow of the Government by force or other unlawful means" should be expanded by adding the phrase, "from domestic groups or individuals whose activities he deems inimical to the internal security of this country."[24] The FBI feared that the general language would not permit its agents to tap or bug domestic Communists and subversives. Congress declined to add the bureau's proposed language to Title III. Hoover ultimately agreed that the two provisions of the act that concerned national security intercepts would "fulfill the Bureau's needs in the security field" if, and only if, "these portions of the Act are held constitutional by the Supreme Court."[25] (Hoover's concerns about the Supreme Court came to pass, but not until 1972, when the Court ruled in *U.S. v. U.S. District Court* that the president had no authority to wiretap domestic subversives without a judicial warrant.[26])

The White House signaled to Congress that it would not veto the Omnibus Crime Control and Safe Streets Act of 1968, even though it allowed for the non-national security electronic snooping opposed by the president and Attorney General Clark.[27] Before President Johnson signed the bill into law on June 19, 1968, a copy was sent to Justice Fortas for his "comment."[28] At the signing of the bill, Johnson denounced the broad electronic surveillance provisions as "unwise and dangerous" and urged Congress to repeal that part of the law.[29]

The following week, on June 26, Johnson announced the resignation of Warren and the nominations of Fortas as chief justice and Thornberry as associate justice.[30]

The president had attempted to garner support for Fortas before the public announcement, for he had been warned that the nomination would fail. Johnson simply did not believe there was sufficient opposition to block confirmation.[31] Attorney General Clark was not advised of Warren's resignation until after Warren's talk with Johnson, and Clark was not asked to have the FBI reinvestigate Fortas.[32] There were good reasons for not conducting another FBI investigation of Fortas: Johnson, Hoover, Clyde Tolson, and DeLoach all knew that Fortas had revealed confidential Supreme Court conference discussions to the Executive

Branch. For obvious reasons, that information would not be passed on to the Senate Judiciary Committee. In addition, Clark, who apparently was not aware of Fortas's indiscretions in the *Black* case, believed there would be a separation of powers problem with conducting a background investigation about a sitting justice of the Supreme Court. The Executive Branch should not be investigating the Judicial Branch, according to Clark: "To go to an associate justice and say, 'Okay, now, are you an honorable man? Have you done anything dishonest? Have you taken bribes, or have you done things foolish?' Just can't be done."[33] As a result, the money Fortas had received from Wolfson in 1966 and his unethical behavior during the *Black* case would not surface during the confirmation hearings. Instead, Fortas's advice to President Johnson, his rulings on obscenity and subversive cases, and financial improprieties would become the issues his opponents would seize upon.[34]

Shortly before his appearance before the Senate Judiciary Committee, Fortas phoned DeLoach at FBI headquarters,[35] to tell him that "a 'nose count' " revealed that approximately sixty-five members of the Senate were in favor of his confirmation as chief justice. Some of the dissenters, Fortas told DeLoach, did not realize the strong stand he had taken on several occasions to defend law enforcement interests.[36] After their clandestine work on the *Black* case, Fortas and DeLoach had remained close, close enough that DeLoach had invited Justice and Mrs. Fortas to a small dinner party at his home, along with Attorney General Clark and an assistant attorney general.[37] On another occasion, DeLoach attended a chamber music concert at Fortas's home.[38] DeLoach was being counted on by the White House to help out in the push to get Fortas confirmed as chief justice.[39]

With the cooperation of both the FBI and the White House, Fortas did not have to worry about the *Black* case haunting him during his Senate Judiciary Committee testimony. He looked Judiciary Committee members in the eye and said: "[S]ince I have been a Justice, the President of the United States has never, directly or indirectly, approximately or remotely, talked to me about anything before the Court or that might come before the Court. I want to make that absolutely clear. [I have participated] in conferences on critical matters having nothing whatever to do with any legal situation or with anything before the Court."[40] Fortas was offended at the intimation that the truth was otherwise. Fortas also lied about his role as presidential speech writer and drafter of legislation while on the Court.[41]

Having no way to know about DeLoach's close relationship with Fortas, a member of Senator Robert P. Griffin's staff visited DeLoach on September 23, 1968.[42] Griffin, a Republican, was one of Fortas's most outspoken opponents. Assuming that Hoover and DeLoach did not want Fortas confirmed, the aide said that Griffin had "received considerable information which he feels represents possible conflict of interests and violation of the . . . separation of powers on the part of Justice Fortas." He had contacted DeLoach because Senator Griffin "is having considerable difficulty in 'running out' [the leads] because of a lack of trained investigative personnel."[43] Griffin needed the FBI's "expertise" in investigating because he knew that Attorney General Clark "fully endorsed Fortas and would not authorize the FBI to conduct [an] investigation along lines which might seek to discredit him." DeLoach said that it was "impossible" to help because an investigation of this type would have to be done at the request of the attorney general.[44] DeLoach and Hoover could have destroyed Fortas's chances of confirmation and provided the Senate with information that would have led to calls for Fortas's impeachment. But the secrets shared by the FBI and Fortas were safely hidden away in Hoover's confidential files.

Even without the help of the FBI, opposition to Fortas escalated beyond Griffin and the southern Senators led by Sam Ervin, McClellan, Robert Byrd, Eastland, and Strom Thurmond. In addition to Fortas's advice to the president and his help in drafting legislation and White House speeches, Fortas had received a $15,000 fee paid by five wealthy benefactors who had been solicited by Fortas's former law partner, Paul Porter. Fortas had received the money as payment for a series of lectures he had given during the summer of 1967 at American University.[45] According to Porter, Fortas was not told the source of his lecture fees.[46] During the Judiciary Committee hearings Thurmond pointed out that all of the donors were successful businessmen who held important posts in the banking and insurance industries and whose business controversies might some day reach the Supreme Court.[47] Three of the five donors were former Fortas clients, and all were friends of the justice.[48]

The conservative opposition also pounced on Fortas's rulings in obscenity, criminal, and subversive cases as evidence of his hard-core liberal values. Thurmond claimed that Fortas had an "appalling record" in obscenity cases, even worse than the full Court's record. Thurmond said that Fortas voted thirty-five out of thirty-eight times to reverse obscenity convictions of the lower courts, with one case held moot and two convictions affirmed. The opposition also put in the record that "Fortas joined in the majority [when it] stripp[ed] the State of New York of its rights to prohibit Communists from teaching in its educational institutions" and that he joined the Court's ruling that a portion of the Subversive Activities Control Act "which prohibited Communists from working in defense plants" was "unconstitutionally broad" and violative of the right of association.[49]

The Fortas confirmation could have survived his judicial rulings and his friendship with the president. As pro-confirmation forces had repeatedly pointed out, Justice Felix Frankfurter had advised Franklin Roosevelt while Frankfurter was on the bench.[50]

Not publicly known at the time, Chief Justice Fred Vinson had often advised President Harry Truman about political matters.[51] Like Vinson and Frankfurter, Fortas's relationship with his president had predated his days on the Court. Neither supporters nor opponents of Fortas knew that he was not the only justice to moonlight for Johnson. In 1965 Justice William O. Douglas had prepared a legal memo for the president at Fortas's prompting.[52] That same year Justice Arthur Goldberg had sent Fortas a list of attorneys names for the president's crime panel.[53] The opposition also could not know that as a private lawyer Fortas had received confidential Internal Revenue Service documents about Bobby Baker's tax troubles.[54] Despite the fact that Justice Fortas often crossed the separation of powers line drawn by the Constitution, he had scrupulously avoided sitting on cases that involved his former law firm, Arnold & Porter.[55]

But it was Fortas's perceived ethical failings, the American University revelation in particular, that turned the tide against him. On October 1, a Senate vote on a procedural point failed to force a final vote on the confirmation. Never before had the Senate attempted to filibuster a Supreme Court nomination. President Herbert Hoover's 1930 nominee Federal Judge John J. Parker was the last Supreme Court nominee to be rebuffed by the Senate.[56] Within days of the Senate vote, Johnson withdrew the nomination at Fortas's request.

The year 1969 saw a new president, Richard M. Nixon, a new attorney general, John N. Mitchell, and, within six months, a new chief justice. Mitchell, a Wall Street lawyer who had graduated from Fordham Law School in 1937, had been a partner in Nixon's law firm. After Nixon announced his selection for attorney general, the bureau ran a record check on Mitchell that came up blank—the FBI had *no* information in its regular files about him.[57] Mitchell celebrated the fact that not even *Who's Who* had listed him before he was tagged for the "top-cop" job in the country.[58] Before he took office, Mitchell told the press, "I've somehow got to dispel the notion that I'm a tough cop and an arch-conservative."[59] However, his tenure only confirmed that notion. When asked whether the Fifth Amendment—the constitutional privilege against compelled testimony—should be repealed, as some Nixon supporters had suggested, Mitchell answered, "When you start tampering with the

Bill of Rights that raises a lot of other considerations down the road."[60] But Mitchell, as campaign manager, as attorney general, and as close personal friend and political adviser to the president, had his own share of scrapes with the Constitution and federal criminal laws.

To avoid a showdown with the new Nixon administration, Warren had promised to resign at the end of the Court's term in June, thereby avoiding a fight over whether he had "resigned" in June 1968.[61] But until then, it was business as usual.

Edward Boykin, Jr., a twenty-seven-year-old black man, had his Alabama death sentence overturned by the Supreme Court, even though he had pleaded guilty to murder and had had a court-appointed lawyer. The Court said that the lower court record did not affirmatively show that Boykin's decision was made voluntarily and intelligently.[62] In *Spinelli v. U.S.* the High Court elaborated upon the requirements for establishing probable cause necessary for the issuance of a search warrant based on information supplied by a confidential informant; in so doing, it reversed the conviction of gambler William Spinelli after the FBI's search warrant application was held to be deficient.[63] In *Tinker v. Des Moines* Justice Fortas, writing for the Court, gave high school principals a civics lesson on the First Amendment. Student protesters who had worn black armbands decorated with peace symbols in opposition to the war in Vietnam did not "shed their constitutional rights to freedom of speech or expression at the schoolhouse gate."[64] Likewise, the justices ruled that an Ohio Ku Klux Klansman had a First Amendment right to preach racial hatred in his calls for vengeance—for sending "niggers" back to Africa and Jews to Israel—during a cross-burning at which other hooded Klan members carried firearms.[65] And a divided Court overturned Sidney Street's conviction for "malicious mischief" after he burned an American flag while shouting "We don't need no damn flag."[66] Criminal convictions of civil rights demonstrators in Chicago, Illinois,[67] and Birmingham, Alabama,[68] were likewise struck down as violations of the Constitution.

John Mitchell v. the Supreme Court

By March 1969 the *Alderman* electronic surveillance ruling had been pending for over a year. On March 10, the Court issued its long-awaiting decision in a trilogy of cases, *Alderman, Ivanov,* and *Butenko.*[69] (Willie Israel Alderman of Chicago had been convicted of conspiring to make murderous threats, but his case did not involve espionage. In an unrelated case, Igor A. Ivanov, a Russian secret agent, and John William

Butenko, an American citizen who had access to classified information about an Air Force command and control system,[70] were convicted of conspiring to give the Soviet Union information about U.S. national defense.)

At least twenty cases possibly tainted by illegal electronic surveillance, including Muhammad Ali's and Jimmy Hoffa's, were awaiting the triple ruling that would come to be known simply as *Alderman*.[71] *Alderman* was so important to the Nixon administration that the Justice Department, in violation of legal ethics and established protocol, sent an emissary to the Supreme Court to ask the justices to reverse their decision.

Alderman set forth the "standards and procedures" that the federal district courts were required to follow in determining whether criminal convictions were tainted when the FBI illegally intercepted conversations. The government was primarily concerned that criminal defendants in espionage cases not obtain access to the wiretap transcripts. The Justice Department argued that the courts should trust the word of prosecutors that a particularly sensitive ELSUR (such as one directed at foreign embassies) did not affect the fairness of the trial. Under this scenario, the wiretap or bug transcript would *not* be given to the defendant *unless* the judge first determined that the evidence was arguably relevant to the prosecution. The defense lawyers would be at a disadvantage by not having access to the documents and the chance at an adversarial hearing.

The Supreme Court rejected the government's position. Justice White's plurality opinion was joined by Warren and Douglas. Marshall disqualified himself.[72] Black dissented, with Stewart, Fortas, and Harlan dissenting in part. The Court ruled that the FBI had to turn over the logs (the written transcripts) of the unlawful ELSUR to all criminal defendants, thus enabling defense lawyers to make informed arguments about whether the trial had been tainted.

Justice Fortas agreed with part of the Court's decision, but dissented when it came to "national security material," activities specifically related to "acts of sabotage, espionage, or aggression by or on behalf of foreign states." These transcripts, he wrote, should not be "turned over to the defendant or his counsel for their scrutiny" when the "Attorney General has personally certified that specific portions of the unlawfully obtained materials are so sensitive that they should not be disclosed." Fortas argued that the trial court should review this electronic surveillance evidence *in camera* and determine whether any of the information is relevant to the prosecution. Fortas the presidential adviser and FBI informer was winning out over Fortas the criminal defense lawyer.

Two days after the *Alderman* ruling, the director of public informa-tion at the Justice Department, Jack C. Landau, an acquaintance of Justice William Brennan's, made an appointment to see him about "an extremely important matter."[73] Landau told Brennan that he had been sent by Mitchell to talk about the ramifications of *Alderman*. (Mitchell had selected Landau because he had been acquainted with Brennan while he was a newspaper reporter, prior to being hired by the Justice Department.) Landau said that due to the *Alderman* ruling the president, the attorney general, the solicitor general, the FBI, and the CIA were very concerned that the government might have to dismiss a number of prosecutions in which criminal defendants had been inadvertently overheard by ELSUR devices directed at the 125 foreign embassies in Washington, D.C. He said that this had not been revealed to the Court because the solicitor general thought that the recent Court appointees who had served in the Justice Department, Thurgood Marshall and Byron White, were no doubt aware of this and would presumably pass this information on to the other justices. The solicitor general and the attorney general, Landau said, did not know how to bring this informa-tion to the Court's attention without it being made public.

Brennan told Landau that he would have to speak with the chief justice. Landau was apprehensive, but eventually agreed. In the chief justice's chambers, in addition to repeating what he had told Brennan, Landau said that Mitchell wanted to assure the Court that he would do everything in his power to stop congressional moves to limit the Supreme Court's jurisdiction concerning national security surveillances. There were no pending bills to limit the Court's jurisdiction, however, and the chief justice took this statement to be a threat: if the Court did not reverse its *Alderman* ruling, legislative action might be forthcoming at the behest of the Nixon administration.

The chief justice explained that this contact with the Court was improper. He would listen to any argument the Justice Department had to make *in* the courtroom, not in secrecy without defense counsel present.

After Landau left, Warren called a conference and related Mitchell's message to the other justices. The Court decided that the Justice Department's overtures would not be made public, a decision the chief justice later came to regret in the wake of Watergate. Warren wrote in his memoirs that this was the only incident he was aware of in which the Executive Branch had illicitly tried to influence a Supreme Court decision.

Two weeks later, on March 24, the twenty other cases involving electronic surveillance were accorded "*Alderman* treatment," despite the Justice Department's subtle threats. All of the cases, Hoffa[74] and Ali included, were sent back to various district courts for hearings to determine whether tainted evidence from the unlawful wiretappings or buggings had crept into evidence at the trials.

It was during this time that Justice Douglas again voiced his conviction that his chambers had been bugged. He insisted that Dagmar Hamilton, the editor of his autobiography, walk with him outside the Court building before discussing his book when she visited.[75] As early as 1967 Douglas had suggested to his clerks that his chambers were being bugged.[76] Douglas would continue to believe that the Court had been targeted. At the time of the Watergate hearings, Justice Douglas proclaimed in a dissenting opinion: "I am indeed morally certain that the Conference Room of this Court has been 'bugged.' "[77] (Chief Justice Warren Burger, also concerned about wiretaps and electronic bugs, had asked the FBI to conduct a sweep of the conference room for listening devices before proceedings "at the Court regarding Watergate."[78])

With—or without—the help of ELSUR, the new occupant, Richard Nixon, would soon have Fortas in his sights. But the FBI was not going out of its way to help Nixon—or Mitchell—load their guns.

Exit Abe Fortas

The Department of Justice housed several individuals who were more than willing to help Nixon force Fortas from the Court. Will Wilson was one of them: a longtime Texas Democrat, Wilson had had a falling out with Johnson and owed his job in the Nixon administration to the help he had given the Republicans at election time.[79] On April 14, 1969, Wilson, assistant attorney general of the Criminal Division, wrote to Hoover that "reliable information" had been received, showing that convicted[80] stock manipulator Louis Wolfson had sent Justice Fortas a check for $20,000 in 1966 and that Wolfson had claimed that "Fortas would make efforts on his behalf to block the Securities Exchange Commission prosecution."[81] Wilson also said that he had other "reliable information that during 1966 Mr. Fortas did go to Florida and spent two or more days with Wolfson on the latter's farm or ranch." Did Hoover have "any [FBI] information relating to this matter"? The FBI director replied that a search of FBI files found no information about an association between Fortas and Wolfson.[82] (In the hour before Fortas had flown down to Florida to meet with Wolfson, DeLoach had met with Justice Fortas during breakfast on June 14, 1966. FBI documents in the offices of Hoover, Tolson, and DeLoach recorded that Fortas was flying to Florida after he met with DeLoach. But, as was customary, the confidential office files of the director and his top assistants were not searched in response to Justice Department requests.)

An enterprising reporter for *Life* magazine, William Lambert, had known about Fortas's connection to Wolfson since the fall of 1968 by way of a tip from a career employee at the Internal Revenue Service.[83] Lambert's notes of his October 29, 1968, conversation record that the IRS was aware that Fortas had been involved in a "situation involving money" received "in a 'slippery' act," which his source believed was "a law violation."[84] Paul Porter, one of Fortas's former partners at Arnold, Fortas & Porter, confirmed to Lambert that Fortas had received $20,000 from the Wolfson Family Foundation. Fortas did not list it as income on his tax return, Porter told Lambert, because he paid the money back during the same tax year. Through interviews with government prosecutors and Wilson, in April 1969, Lambert reconfirmed some dates in his story; in return Wilson used Lambert's information to build his case.[85] Lambert says that he when he first spoke with Wilson about Wolfson and Fortas, it appeared to him that Wilson had not known about the $20,000 payment.[86] As for reports that the Nixon administration had leaked the Fortas story, Lambert said, "If anything, I leaked it to the Nixon administration."[87] Lambert said he "stayed the hell away from the bureau on this," even though he had sources at the FBI, because the bureau at the time was politicized by Hoover.[88]

No matter who was doing the helping, with Justice Fortas the subject of Executive Branch interest, Wolfson, who was represented by former Justice Department prosecutor William Bittman, was in a good position to make a deal. If Wolfson talked about Fortas, Wolfson might get his sentence reduced. Bittman approached Wilson in Washington because holdover Democratic U.S. attorney Robert Morganthau in New York City did not want to cut a deal.[89] Morganthau had no motive to help Wolfson in exchange for information about Fortas.[90]

"The effort that led to Fortas's resignation didn't come from the FBI. It came from Bill Bittman," Wilson remembered. Before the *Life* magazine article came out, Bittman went to see Wilson "about trying to work out a plea bargain" in exchange for giving up "alot of dope on [Justice Fortas.]"[91] According to Wilson, "[T]he overriding nature of this thing was to get Fortas off the Court. From the standpoint of the [Nixon] Administration, Fortas was an impediment on the Court. He was the number one guy in the way [voting] pretty steadily against the Government on law enforcement issues."[92] DeLoach agreed with Wilson about the FBI's role vis-à-vis Fortas. "Mr. Hoover took no action and made no comments concerning the resignation of Justice Fortas," DeLoach remembered. "[H]e meticulously avoided being involved in the matter."[93]

This was true, even though it was DeLoach who had been on personal terms with Fortas, not the director.

On April 23, 1969, Hoover and Nixon discussed Lambert's upcoming *Life* magazine exposé on Fortas. Hoover recorded a memo for his top assistant directors, including Tolson and DeLoach, about his conversation.

> The President said . . . *Life* is coming out with an expose on Abe Fortas. I said they have a story by [William Lambert] and the President said that I knew about it then. I said it is a very strong story as they went to see Fortas to see what answer he was going to make, if any, in order to protect themselves from libel. I said . . . so if he has the facts, and I understand he does, it [the story] ought to do something. The President asked why a man like Fortas, who does not need the money would do such a silly thing.[94]

The director, eager to please the new president, told Nixon that he was also looking into a possible real estate conflict of interest concerning Justice Fortas and liberal Federal Judge David Bazelon, about which he was "hoping to dig something up." Fortas should be off the Court, Nixon replied.[95]

Strangely, Hoover did not mention Wilson's memos about Wolfson and Fortas. The director must have had mixed feelings about moves to force Fortas off the Court. DeLoach was torn by the information from the Justice Department and his relationship with Fortas. He remembered that Hoover "respected Justice Fortas's keen mind." DeLoach himself "respected Justice Fortas for his brilliance and compassion," as a "strict disciple of the law," and not someone who was pro–criminal defendant.[96] DeLoach's opinion of Fortas did not change over the years.[97]

But the battle over the Supreme Court was bigger than the allegiance of an agent for his star informer. Less than a week later, Nixon and Hoover talked again about the Supreme Court. Hoover complained that at times he was almost "despondent" about whether anything could be done about the Supreme Court rulings. The president said it was "going to take at least four years or more to get the Court changed." Hoover disagreed—he felt that "some progress" could be made because there would be four vacancies. Surprised, Nixon asked Hoover how he came up with four. "The fellow from New York," Hoover said. "Harlan?" Nixon asked. "Yes," Hoover said. "He's deaf and can't hear anything and is planning to retire, and, of course, Warren will be going off and Black's health is getting worse. . . . Douglas, of course, is crazy, and is not in too good health. That makes Harlan, Douglas, Black and Warren."[98] Once again, neither Nixon nor Hoover included Fortas on their list of justices soon to be leaving the Court. Twenty-one years later, Wilson recalled that the FBI did not seem to be particularly eager to go after Fortas, unlike their zealous help in pursuing Justice Douglas the following year. Privately, Hoover would accuse someone in the Justice Department of leaking information to the press about the Fortas-Wolfson matter.[99]

Lambert's article in *Life* had been released to the press on May 4.[100] Fortas, in a desperate move, called the Justice Department himself, asking to speak to Mitchell. Wilson advised Mitchell against talking to Fortas. Earlier, Wilson and Mitchell had discussed "arranging [an] appropriate contact with Fortas" to determine if he were ready to resign.[101] Now Wilson advised his boss that it would be more effective to squeeze Fortas if Mitchell dealt only with the chief justice.[102]

After the *Life* article, the Fortas investigation snowballed. The FBI was called in to interview Wolfson, who was imprisoned at Eglin Air Force Base in Florida. Wilson told the FBI that the administration "hoped that . . . a statement from Wolfson would . . . cause Fortas to submit his resignation from the Supreme Court."[103] To that end, Mitchell had already advised the chief justice that the FBI was being sent to interview Wolfson.[104] But the bureau was hesitant to become involved in interviewing Wolfson, contending that the investigators from the Security and Exchange Commission (SEC) "would have more background information available." Wilson and the attorney general insisted that the FBI conduct the interview.[105]

On May 10, 1969, five days after the *Life* article, Wolfson signed a nine-page, double-spaced affidavit.[106] While his attorneys listened, Wolfson explained to two FBI special agents that in 1965 he had read in the papers that President Johnson was considering nominating Fortas to the Supreme Court. Wolfson remembered telling Fortas that he "would be agreeable to furnishing [Fortas] any financial assistance that he felt necessary" to enable Fortas to accept a Court appointment and not take such a large pay cut to serve his country. Fortas declined this offer. Later, after Wolfson had read that Fortas had been nominated to the Supreme Court, he called Fortas to congratulate him. This time Wolfson mentioned that Fortas's "services might be utilized as an adviser to the Wolfson Family Foundation." Fortas listened intently while Wolfson described one of the foundation's programs—"to promote racial and religious understanding and coexistence."[107]

Soon after taking his seat on the Court, in October 1965, Justice Fortas agreed to serve as a consultant to the Wolfson Foundation. Abe Fortas's annual compensation from the foundation was $20,000 a year plus expenses for the rest of his life; should Mrs. Fortas survive him, she would receive the money. At this meeting, Wolfson mentioned that he was alarmed about the SEC investigation. Fortas told him not to worry, for the investigation concerned "technical violations" and were not of a "serious nature."[108]

Wolfson sent Fortas his first check on January 1, 1966, after the Wolfson Foundation board approved of the arrangement. Fortas attended one meeting of the Wolfson Family Foundation, in Jacksonville, Florida, on June 15, 1966, and then visited Wolfson's horse farm in Ocala. While Justice Fortas was in Florida, the president tried unsuccessfully to reach him by telephone. Late in the evening, still looking for Fortas, the White House phone operator called a Fortas law clerk, Daniel Levitt,[109] who reported that Fortas was visiting Wolfson. The next day Levitt mentioned the call to Fortas's secretary, Gloria Dalton, and she told him that earlier in the year Fortas had received a large check from Wolfson. Levitt was concerned, for he knew that Wolfson was being investigated by the SEC.[110] He suggested that Dalton tell Fortas that his association with Wolfson might be misconstrued as practicing law.[111]

During Fortas's Florida trip, Fortas and Wolfson had discussed the foundation's work as well as the SEC investigation. Fortas again told Wolfson not to worry because the violations were technical and that "he had or would contact Manuel Cohen of the Securities and Exchange Commission" about the investigation. Justice Fortas said that he was "somewhat responsible for Cohen's appointment to the Commission as chairman."[112]

When Fortas returned to Washington on June 16, he was incensed that Levitt was questioning his judgment and told Levitt to stay out of his business.[113] But after thinking about his law clerk's warning, Fortas resigned as adviser to the Wolfson Foundation, though he did not immediately reimburse it for the $20,000 he had received.[114]

A telephone call did go out. Manuel Cohen called Fortas on September 26, 1966, a week after Wolfson's indictment for selling unregistered stock.[115] In a sworn statement to the FBI, Cohen said he could not recall whether the call went through and, if it did, what the conversation was about.[116] Less than a month after Cohen's call to Fortas, Wolfson was indicted for perjury, filing false SEC reports, and conspiracy to obstruct the investigation of the purchase of Merritt-Chapman stock. Members of Fortas's former law firm, Arnold & Porter, kept Fortas current on Wolfson's troubles.[117]

Although Fortas had resigned from the Wolfson Foundation by a letter dated June 21, 1966, he did not repay the $20,000 until almost six months later. Fortas sent the check to the foundation on December 15, 1966.[118] Wolfson denied that Fortas had agreed to exercise his influence at the SEC to have the investigation halted. According to Justice Department interviews with one of Wolfson's associates, Wolfson had "made the repeated claim . . . that he was going to stop this whole [SEC] matter in Washington and that Fortas was going to help him do it."[119] Ultimately, Mitchell ordered the marshaling of all documents that supported the case against Justice Fortas. The implicit purpose was that if Fortas remained on the Court, his next case was going to be as a defendant in *U.S. v. Fortas*. The threat of prosecution was a bluff, but a successful one.[120] Fortas asked one of his law clerks to research whether he could be prosecuted.[121] More likely were impeachment proceedings at the behest of House Republicans. The Justice Department package of documents, designed to convince Fortas to resign, was delivered to the chief justice. Wolfson's sworn affidavit and Wolfson Foundation documents were included, but a more impressive document, called the "Wolfson–Fortas Matter" chronology, was not.[122]

Three days after Warren received Mitchell's Fortas-Wolfson package, Fortas still had not resigned—and Justice Douglas argued strenuously that he should not.[123] Fortas's wife disagreed.[124] The Nixon administration then announced that the Justice Department would cooperate with an investigation of Fortas by the House Judiciary Committee.[125] Calls for Fortas's resignation were coming in from Democratic politicians, including Senator Robert C. Byrd of West Virginia, and from Republicans, such as Ronald Reagan, governor of California.[126]

On May 14, 1969, Justice Fortas resigned from the Court in a four-page letter to the chief justice. "[I] have not interceded or taken part in any legal, administrative or judicial matter affecting Mr. Wolfson or anyone associated with him," Fortas wrote. "There has been no wrongdoing on my part."[127] He became the first Supreme Court justice to resign in disgrace. But his greatest improprieties on the Court had not yet come to light—nor would they, in his lifetime.[128]

The Nixon–Hoover–Burger Axis

Despite the FBI's ambivalence about losing its gateway to the Court via Fortas, Nixon had a vacancy on the High Court, to fill with a conservative jurist. Before Fortas's resignation, Nixon had named Warren E. Burger as chief justice at the end of the Court's term. Burger was described as a Republican Horatio Alger, who had risen from humble origins by hard work. Hoover and his FBI were overjoyed by the selection of Burger[129] and confirmed Burger's pro–law-and-order and anti-Communist credentials, based both on Hoover's personal dealings with Burger and the prenomination search of FBI files.[130] Burger had been a willing foot soldier in Hoover's war on domestic Communists, going back to *Peters v. Hobby* in the 1950s and continuing during his tenure as a federal judge.[131]

In 1955 Warren Burger was a U.S. assistant attorney general, preparing for oral argument before the High Court in the case of *Peters v. Hobby*.[132] The case concerned the government's use of anonymous informers in loyalty review board proceedings. Solicitor General Simon Soboloff, who was to argue the government's case before the Court, refused to sign the Justice Department's brief, believing that the dismissal of John Peters as a special assistant to the surgeon general was baseless.[133] Burger wanted to impress upon the Court the importance of confidential sources and presumably use examples of the justices themselves providing confidential information to the FBI. Burger asked "if [the FBI] had ever interviewed a Supreme Court Justice who had furnished . . . information in confidence."[134] Assistant FBI Director Louis Nichols recalled that one justice had "furnished information to [him] in confidence." Hoover and Nichols named a few other such judges.[135] Hoover agreed that top bureau officials would be polled about information received from justices and the result was to be given to Burger. In spite of (or possibly as a result of) his unusual method of preparing for oral argument, Burger offended some of the justices by arguing that he had the right to see the confidential evidence that the review board relied upon but that the Court did not.[136] The Court ruled against Burger on technical grounds, refusing to deal with the constitutional issues.

Fourteen years later, in 1969, the initial phase of Nixon's campaign promise to dismantle the liberal Warren Court was being fulfilled with Burger's appointment. The president would have three more appointments to construct a "Nixon Court," as White House counsel John Ehrlichman referred to it.[137] From all appearances, Hoover had his best chance to bring the FBI's Supreme Court program to a successful conclusion with Nixon's help.[138] Both the president and the director believed that to institute a new conservative political order in America, the federal judiciary had to be remade.

The FBI's close ties to Nixon went back to the late 1940s, when he worked with Nichols to break the Alger Hiss case.[139] The bureau helped create Congressman Nixon's Communist fighting persona by leaking confidential information to him.[140] A Nixon-Hoover team should have been a blissful union for the White House and the FBI. But a problem developed: "[B]y 1970, [Hoover] was reluctant to allow his agents to break into embassies, tap telephones, or open other people's mail," FBI Assistant Director William Sullivan wrote in his memoirs, "even though these were the very investigative techniques to which he owed his publicized successes"[141] and to which Sullivan himself had continued to subscribe. Nixon was not yet prepared to give up the dirty tricks he had come to expect from the FBI. Despite the president's zeal, Hoover was increasingly afraid of being blamed for agents caught breaking the law. Times had indeed changed.

Despite their differences, Hoover and Nixon still worked to further their common goal of tilting the federal courts as well as on other presidential political objectives.[142] Both men agreed that law-and-order justice demanded ideological appointments to the federal bench of persons who supported the death penalty and opposed the criminal law decisions of the Warren Court.[143] And the Executive Branch now had the help of the Judicial Branch. Chief Justice Burger was chief of the U.S. Judicial Conference, the administrative rule-making body for the federal courts.[144] The program to remake the lower federal courts was a White House–Justice Department–FBI–Burger united front.

President Nixon announced that he would not seek racial, religious, or geographical balance in making his appointments to the Supreme Court. Presidential speechwriter Patrick Buchanan told Nixon that he was "right in ending the 'Jewish seat,' " in which the torch had been passed over the decades from Justice Louis Brandeis to Benjamin Cardozo to Felix Frankfurter to Arthur Goldberg and finally to Abe Fortas. Buchanan argued for an Italian-American justice because they "have never had one of their own" on the Supreme Court. "Politically, the elevation of a Catholic Italian-American to the Jewish seat on the Court would mean ten million Italians would light candles in their homes for the President" and remove "some of the hurt Italian-Americans constantly feel as a result of Italian-Sicilian control of organized crime in the United States."[145] But an Italian-American appointee would have to wait for President Ronald Reagan. William Safire, another Nixon speechwriter, also debated the " 'Jewish Seat' problem." "If the President is *not* going to appoint a Jew, nothing he says beforehand is going to placate that community," Safire wrote to H.R. Haldeman, White House chief of staff.[146]

Despite White House protestations, President Nixon also had a southern strategy for the Court. Within the space of a year, Nixon had asked the Senate to confirm two southerners to fill Fortas's spot. But while Nixon could select, he could not confirm.

The days of the Nixon White House's unquestioned reliance on an FBI report were ending. The FBI's politically slanted background checks on Supreme Court nominees helped torpedo two confirmations. Federal Judges Clement Furman Haynsworth, Jr., and G. Harrold Carswell were victims of Mitchell's and Hoover's failures to change with the times.[147] Race and partisan politics were more powerful than an FBI clean bill of health. The FBI's background checks on Haynsworth and Carswell uncovered "no derogatory information,"[148] but the bureau did not consider a segregationist background to be derogatory. Although the bureau collected information regarding the racial attitudes of southern congressmen, judges, and others, this information was not regularly passed along to the White House, attorney general, or the Senate Judiciary Committee.[149] When liberals were appointed to the federal bench, every "subversive" reference that could be dredged up was included.[150] By 1971 the White House had learned a hard lesson. John Ehrlichman, chief domestic affairs adviser to the president, received an *"Eyes Only"* memo from his assistant, Egil "Bud" Krogh, saying that the White House could no longer rely on the FBI alone to investigate Supreme Court nominees.[151] "[A]n *independent* check of potential nominees should also be undertaken" by a very secret White House unit, Krogh wrote. The suggested names for the secret unit included Ehrlichman, special counsel to the president, Charles Colson, and John Dean. Attorney General Mitchell, William Rehnquist, and the FBI were responsible for "flush[ing] up names," according to the Nixon criteria of "integrity, ideology, intellect, age, ethnicity, sex, region, politics and professional background." But "the FBI investigations and a casual luncheon" with the candidate were not sufficient "to extract the kind of information we need," Krogh argued. He believed that something on the order of a three-day "CIA-de-briefing" for the nominee was necessary whenever a Supreme Court candidate reaches the top of the list.[152]

Haynsworth and Carswell:
The Decline of Hoover's Influence

Federal Judge Haynsworth had been nominated to the Fourth Circuit Court of Appeals in Richmond, Virginia, by President Dwight Eisenhower in 1957. A South Carolina native, Haynsworth graduated from Harvard Law School in 1936 and served as a Navy intelligence officer.[153] When he was nominated for the federal appellate bench, Federal Judge George Bell Timmerman told the FBI that Haynsworth was a "good attorney" but that he would "probably be handicapped" as his "experience has been limited almost exclusively to representing large corporations."[154] Federal Judge Cecil C. Wycke said he would not recommend Haynsworth for a district court judgeship, much less an appellate judgeship, because "he is unqualified." Haynsworth rarely tried cases himself because of a speech impediment said the judge.[155] When Haynsworth did try a case himself, he was "unprepared," the judge remembered. Haynsworth was confirmed as judge on the Fourth Circuit and came to be respected by his colleagues on the appeals court.

The FBI appreciated Haynsworth's attitude on the bench. In 1966 Haynsworth, then chief judge of the Fourth Circuit, was writing an opinion in a case the FBI had investigated. Judge Haynsworth phoned the Columbia FBI field office, apparently without notifying the defense lawyers, and said that "he would like to state in his opinion a summary of the Bureau's instructions concerning advising subjects and suspects of their right to counsel, of their right not to make any statements and that any statements they do make must be voluntarily given and that any statements given may be used in court." He wanted a summary of FBI instructions as they appeared in the agents' handbook on "May 29, 1962, the date of the critical interview in this case." The agent in charge of the Columbia, S.C., office advised FBI headquarters that Judge Haynsworth was an ardent supporter of the FBI and that it would be advantageous to the bureau to provide him with the information that he has requested. Hoover ordered that Haynsworth be "give[n] every assistance." Realizing the impropriety of the request and the bureau's response, a blind memorandum, leaving no markings indicating its origin, was given to Judge Haynsworth.[156]

Before President Nixon announced the nomination of Haynsworth, Attorney General Mitchell called Hoover and said that to meet the "requirements of the Judiciary Committee," the FBI needed to conduct a "quiet check to the extent that [you] find it necessary," so the Justice Department could put it in the record of the hearings. Mitchell repeated that the check be "done as quietly as possible."[157] Hoover told Mitchell that he would have the agent in charge in South Carolina give him "a rundown on [Haynsworth's] ability and standing without making any outside inquiries." The attorney general said that would be "excellent." Later in the day the attorney general was told by Hoover that the top agent in Columbia, S.C., Roland Trent, was "acquainted" with Haynsworth and he is "generally regarded as the foremost jurist in the area," is "very conservative, and is well disposed toward law enforcement. He is definitely in favor of law and order." Hoover also reported that "Haynsworth has a slight lisp," a "brilliant mind," and that the bureau "knew of no derogatory information concerning the Judge."[158] Nothing was said about any alleged conflicts of interest while Haynsworth was on the bench. No additional FBI investigation was conducted.[159]

Haynsworth was nominated to the Supreme Court to fill the vacancy left by Justice Fortas on August 19, 1969. Almost immediately, Democrats raised allegations that Judge Haynsworth participated in court rulings about corporations in which he had a financial interest.[160] But the White House was also playing its own version of hard ball. Democratic Senator Birch Bayh of Indiana, who later made Nixon's "enemies list," was one of Haynsworth's main opponents.[161] On October 15, Clark Mollenhoff, Nixon's deputy counsel, called the FBI headquarters to enlist the bureau's help in attacking Bayh.[162] Hoover, Tolson, and DeLoach all created a paper trail that cautioned against helping the White House on this political mission. The FBI file on Haynsworth does not say what steps the bureau took in furtherance of the White House plan to "discredit Bayh," but Attorney General Mitchell was kept up to date on White House efforts.[163] And Assistant Attorney General William H. Rehnquist was in charge of developing materials to support the nomination and to coordinate efforts to "target Senators" to get out the votes needed.[164]

On October 15 the FBI took a broadside shot from columnist Carl Rowan in the Washington *Evening Star*.[165] "[E]ven . . . Republicans are asking how President Nixon could crawl out on such a rotten and risky limb as to try to make a Supreme Court justice of Haynsworth, whose financial manipulations in companies involved in litigation before his court prove him to be forgetful, naive [and] poor of judgment." Rowan said the FBI needed new leadership. "The situation has deteriorated to the point that if you are politically palatable to the FBI and its director, or if you have been cooperating with it, a lot of questionable things get overlooked when your name comes up for a big job." If you are not politically palatable to the FBI, Rowan said, a more painstaking investigation will lead to "digging skeletons out of closets." He argued that FBI investigations reflect Hoover's biases and political views. Hoover wrote on the margin of the newspaper column: "This racist is at it again."

On November 21, 1969, the Senate voted 55 to 45 against the confirmation of Haynsworth. Even Republican Senators Robert Griffin (Michigan) and Jack Miller (Iowa), both of whom voted against Fortas, also voted against Haynsworth. The alleged conflict of interest charges, which were flimsy, and opposition from labor and minority groups doomed the nomination.[166] The first term of the Burger Court was operating at eight-ninths strength.

Federal Judge Carswell was up next.[167] And like Haynsworth, Carswell would go down swinging. Carswell had been investigated by the FBI in 1953 before his nomination as U.S. attorney and again in 1958, when he was appointed a federal judge. According to the bureau, the "investigations were favorable."[168] Mitchell bragged that Carswell was "almost too good to be true."[169] For Nixon's opponents, Carswell's speech eleven years earlier to the American Legion, when he proudly asserted his "vigorous belief in White Supremacy," was definitely too good to be true. Rehnquist was given the task of thinking up arguments to show that Carswell was a moderate.[170] He spent his "time with the undecided and weak Senators" who had been affected by Carswell's "public image" as "anti–civil rights" and by his lackluster qualifications. (Rehnquist's nomination to the Supreme Court would subsequently be attacked as anti–civil rights, also.)

Supporters of the nomination employed creative tactics. Carswell's mediocrity was praised by Senator Russell Long, who said he would rather have a C student who could think straight than an A student whose rulings on the bench would lead to an increase in crime.[171] On April 9, 1970, the Senate voted down Carswell, 51 to 45. Nixon accused his nominee's Senate opponents of anti-southern bigotry, but the president himself looked to the North for a nominee: Federal Appeals Judge Harry A. Blackmun, who would for a time be tagged with the derogatory nickname "Minnesota twin" for his long and close friendship with fellow Minnesotan, Chief Justice Burger. On May 12, 1970, Judge Blackmun became Associate Justice Blackmun by a unanimous vote of the Senate.[172]

The Senate may have tired of partisan fighting about the Supreme Court. In the House of Representatives, however, Republicans had already begun firing at their favorite judicial bogie-man: Justice William O. Douglas. Representative Gerald Ford sounded the battle cry.

CHAPTER 10

Impeach Douglas! Remember Haynsworth and Carswell

> Following the public disclosures last year of the extrajudicial activities and moonlighting employment of Justices Fortas and Douglas, which resulted in the resignation from the Supreme Bench of Mr. Justice Fortas but not of Mr. Justice Douglas, I received literally hundreds of inquiries and protests from concerned citizens and colleagues. . . . I quietly undertook a study of both the law of impeachment and the facts about the behavior of Mr. Justice Douglas. . . . I cannot see how, on the prima facie case I have made, it is possible to object to a prompt but thoroughgoing investigation of Mr. Justice Douglas' behavior . . . [and] for [his] impeachment and removal.[1]
>
> —Representative Gerald R. Ford to the House of Representatives,
> April 15, 1970

Justice William O. Douglas had survived impeachment threats before. After he had issued a stay of execution in the Julius and Ethel Rosenberg cases in 1953, there were calls for his removal. Later his numerous marriages and divorces were cited as evidence of unfitness. But before 1970, Douglas had never faced such powerful and determined foes as Richard Nixon, John Mitchell, and J. Edgar Hoover, men who had the means and the will to attack him through political surrogates in Congress while themselves able to listen electronically on his conversations and on those close to him. As the Justice Department told a federal judge twenty years later, in response to a Freedom of Information Act lawsuit, the FBI had done nothing wrong. Justice Douglas was not the *target* of the wiretaps and the bugs.[2] Nevertheless, to paraphrase a television commercial, when Douglas spoke, the FBI listened.[3] (At some point Mitchell himself was picked up via electronic surveillance directed at an FBI target; no other information about this interception has been made public. After Mitchell resigned in 1972 to run Nixon's reelection campaign, his outspoken wife Martha publicly accused the FBI of tapping her phones.[4]) In addition to information the government had learned about Douglas from wiretaps and bugs, the Central Intelligence

Agency had opened Douglas's mail under its "Hunter Project" and passed it along to the FBI.[5]

With Warren and Fortas removed from the Court, Douglas was the next liberal target of Nixon,[6] Mitchell, and some members of the press.[7] Despite Hoover's recent tendency toward caution, the FBI's Supreme Court program was leading to its logical conclusion, and the bureau believed it could finally help rid the Court of its most reckless, outspoken, and liberal justice. Justices William Brennan and Thurgood Marshall, despite their liberal rulings, did not publicly assail the FBI or the Nixon administration.

Within a week of Fortas's resignation, on May 23, 1969, Will Wilson was headhunting for Douglas. He asked Hoover to send him information from FBI files about the justice and the Parvin Foundation.[8] (That same day John Ehrlichman wrote Nixon that "the Attorney General strongly recommends that you do *not* get into the question of judicial ethics [at your meeting with American Bar Association officials] either as it relates to the Fortas matter or the pending investigation of Mr. Justice Douglas."[9]) The FBI had collected thousands of pages of records about Douglas over forty years. Much of the dossier was rumor and innuendo, other portions could not be released because that would reveal FBI and CIA illegalities, such as warrantless wiretapping and mail tampering. The rest of the file, including information about Parvin, needed further investigation to make the information usable.[10]

Seeing that Clement Haynsworth's defeat was imminent, Nixon instructed Ehrlichman to have Representative Gerald Ford move to impeach Justice Douglas, a man Nixon considered to be practically a criminal.[11] Nixon's wishes were passed along, and eventually Wilson, on orders from Mitchell, gave Ford some of the materials that Wilson had collected about Douglas during the spring and summer of 1969.[12] A blind memorandum was prepared, and Wilson personally carried it to Ford at his congressional office a month after Haynsworth's confirmation bid was defeated.[13] The memo, which Ford later described as "pieces of paper," included information about Douglas's connections to the Parvin Foundation and other derogatory information culled from FBI and CIA files.[14] Ford apparently used this information, without investigation or corroboration, to compose his error-riddled speech attacking Douglas.[15] "Ford just really blew it by giving a speech about impeachment without doing his homework," Wilson recalled. "You don't start down that road without having the facts. He had the payment of the money [to Douglas by Parvin]. . . . [Ford] didn't come close to having the *quid pro quo*—what Douglas did for Parvin." The blind memo was intended to be a starting point for Ford's investigation, according to Wilson, not a finished product.[16]

On April 15, 1970, one week after the defeat of G. Harrold Carswell's Supreme Court nomination, Ford denounced Justice Douglas on the floor of the House and called for his impeachment. He blasted Douglas for five areas of impropriety, which he claimed were sufficient for bringing articles of impeachment. First, Douglas had failed to recuse himself from a case involving Ralph Ginzburg, publisher of the skin magazine, *Avant-Garde,* after Douglas had received $350 for an article about folk singing that had appeared in the magazine following an article on "The Decline and Fall of the Female Breast."[17]

Second, Douglas had written a book entitled *Points of Rebellion,* the thesis of which, Ford claimed, was the "espousal of hippie-yippie style revolution" where "violence may be justified and perhaps only . . . overthrow of 'the establishment' can save the country."

Third, excerpts from *Points of Rebellion* were reprinted in *Evergreen Review,* an artsy magazine of political essays, photographs, fiction, and poetry that Ford described as filled with "hard-core pornography."[18]

Fourth, "[Justice Douglas] was for nearly a decade the well-paid moonlighter for [the Albert Parvin Foundation], an organization whose ties to the international gambling fraternity never have been sufficiently explored." Ford claimed that Douglas, in addition to receiving $12,000 a year from 1961 until May 1969 for the nonprofit purpose of "educating the developing leadership in Latin America," gave legal advice to the foundation. Ford likened Douglas's Parvin connections to Fortas's relationship with Louis Wolfson. "[T]he cast of characters in these two cases is virtually interchangeable," Ford claimed.[19]

> Albert Parvin was named a coconspirator but not a defendant in the stock manipulation case that sent Louis Wolfson to prison. Albert Parvin was again under investigation in the stock manipulation action against Parvin-Dohrmann. This generation has largely forgotten that William O. Douglas first rose to national prominence as Chairman of the Securities and Exchange Commission. His former law pupil at Yale and fellow New Dealer in those days was one Abe Fortas, and they remained the closest friends on and off the Supreme Court. Mrs. Fortas was retained by the Parvin Foundation in its tax difficulties. Abe Fortas was retained by Bobby Baker until he withdrew from the case because of his close ties with the White House.[20]

Finally, Ford impugned Douglas's patriotism for his close "connection with the leftish Center for the Study of Democratic Institutions" (CSDI) based in Santa Barbara, California, after "he gave up his open ties with the Albert Parvin Foundation." Ford noted that the Parvin Foundation had often funded CSDI and its "intellectual incubators for the New Left and the SDS." The center financed and sponsored a conference in 1965 during which, Ford alleged, "plans were laid for the violent campus disruptions of the past few years."[21]

"I cannot see how, on the prima facie case I have made," Ford told his colleagues in the House, "it is possible to object to a prompt but thoroughgoing investigation of Mr. Justice Douglas' behavior . . . [and] for [his] impeachment and removal."[22]

Douglas's legal team consisted of Simon H. Rifkind, former Attorney General Ramsey Clark, Abe Fortas's former law clerk, Daniel Levitt, as well as Douglas's former law clerks, Professor Vern Countryman, Warren Christopher, and Charles Miller, among others.[23] Rifkind forcefully and unapologetically countered Ford's speech, point by point, in a letter to the House Judiciary Committee. Yes, Justice Douglas sold an article about folk singing to *Avant-Garde,* but he had no reason to "believe the magazine had anything to do with Mr. Ginzburg" and had no need to disqualify himself from Ginzburg's case. Ford's attack on Douglas's book *Points of Rebellion* was "profoundly subversive of the First Amendment" and is "an inexcusable distortion of what the Justice actually wrote." And Douglas did not authorize the editors of *Evergreen Review* to reprint a portion of his book. It was Random House, his publisher, that made the decision.

The hardest to point to defend was Douglas's taking money from the Parvin Foundation. So Rifkind wisely tossed conservative Chief Justice Warren Burger into the fray. He argued that Douglas's service as director of the Albert Parvin Foundation and receipt of "modest compensation for such services" had precedents, including the work of Chief Justice Burger and Justice Harry Blackmun with the Mayo Foundation. The rest of Ford's allegations about Douglas and Parvin were simply untrue. "Justice Douglas does not know the alleged underworld persons named in the attacks upon him. He was not in Las Vegas when it was insinuated he was, he has never been associated with Bobby Baker, and he did not attend the inauguration of President Bosch [of the Dominican Republic] as alleged." Neither did Justice Douglas engage in the practice of law. As for Ford's Red-baiting, Rifkind wrote that Justice Douglas proudly participated in the activities of the Center for the Study of Democratic Institutions, "one of the free world's great academic institutions." He pointed out that even Chief Justices Warren and Burger participated in the center's programs.[24]

The White House carefully maintained a public policy of distance from Ford and House Republicans who were calling for Douglas's impeachment. The official line was: "It is a Constitutional matter solely for the House to decide and it would be improper for the White House to comment."[25] Ehrlichman suggested that the White House actively "disassociate . . . even more clearly."[26] Daniel P. Moynihan wrote back, "I only hope, against hope, that it does not soon appear in the press that we were involved [in the move to impeach Justice Douglas]."[27]

As with the failed efforts to bolster Haynsworth and Carswell, William Rehnquist was called in to prepare the White House response to the request of the House Committee on the Judiciary for all Executive Branch records about Douglas.[28] On May 15, 1970, Nixon wrote to Emanuel Celler, chairman of the Judiciary Committee, telling him that he would order Executive Branch agencies to cooperate by furnishing relevant information about Douglas.[29]

Nixon wanted to make sure that the FBI provided Ford everything he needed to be successful, so he personally contacted Hoover. On June 5 Nixon phoned Hoover; he started by asking if the death penalty could be imposed on plane hijackers. Hoover said it could not, unless someone had been harmed; he continued, noting that the Supreme Court has "several cases involving capital punishment and I would imagine the court is going to be 5–4." "To knock it out completely?" Nixon asked. "I would not be surprised," Hoover replied, "unless we get another vacancy to be filled by a real man." "If we get one, we will do it," Nixon promised. Hoover said they had the "same problem in [the] obscenity" area and that the current Court "will not declare obscene even . . . raw obscenity." "[T]he country is sick of that crap they see in the newsstands," Nixon said. "I'm no prude, but my God, . this stuff they are doing now—that's what is getting kids on dope and everything else. Justice Douglas had an article in one of those [pornographic] magazines." Hoover chimed in, Justices Douglas and Black "won't look at a pornographic motion picture like 'I Am Curious—Yellow' and they still rule it's not obscene. The president asked "if he had Jerry Ford call [him], would [he] fill [Ford] in on this; . . . he is a good man." Hoover agreed to help Ford on the Douglas impeachment.[30] This was Hoover's last chance to realize his goal of remaking the Supreme Court. Although the director viewed the Burger Court as better than the Warren Court, it was still too liberal and was certainly no reflection of the Nixon-Hoover values.[31]

At the same time the bureau was helping the anti-Douglas forces, Chief Justice Burger was conferring privately with Hoover. Burger seemed to genuinely like Hoover, and he called on the director to complain about his sore back—and for political and security services.[32] In turn, Hoover sent Burger classified FBI reports, such as "Extremists Attack the Courts," which were little more than political diatribes against the courtroom antics of New Leftists and their lawyers. Leonard Boudin, Leonard Weinglass, and William Kunstler were singled out as "attracted to the defense of those who oppose the capitalist system or who have chosen to resort to violence to change it."[33] Hoover also helped Burger get what he needed from the White House: a government plane for when he traveled around the country at the request of the president, making appearances at conventions, for instance.[34]

Meanwhile, for President Nixon, crime had become synonymous with dissent. The invasion of Cambodia by U.S. troops set off often violent antiwar demonstrations on college campuses. Four students were shot down by National Guardsmen at Kent State University. Jackson State students had been gunned down, too. There were four hundred bomb threats in New York City during one twenty-four-hour period. In response to the continuing threat of violence, in June 1970, President Nixon asked for a review of current intelligence collection practices to pinpoint ways to obtain better information about dissenters.[35] A lengthy special report was presented to the president, and shortly thereafter a proposal was made for escalation of aggressive intelligence tactics against American citizens, which came to be known as "the Huston Plan." Tom Charles Huston, White House counsel who had recently been discharged as an Army intelligence officer, wrote to H.R. Haldeman in July 1970 about a plan to coordinate the efforts of the FBI, CIA, the National Security Agency, the Defense Intelligence Agency, and other military services. The Huston Plan, the preparation of which was aided and abetted by FBI Assistant Director William C. Sullivan (who replaced Cartha DeLoach after his retirement in 1970) in order to avoid Hoover's new strictures, would authorize intelligence and counterintelligence agents to: (1) monitor the international communications of U.S. citizens; (2) intensify the electronic surveillance of domestic dissenters and selected establishments; (3) read the international mail of American citizens; (4) break into specified establishments and into homes of domestic dissenters; and (5) intensify the surveillance of American college students.[36]

Everything that Huston recommended had been done in the past or was still being done by intelligence agencies. The only difference was that previously it had been done without specific White House authorization. Huston recommended that conducting illegal intelligence activities become the official policy of the Nixon White House. Hoover vehemently objected to the plan not because he viewed it as inherently wrong or illegal but because its construction made the FBI, not the president, the responsible agent if the plan were to be made public. Nixon, Haldeman, and Sullivan agreed with Huston that the entire intelligence community needed to be unleashed, just as the FBI had been prior to 1966, to protect the nation from the "indigenous revolutionary activism" responsible for bombings and violence on campuses and elsewhere, which was "determined to destroy our society."[37]

Huston may have written Hoover off as a tired, old man, "worried about his legend,"[38] but others, like CIA veteran James Angleton, believed that after the Senate's Long Committee hearings and the *Black* case, the director "had no recourse but to gradually eliminate activities which were unfavorable to the Bureau and which in turn risked [reducing] public confidence in the number one law enforcement agency."[39] No one believed that Hoover was opposed to engaging in burglaries, mail openings, or warrantless electronic surveillance because it was illegal; he simply would not "accept the responsibility" any longer.[40] If the president or attorney general would agree to sign the Huston Plan, Hoover would go along.

Nixon, as Johnson before him, was of the opinion that the domestic protesters had connections to foreign Communists in Cuba, China, and Eastern Europe.[41] The Huston Plan, like the FBI COINTELPRO, was an intelligence operation in which the ends—stopping the radical bad guys—justified the means.

The Huston Plan was doomed when Hoover disclosed the plan to Mitchell, making it clear that the FBI would not break the law unless the attorney general gave specific written instructions prior to each illegal break-in or phone tap.[42] Neither Mitchell—nor Nixon—wanted any record that they had authorized specific illegal intelligence activities.[43]

Less than a month after the birth of the Huston Plan, Nixon rescinded it. (Nixon's approval of the Huston Plan formed the basis of Article II of the Articles of Impeachment against him in 1974.[44]) The FBI, CIA, and NSA continued their illegal and extralegal programs, which they had been engaging in without White House approval. The FBI's COINTELPRO continued until 1971.[45] NSA's "watch list," which targeted the international phone calls of Americans, continued until 1973.[46] The CIA's Operation CHAOS, designed to gather information about foreign links to domestic racial, antiwar, and protest movements and its mail opening programs, continued until 1974.[47] By mid-1971, after the New York *Times* began publishing the "Pentagon Papers," the White House would create its own "plumbers' unit" to "stop security leaks and to investigate other sensitive security matters."[48] Burglaries and warrantless wiretapping against domestic targets would be directed from the White House itself. And Justice Douglas would continue to claim that Nixon and the FBI were employing electronic surveillance measures against him.

The House Judiciary Subcommittee's investigation of Douglas dragged on until December 1970, when it issued a report in excess of nine hundred pages. Although the subcommittee found that no grounds for impeachment existed, its findings about Douglas's non-judicial sources of income raised questions about the propriety of Douglas's actions.[49] But Douglas had not committed "treason, bribery, or other high crimes and misdemeanors," the crimes the Constitution lists as warranting impeachment.

CHAPTER 11

From Burger to Rehnquist: Court Administration from the Right

Judge Tamm [said] that the Chief Justice thinks men with FBI training would be admirably situated [as federal court administrators] and his, Tamm's, interest is that he thinks men in these key positions could influence these judges who are so completely inexperienced and unlearned in the practicalities of law enforcement. [A]side from their executive duties, they could be a tremendous force for keeping some of these stupid appellate opinions from coming out.[1]

—J. Edgar Hoover to his assistant directors, 1971

Justice Hugo Black died on September 23, 1971, and Justice John Harlan died three months later, on December 29.[2] Both men had already submitted their resignations.[3] President Richard Nixon had two more slots to fill on his Court. Virginian Lewis F. Powell, Jr., and Assistant Attorney General William H. Rehnquist were selected to sit on the High Court.

J. Edgar Hoover was generally pleased with the selection of Powell, who had been president of the American Bar Association and "had generally concurred with Hoover's beliefs concerning crime."[4] Powell had also publicly supported warrantless FBI wiretapping of domestic subversives upon presidential authority.[5] A proverbial southern gentleman from a wealthy family of influence, Powell had chaired the Richmond Public School Board's integration of schools in 1959 and had practiced law with the city's most prestigious firm.[6] With the support of the National Association for the Advancement of Colored People (NAACP), Powell was confirmed by the Senate with only one dissenting vote.

Nixon's other selection was not so fortunate. Rehnquist, who might have been Hoover's soulmate on criminal law, national security,[7] and racial issues, was as welcomed by the FBI as he was opposed by the NAACP and liberal groups. In the Justice Department Rehnquist had been an ardent supporter of wiretapping and other means of keeping an ear or an eye on dissenters.[8] During his confirmation hearings, Rehnquist was described variously as a racial bigot, a shy but personable intellectual, a right-winger, and a dedicated foe of civil liberties. He had been a vocal critic of the Warren Court during his entire legal career, even though—or perhaps because—he had served as law clerk to Justice Robert Jackson during Earl Warren's first year on the Court.[9] In 1957 Rehnquist, then an attorney, joined the ideological debate about the alleged leftish tendencies of the Supreme Court law clerks. He wrote in *U.S. News and World Report:* "Some of the tenets of the 'liberal' point of view which commanded the sympathy of a majority of the clerks I knew were: extreme solicitude for the claims of Communists and other criminal defendants, expansion of federal power at the expense of state power, great sympathy toward any government regulation of business—in short, the political philosophy now espoused by the Court under Chief Justice Earl Warren."[10] Although his comments about the Warren Court may have been considered humorous by some and ill-advised by others, his 1953 memo to Justice Jackson on *Brown v. Board of Education* was no laughing matter. The young law clerk had written that the separate but equal doctrine was correct and should be upheld.[11] Another allegation, this one by the NAACP in Arizona, impugned Rehnquist's integrity, not just his commitment to civil rights. It was alleged that Rehnquist harassed and intimated minority voters in Arizona.[12] Rehnquist denied that he had ever "harassed or intimidated voters, or encouraged . . . or approved the harassment or intimidation of voters by other persons."[13]

In a letter to Senate Judiciary chairman James O. Eastland, Judge Charles L. Hardy described the tactics of Republican party vote challengers in Phoenix during 1962:

[A]mong the statutory grounds for challenging a person offering to vote [was] that . . . he was unable to read the Constitution of the United States in the English language. In each precinct *every* black or Mexican person was being challenged on this . . . ground and it was quite clear that this type of challenging was a deliberate effort to slow down the voting . . . and leave without voting. In addition, there was a well organized campaign of outright harassment and intimidation to discourage persons from attempting to vote. In the black and brown areas, handbills were distributed warning persons that if they were not properly qualified to vote they would be prosecuted. There were squads of people taking photographs of voters standing in line waiting to vote and asking for their names. There is no doubt in my mind that these tactics of harassment, intimidation and indiscriminate challenging were highly improper and violative of the spirit of free elections.[14]

In response to Judge Hardy's letter—which did state that Rehnquist himself had not been a vote challenger—Rehnquist wrote to the Senate Judiciary Committee that he was chairman of the county Republican

"Lawyers Committee" during the 1962 election, not a vote challenger, and that he "neither advised nor suggested that scattergun challenges be made on the basis of literacy" and that he "neither advised nor suggested the handing out of handbills nor the photographing of voters at the election places."[15]

(In 1986, during Rehnquist's hearings to become chief justice, James J. Brosnahan, a successful San Francisco attorney, and four others came forward with information about the voting allegations. Brosnahan, who was an assistant U.S. attorney between 1960 and 1964, testified that he believed that Rehnquist, as a lawyer for the Republican party, had challenged the eligibility of minority voters.[16] In his official capacity as a Justice Department lawyer, Brosnahan, accompanied by an FBI agent, had been "summoned by panicky voters and officials to a precinct where Rehnquist was a challenger." Although Brosnahan had not personally seen Rehnquist challenging voters, he "assumed that it was Rehnquist's 'blanket' challenges of black and Hispanic voters that had led to the tense situation."[17] He believed that "this matter was not fully handled by the bureau in 1971. They did not contact me."[18] Brosnahan speculated that "lots of other people who had information on Rehnquist's role" were not contacted by the FBI in 1971.[19])

According to the majority report on Rehnquist's 1971 nomination, Rehnquist "was not mentioned in the [FBI] investigative report as either a participant in or as a witness to the incidents under investigation."[20] The voter harassment charges are . . . wholly unsubstantiated [and] at the very most a case of mistaken identity."[21] A Democratic minority report from Senators Birch Bayh, Philip A. Hart, Edward M. Kennedy, and John V. Tunney concluded that the Senate Judiciary Committee lacked "either the motivation or machinery to conduct the type of fact-finding which is needed" to verify or disprove the allegations.[22] Of course, digging into a friendly nominee's background on the issue of race was not of interest to Hoover or Mitchell. And there were allegations that during the course of the FBI background investigations of Rehnquist and Powell, agents were interested in supporting the president's candidates and had asked some opponents "whether they plan[ned] to fight the confirmations."[23]

Despite the vitriolic debate about the nominee and a filibuster attempt, Rehnquist was confirmed by a vote of 68 to 26.[24] Rehnquist and Powell were sworn in during a joint ceremony on January 7, 1972. The liberal backbone of the Warren Court was now down to three: William Brennan, Thurgood Marshall and the sickly and aged William Douglas. Rehnquist joined the chief justice and Byron White (on criminal law and national security issues) on the right-flank of the Court.

The fluctuating middle ground was filled by Potter Stewart, Harry Blackmun and Lewis Powell.

In the meantime, Hoover had become an outsider at the White House: Nixon's aides sent memos to the president reminding him to get together with the FBI director every three months or so.[25] Nixon needed no reminder to stay in touch with Warren Burger. As Justice Fortas had done with Lyndon Johnson, Chief Justice Burger gave political advice to Nixon and was a cheerleader for the Vietnam War.[26] They also discussed Court matters. On one occasion, Burger had suggested to the president that the attack against Justice Douglas had harmed the Court.[27] Other times, as described by John Ehrlichman in his White House memoirs, Ehrlichman, Nixon, and Mitchell talked with Burger about the "pros and cons of issues before the court." At another meeting, Burger complained that Justices Douglas and Black had participated in the "landmark cases." The president reassured Burger that the school busing cases were extremely important to the White House. At other meetings, Nixon and Burger had discussed the death penalty, criminal procedure, and other issues related to crime.[28] Burger also provided Mitchell with his recommendations for judicial nominations.[29] Later, during the Watergate scandal, Attorney General Richard Kleindienst told the president that he would consult with his "close friend," Chief Justice Burger, about whom to appoint as special prosecutor.[30]

Burger continued to team up with Hoover and Federal Judge Edward Tamm, a former FBI assistant director, in their plans to make the federal judiciary more responsive to law enforcement issues. One such scheme was to hire retired FBI agents as court administrators to track cases that were important to the FBI and "educate" naive federal judges about law enforcement problems.[31] According to Judge Tamm, these court administrators would be in charge of each of the federal circuits, and FBI agents in "these key positions could influence these judges who are so completely inexperienced and unlearned in the practicalities of law enforcement"; "they could be a tremendous force for keeping some of these stupid appellate opinions from coming out."[32] These same people could also spot cases, like those involving Bobby Baker and Cassius Clay, "and have them moving through," providing an "unlimited opportunity for good," Hoover quoted Judge Tamm as saying. Tamm told Hoover that he had already spoken to the Burger and that the chief justice would be calling Hoover soon to ask whether Hoover would consider "recommending to him or to Rowland Kirks of the Administrative Office, FBI men who are retiring or are on the verge of retiring or are otherwise available who . . . would become court executives."

Tamm had in mind a cadre of "600 trained administrators" for the federal and state courts.[33]

Chief Justice Burger's efforts at reforming the federal courts[34] included a hidden political agenda as well.[35] Within the Court, Burger had subverted the time-honored protocol at conference by voting with the majority in order to give himself the power to assign cases in which he was actually a dissenter.[36] Similar power plays were set in motion outside the Supreme Court. In 1970 the chief justice had hired his close friend, Rowland Falconer Kirks, as director of the Administrative Office of the U.S. Courts, a judicial agency that supervises all administrative matters concerning the offices of clerks and other personnel of the federal courts nationwide.[37] Other Burger friends were hired in high administrative positions in the federal judiciary.[38] Kirks, a major general in the U.S. Army Reserve and a former Justice Department attorney, was on Hoover's "Special Correspondents' List" of most favored persons.[39] Kirks himself had applied to become an FBI special agent in 1940, but later withdrew his application.[40] If former agents were to be hired to infiltrate the judiciary as court administrators, Kirks was in a position to make it happen.[41] When a court executive position was created in the District of Columbia in 1970, Judge Tamm had suggested to Hoover that Kirks be given the names of a current FBI employee who "could go into a job like this and knock some sense into the heads of freaks" they have on the bench.[42] Tamm said that a "gutsy" fellow "who had no obligation to any of those Judges could do a whale of a job" and might ultimately "become a Judge."[43] Hoover said he would think about it and get back to him. Tamm concluded that "Kirks would be tickled to death" if Hoover recommended someone. FBI records either were not kept, were censored, or do not exist about any follow-up discussions of these plans for court administration.

At age seventy-seven, John Edgar Hoover died of a heart attack in his sleep on May 2, 1972. Hoover had named Clyde A. Tolson, his colleague and companion, as the executor of his estate and its principal beneficiary.[44] The ensuing revelations of the Watergate scandal and cover-up, the Senate's Church Committee report in 1976, and the amendments to the Freedom of Information Act, which opened up millions of FBI records to public inspection for the first time, were subsequent body blows to the once proud bureau.

Epilogue

During the course of the late 1970s most of the FBI's domestic political surveillance ceased. Certainly with respect to the federal courts, the bureau's interactions were much more circumspect, as far as can be learned from FBI documents released under the Freedom of Information Act. Yet some aspects of J. Edgar Hoover's federal court program continued after his death and are still in place today. The FBI's public relations activities with the Supreme Court[1] as well as favors to Chief Justice Warren Burger and other favored federal judges continued under FBI Directors L. Patrick Gray, Clarence Kelley, and William Webster. In 1974 the chief justice had special agents from the Washington field office working for him to find out the names of Court employees who had leaked memos to the press about labor problems and union organizing at the Court. All "officers of the United States Supreme Court Police Department . . . [were] considered suspects." This union-busting investigation during Kelley's directorship included fingerprint comparisons of all police employees with the latent prints taken from the memos that were leaked.[2]

Under Burger, the FBI presence was institutionalized in employee selection by placing an FBI agent on the Supreme Court Employee Selection Board along with the marshal of the Supreme Court, who sits as chairman (other members include a member of the U.S. Capitol Police, U.S. Secret Service, and the Executive Protective Service).[3] The post-Hoover FBI directors continued to work with Burger to ensure the security of the Court building and the telephone and computer systems,[4] though this was the job of the marshal of Court as delegated to the Supreme Court police.

One FBI program still operating with the Rehnquist Supreme Court and the federal judiciary under Director William Sessions is the so-called liaison program. One beneficiary of this program is former New York Yankees' owner, George Steinbrenner. In the liaison program Steinbrenner received bureau help in obtaining a presidential pardon, getting agency record checks on his employees and associates, and other favors not within the jurisdiction of the bureau.[5] The FBI has long had similar arrangements with favored federal judges, court personnel, and even Supreme Court justices.

The documented interaction between the bureau and the justices in the post-Hoover era is generally innocuous.[6] Yet, even under Webster, the FBI's Liaison Unit at headquarters helped longtime bureau friend, Chief Justice Burger, bring Oriental rugs from England in 1985.[7] The bureau's current liaison program at the Supreme Court is described in internal memos as an effort to be aware of "all violations of Federal law within our investigative jurisdiction and liaison sources are important sources of any new cases."[8] As part of the program an "administrative matters" file is opened and the judicial branch "source" is "assigned to a primary contact Agent with an alternate contact Agent, who will handle the source in the absence of contacting Agent."[9] These files are given a classification number, "66," which reflects that they are a repository for records about "supplies, automobiles, salary matters and vouchers."[10] Unofficially, it is believed that vouchers for informers sometimes end up in these administrative files.[11]

Bureau liaison with the judiciary was never limited to justices and judges. Secretaries, court security personnel, and law clerks were often valuable sources of information or help. In the Ninth Circuit the FBI liaison agents had arranged for the clerk of court's office to flag appeals in criminal cases and provide an early warning system for agents— essentially doing the Justice Department's work in letting the bureau know what was going on with the case. All "briefs and official communications" filed with the Circuit Court were "furnished [to] the San Francisco [FBI] Office" by the clerk's staff.[12]

There were other public relations and liaison schemes originated by Hoover that were designed to turn judicial employees into informers and sources, as happened when the Julius and Ethel Rosenberg case came before the Supreme Court. Twenty years later, in the 1970s, Supreme Court employees frequently contacted by FBI agents were described as "very cooperative," even though the stated purpose of the visit was simply to obtain copies of public documents that these employees are required to give to any member of the public.[13]

The current FBI version of liaison with judges and court personnel includes the provision of security-related services to federal judges, such as file checks on prospective law clerks and other employees if this is requested through the Administrative Office of the U.S. Courts, as well as arranging social or educational functions during which agents can get to know the judges or justices.[14] FBI agents still take and develop

8 x 10 color photographs for federal judges at taxpayer expense to give as public relations gifts to the men and women who preside and rule on FBI-investigated criminal cases.[15] The liaison programs are not simply a way to obtain publicly available information and become aware of violations of law—they are attempts to obtain favors by providing them first or giving them in return.

Other public relations programs with the judiciary have similar purposes, as can be seen by viewing them from a historical perspective. These programs are Hoover's inventions, passed on to a new generation of special agents in the field. Sessions's FBI follows the Hoover credo that it has the right to routinely initiate releases of personal information from its files to federal judges about law clerks or others "where disclosure appears relevant to the authorized function of the recipient judicial office or court system."[16]

And when looking at the FBI's current programs directed at the judiciary, one must consider the recent movement of the bureau toward the old ways of conducting business. The bureau engages in a "Library Awareness Program," which seeks to make unpaid informers out of librarians by asking them to report suspicious activity or reveal the names of patrons who might be helping Soviet agents obtain technical information.[17] It conducted a wide-ranging "terrorism" investigation of the Committee in Solidarity with the People of El Salvador (CISPES) from 1981 to 1985 and used informers and agents to keep tabs on lawful demonstrations, seminars, and marches.[18] Other problems at the FBI, such as institutionalized racism, are still present. Job discrimination lawsuits brought by an African-American and a class action suit brought by a group of Latino agents have been settled out-of-court after initial findings of discrimination.[19] Black agent Donald Rochon settled his racial harassment suit for almost one million dollars, and eleven FBI supervisors and agents face disciplinary action as a result. The racial problems within the bureau had reached such a level that in April 1991 Sessions and his top aides met with 250 black agents from around the country to work on ways to avert a lawsuit charging the FBI with racial discrimination.[20]

Some believe that the FBI may still be up to its old ways in the political surveillance area. Twenty-one-year FBI veteran John C. Ryan was fired for insubordination in 1987 for refusing to conduct a "terrorism" investigation of peace activists who were breaking the law to show their opposition to U.S. intervention in Central America. In a 1987 interview Ryan sounded like a 1960s protester when he called the FBI "an internal arm to quell dissent."[21] And former Senator Robert Morgan, who was a member of the Senate's Church Committee that investigated intelligence agency abuses, said that "the FBI and most other federal agencies, and some state agencies, are still doing the same thing."[22] Morgan, who served as director of the North Carolina State Bureau of Investigation, said that money used to pay informants continues to breed unaccountability in the FBI and other agencies.[23]

In the 1990s the fear of international and domestic terrorism as a result of the Persian Gulf War led to greatly increased FBI counterterrorist efforts.[24] Some of the FBI's tactics were criticized as violations of civil liberties.[25] As is true with most classified FBI programs, it will take years, if not decades, to learn the scope of the bureau's actions.

Apart from the issue of whether bureau infringements on citizens' First Amendment and privacy rights are continuing, when it comes to the federal judiciary, neither the FBI nor any other litigant or interested party should have special access to court personnel, judges, or justices. The average citizen's distrust of lawyers, judges, and the judicial system in general is fostered by even the appearance of an "old boy" system in which prosecutors, law enforcement officers, and judges appear to be more than simply cordial and respectful of each other. An informal arrangement in which FBI agents and U.S. attorneys are more welcome in the chambers of justices and judges than defense lawyers or citizens does not inspire confidence and leads to the appearance that cases have been discussed and resolved beforehand, no matter how untrue this may be. This appearance itself is contrary to both the high ethical standards required of judges and to basic notions of fair play and good citizenship.

In the 1980s, under the administration of President Ronald Reagan, once an FBI "confidential informant" himself, the Executive Branch again empowered the FBI, this time to fight terrorism.[26] The Freedom of Information Act was greatly weakened in 1986.[27]

The Supreme Court has also changed. The combined nominations of Presidents Reagan and George Bush transformed the "moderate" Burger Court into the "conservative" Rehnquist Court of 1991.[28] Thurgood Marshall's retirement and replacement by Clarence Thomas might well make the Rehnquist Court the High Court for which Hoover had plotted, worked, and hoped. Had the FBI not interfered with the Supreme Court for decades—with the help or acquiescence of liberal and conservative justices alike—the Supreme Court might be a different institution as it goes into the twenty-first century. If William O. Douglas had been appointed chief justice in 1946, Earl Warren would not have gotten the job in 1953 nor Warren Burger in 1969, since Douglas did not retire until 1975. The appointment of Douglas's successor would have gone to President Gerald Ford—and the chief justice of the United States today would probably be moderate John Paul Stevens rather than the conservative William Rehnquist.[29]

Despite the FBI's history of covertly manipulating the High Court, the bureau's background investigation remains a routine but highly important element of the confirmation process, as the confirmation hearing of Justice Thomas attests. As has been shown, the background investigation itself is rife with potential conflicts of interest for the FBI, whose client is the White House, not the Senate.

The Senate Judiciary Committee's unprecedented hearings on charges that Thomas had sexually harassed a female employee underscores the questionable role that the Judiciary Committee still allows the FBI to play in the confirmation process. To the extent that the Senate relies upon the FBI, it de facto delegates its right to investigate the president's judicial nominees back to the Executive Branch.

The original FBI background investigation of Judge Thomas for the position of associate justice did not uncover Professor Anita Hill's sexual harassment allegations.[30] Neither did prior FBI investigations of Thomas uncover these charges when he was nominated to head the Equal Employment Opportunity Commission nor when he was named to serve on the D.C. Circuit Court of Appeals. *Newsday* reporter Timothy Phelps learned of the harassment charges almost two months before the Senate or the FBI did. Phelps said that the "FBI and Senate could have done the same."[31] Nina Totenberg of National Public Radio also learned of Hill's allegations. Only after the liberal lobbying group, Alliance for Justice, brought Professor Hill to the attention of the Judiciary Committee did committee chairman, Senator Joseph Biden, ask the White House to have the FBI investigate the charges.[32]

Had the Judiciary Committee been interested in a thorough, independent investigation of the sexual harassment charges, it would have conducted its own investigation rather than initially relying on the FBI, an agency of the Executive Branch. Without the leak to the press of Professor Hill's affadavit, no full Judiciary Committee investigation would have occurred.

The FBI's conflict of interest in the Thomas-Hill scandal was clear. White House counsel staff, with help from Justice Department lawyers and Senate Republican staffers, amassed information to attack Hill's credibility.[33] Meanwhile, the FBI, a component of the Justice Department, had investigated the sexual harassment charges.

All information is shaped by the biases of those who assemble and provide it, whether it is the FBI under Director William Sessions or Hoover or the leadership of the NAACP. The Senate's reliance on FBI background investigations of Supreme court nominees was and is a bad idea.

It discourages the Senate from doing its own investigation and has in the past been used to mislead the Senate Judiciary Committee— deliberately.

It is the president's constitutional prerogative to nominate candidates, but the Senate must make the final decision on their fitness to serve. As such, the Senate is ultimately responsible for conducting an independent investigation. Advice and consent require nothing less.

A number of steps should be taken by Congress, the White House, and the Supreme Court in an attempt to prevent the abuses described in this book.

(1) The Senate, which has the constitutional responsibility of advising and consenting to all federal judicial nominations by the president, should increase its investigative staff to enable it to conduct its own independent background investigations of nominees. If the Senate Judiciary Committee chooses to accept a report based upon an FBI investigation, it should request all FBI records, including all documents concerning a nominee's contacts with the bureau. An FBI report on a nominee's background should be viewed with as much skepticism as reports submitted by other interest groups. With regard to the Supreme Court, the FBI was, is, and will remain an interested party that serves the president.

(2) The attorney general and director of the FBI should end the FBI's liaison program with the courts. Liaison with the judiciary or the court administration is ethically questionable, raising an appearance of impropriety.

(3) Concomitantly, court and clerk of court employees, law clerks, and judges should not participate in the FBI liaison program. Additionally, the lower federal courts should consider hiring guards accountable to the judiciary for security in judges' chambers and not rely solely on the U.S. Marshal's Service, which is within the Department of Justice.[34] In addition, the judiciary should hire its own employees with security expertise, so that the judiciary need not rely solely on the FBI or the Marshal's Service, both within the Executive Branch, to secure their computer systems, phones, and buildings.[35]

(4) An FBI charter should be enacted that specifically sets out its lawful authority, outlaws infringements of First Amendment rights and violations of the separation of powers, and bans lobbying and propaganda activities.[36]

(5) The Freedom of Information Act and Privacy Act should be strengthened by Congress, and the president should issue a new executive order dealing with the declassification of documents and collection and dissemination of information about citizens.

(6) Congress itself should more vigorously engage in overseeing the activities of the FBI.

(7) The Supreme Court should enact its own rules, treating its interchambers memoranda, bench memoranda, and case files as public records within a reasonable time after a decision is rendered in a case. The personal conference notes of the justices might be treated differently as they sometimes contain personal comments about one another.

Supreme Court justices are no less corruptible than presidents, lawyers, FBI agents, representatives, or senators. When the High Court has been "conservative" and when it has been "liberal," secrecy has been used as a cover for unethical, inappropriate, and unconstitutional behavior by certain justices. Only by making the High Court more open to public scrutiny, while being mindful of the function of the Court in our constitutional system, can we guard against similar judicial misdeeds. Without the Freedom of Information Act, to which neither the Supreme Court nor Congress is subject, the improprieties documented in this book could not have been uncovered. It is time for the Supreme Court to shed its pious facade and face the need for open doors. Nine black-robed justices looking down from the bench and a Court crier's incantation— "Oyez, oyez, oyez. God save the United States and this Honorable Court"—neither create a secular writ of infallibility nor preserve the honor of the Court.

Notes

Preface

1. *Public Citizen v. U.S. Dept. of Justice,* 109 S.Ct. 2558, 2573 (1989) (Kennedy, Rehnquist, and O'Connor, concurring, citing *The Federalist,* Nos. 47–51 (J. Madison)).

2. A. Hamilton, J. Jay, and J. Madison, *The Federalist Papers* (Pocket Books 1964), No. 48 (J. Madison), pp. 111, 116.

3. *See, e.g.,* Q. Tamm to Tolson, Classification of Documents, 6/5/57, 66-7225-1195 ("Department has in the past questioned classifications of documents sent to them from SOG."); *see* Sanford J. Ungar, *The FBI* (Atlantic Monthly Press 1976), p. 660.

4. Athan Theoharis and John Stuart Cox, *The Boss: J. Edgar Hoover and the Great American Inquisition* (Temple University Press 1988), p. 17 (hereafter cited as *The Boss*).

5. Clark Clifford with Richard Holbrooke, *Counsel to the President: A Memoir* (Random House 1991), p. 182 (hereafter cited as *Counsel to the President*).

6. *The Federalist Papers,* No. 78 (A. Hamilton).

7. *See gen.* Michael Tigar, "The McCarthy Era: History as Snapshot" (review of David Caute's *The Great Fear: The Anti-Communist Purge under Truman and Eisenhower* [Simon and Schuster 1979]), *Harvard Civil Rights Civil-Liberties Law Review* 15, No. 2 (Fall 1980), pp. 507 *et seq.*

8. *See* infra pp. 7–10.

9. Ungar, *The FBI,* pp. 407–408. Hoover's comments were made at a cabinet meeting.

10. C. 678, §2, 70 stat. 623 (1956) (current version at 18 U.S.C.A. Sec. 2385 1962). In addition to the conspiracy provision (18 U.S.C.A.§. 2384 [1956]), the Smith Act also outlawed membership, "knowing the purposes thereof" in any group that advocates "overthrowing or destroying" the government and also the printing, publishing, selling, editing, or circulation of printed materials with the intent to cause the "overthrow or destruction" of the government.

11. Senate Select Committee on Governmental Operations, Book III, Supplementary Detailed Staff Reports on Intelligence Activities and the Rights of Americans, 94th Cong., 2d Sess., Report No. 94-755 (1976), p. 10 (testimony of

FBI Deputy Associate Director Adams), hereafter cited as Senate (Church) Committee, Final Report, Book III.

12. Morton Halperin, Jerry Berman, Robert Borosage, and Christine Marwick, *The Lawless State: The Crimes of the U.S. Intelligence Agencies* (Penguin Books 1979), p. 111. *But see,* Henry Abraham, *Freedom and the Court: Civil Rights and Liberties in the United States* (Oxford University Press 1988), p. 246 (listing the number of Smith Act convictions as of June 1957 at 89).

13. Senate (Church) Committee, Final Report, Book III, p. 3.

14. *Id.,* at p. 4.

15. Frank J. Donner, *The Age of Surveillance: The Aims and Methods of America's Political Intelligence System* (First Vintage Books Edition 1981), pp. 177–181.

16. According to the FBI, there were twelve COINTELPROs: "Communist Party," "Socialist Workers Party," "White Hate," "Black Nationalist," "New Left," "Special Operations," "Soviet-Bloc," "Border Coverage," "Yugoslav," "Cuban," "Puerto Rican," and "Hoodwink." Emil Moschella memo to all agents *inter alia,* re: COINTELPRO, No. 11, 12/12/88, HQs Policies Relating to implementation of the FOI–PA, numbered memoranda (unclassified). Scholars have indicated that COINTELPRO-type actions were also directed at the Reverend Martin Luther King, Jr. *See* David Garrow, *The FBI and Martin Luther King, Jr.* (Penguin Books 1985), pp. 182–183, and the Los Angeles–based National Committee to Abolish HUAC. *See also* Kenneth O'Reilly, *Hoover and the Un-Americans: The FBI, HUAC, and the Red Menace* (Temple University Press 1983), pp. 255–281.

17. Richard E. Morgan, *Domestic Intelligence: Monitoring Dissent in America* (University of Texas Press 1980), p. 48. *See* Kenneth O'Reilly, *"Racial Matters": The FBI's Secret File on Black America, 1960–1971* (The Free Press 1989), p. 301 (hereafter *Racial Matters*).

18. *Racial Matters,* pp. 299–324.

19. In response to the author's 1984 request for records about the Supreme Court and COINTELPRO, FBI headquarters failed to locate any documents with that heading. In the course of litigation, which began in February 1988, no documents have been released by the FBI captioned COINTELPRO–Supreme Court. Hundreds of records concerning the justices and the Court have been censored or withheld altogether, under claims that they are classified or protected under the law enforcement exemptions. This litigation is continuing in the Middle District of North Carolina.

20. (*Court*) *E.g., infra,* ch. 3 (Justice Fortas as informer and lawyer for the FBI at conference discussions on *Black*). (*Law Clerks*) *infra,* ch. 1. (*Justices*) *infra,* ch. 1. (*Congress*) *E.g., infra,* ch. 1 (the FBI's role in the Warren confirmation) and ch. 9 (the FBI's role in the impeachment moves against Justice Douglas). (*White House*) *E.g., infra,* ch. 4 (the FBI bypassing the attorney general's office in *Black* and going directly, albeit clandestinely, to the White House) and ch. 9 (FBI help to the Nixon administration during the Douglas impeachment moves). (*"Subversives"*) *E.g.,* FBI COINTELPRO actions sometimes directly interfaced with Court business. In 1961 the Supreme Court upheld the convictions of activists Frank Wilkinson and Carl Braden for refusing to answer questions

posed by House Un-American Activities Committee (HUAC) interrogators about Communist infiltration of the textile industry in the South and Communist propaganda activities. 365 U.S. 399 (1961) and 365 U.S. 431 (1961). Wilkinson was an FBI COINTELPRO target, his reward for being the "brains and energy" of the National Committee to Abolish HUAC. Hoover took special interest in Wilkinson's Supreme Court case. After the Court upheld Wilkinson's conviction (pending his lawyer's request for a rehearing), Wilkinson continued to tour the country attacking HUAC. Incensed, Hoover asked his assistants if they could "expedite" Wilkinson's date for reporting to prison for contempt of Congress. J.F. Bland to A.H. Belmont, Frank B. Wilkinson, IS–C, 3/21/61, 100-112434-107, filed in *Wilkinson v. FBI*, C.D.CA., Civ. 80-01048 AWT (Tx), Declaration of Douglas E. Mirell in Opposition to Defendants' Motion for Judgment on the Pleadings, Exhibit 5; Richard Criley, *The FBI v. the First Amendment* (First Amendment Foundation 1990), p. 52. The Washington field office was ordered to follow the progress of the Wilkinson case at the Supreme Court. Using established FBI sources at the Court, agents were provided with a copy of Wilkinson's petition for rehearing immediately after it was filed. A Court employee told the FBI liaison agent that the Court would not rule for a month or so. SAC, WFO, to Hoover, Frank B. Wilkinson, IS–C, 3/24/61, 100-112434, filed in *Wilkinson v. FBI*, C.D.CA., Civ. 80-01048 AWT (Tx), Declaration of Douglas Mirell, Opposition to Defendants' Motion for Judgment on the Pleadings, Exhibit 9.

Also, the FBI's COINTELPRO–Communist party came to the Supreme Court, unbeknownst to the justices, in a pending case involving the Communist Party of the USA, in which the FBI had done the investigation for the Subversive Activities Control Board (SACB). But Supreme Court litigation did not stop the bureau from violating the constitutional rights of the Communist party members by interfering with the party's Washington state affiliate, which was organizing activities to coincide with a planned Justice Douglas trip to Seattle. Hoover to SAC, COINTELPRO, Seattle, Citizens Committee for Constitutional Liberties, re: WOD meeting 8/28/61, IS–C, 8/11/61. 100-3-104-2792. FBI headquarters ordered the Seattle field office to disrupt the party's plans.

The Supreme Court ruled against the FBI's COINTELPRO targets in *Communist Party v. S.A.C.B.*, 367 U.S. 1 (1961). Congress had determined that there existed "a world Communist movement . . . directed by the Communist dictatorship of a foreign country" and that it was bent on the "establishment of a Communist totalitarian dictatorship throughout the world." *Id.*, p. 112. The Court ruled that because of the congressional findings, the requirement of the Subversive Activities Control Act—that party officers and members register their names and addresses with the attorney general—was not inconsistent with the First Amendment's protection of freedom of speech and association. Frankfurter's opinion was joined by Clark, Harlan, Whittaker, and Stewart. Warren, Black, Douglas, and Brennan dissented.

(*General Public*) *See, infra*, ch. 1.

21. One could argue that Hoover intended to remake all of America in his own image and that the FBI's program with respect to the Supreme Court was

different in form but not in substance from all other bureau activities designed to increase FBI prestige and power by maintaining high public visibility through aggressive public relations, encouraging an antiradical, conservative political culture through alliances formed with important business, media, and government leaders, and adopting a "carrot and stick" system of reward and punishment. Yet the Warren Court, even with some pro-FBI justices and informers, was perceived as a unique and powerful enemy of Hoover's, as is shown by the contents of the FBI's subject files entitled "U.S. Supreme Court," portions of Hoover's "Official & Confidential" files, and the files of every individual Supreme Court justice who served between 1935 and 1972. (Files on Justices William Brennan, Byron White, Thurgood Marshall, Harry Blackmun, Lewis Powell, and William Rehnquist cannot be obtained, due to the restrictions of the Privacy Act. Portions of Warren Burger's file were released to the author after litigation. Arthur Goldberg's file was requested after his death, but was not received before publication of this book.)

22. Domestic Antiterrorism Prevention Efforts in Selected Federal Courts, GAO Report to the Chairman of the Subcommittee on Civil and Constitutional Rights, Committee on the Judiciary, U.S. House of Representatives, June 1988 (GAO, PEMD-88-22), pp. 25–26.

23. Senate (Church) Committee, Final Report, Book III, p. 178.

24. See gen., Senate (Church) Committee, Final Report, Book III; The Boss; Racial Matters; Age of Surveillance; Alexander Charns, "How the FBI Spied on the Supreme Court," Washington Post 12/3/89, C1. For example, Hoover used Federal Judge Edward A. Tamm, a former FBI assistant director, to spread derogatory information about judicial enemies. In 1958 Hoover sent Tamm six copies of a blind memorandum, prepared by the FBI, about Judge George Edwards. The memo accused Edwards of having been a socialist in his youth and claimed that Edwards's father, a Dallas attorney, "was a Socialist nominee for Governor of Texas." Edwards had drawn the ire of Hoover when he supported a resolution, adopted by the Advisory Council of Judges, National Probation and Parole Association, which was critical of Hoover. Hoover to Tamm, letter by special messenger, 10/7/58, 94-44876-31. The blind memo about Edwards had no markings revealing its source, so Tamm could pass it to other judges or to the press.

25. E.g., Edward Scheidt, the SAC, Charlotte, from 1937 to 1946, was asked by the Justice Department to recommend the best federal judge in North Carolina to preside over an antitrust prosecution of a fertilizer manufacturer. Scheidt recommended Judge Hayes, and this was accepted. "In my humble way, I did select the judge," Scheidt recalled. Scheidt interview with author, 10/14/90.

26. E.g., FBI agents regularly attended the annual Federal Judicial Conference for the Ninth Circuit, where agents met with the judges and lobbied for positions on criminal procedure and other matters of interest to the bureau. "I cannot stress too strongly my personal belief that the Bureau's attendance and participation with this group is in the very best interests of the Bureau." SAC, SF, to Director, 9th Cir. Judicial Conference, Portland, Oregon, 7/13/61, Information Concerning, 7/21/61, 94-33476-NR. Attendance of agents at Federal Judi-

cial Conferences became systematized throughout the country, where possible, due to its perceived salutary effects.

27. *E.g.*, nine years later, during one of Hoover's long-running battles with Warren Olney III, director of the Administrative Office of the U.S. Courts (this one about FBI agents orally providing information to federal probation officers for use in court), Hoover had the SAC in Cincinnati contact Federal Judge John H. Druffel and provide him with information about the feud with Olney. "Judge Druffel responded to the Director that it is no problem for him to cooperate with the FBI because the Judge has such a high regard for the Director and his entire staff." SAC, Cinci., to Hoover, re: Warren Olney, III, Dir., AOUSC, 6/15/60, 62-56933-NR.

An example of what happened to a judicial enemy of the bureau is Federal Judge Charles E. Wyzanski of Boston, the former star law student and confidant of Supreme Court Justice Felix Frankfurter. Judge Wyzanski was targeted by Hoover. The Boston FBI field office plotted to prevent Wyzanski from hearing the case of Michael A. Russo, who, along with four other Smith Act defendants, was charged with conspiracy to overthrow the government. Wyzanski, like Frankfurter, had testified for Alger Hiss and had, according to the FBI, "connections with individuals active in communist front groups." 62-75474-21.

At Russo's arraignment Wyzanski lambasted FBI agents for arresting Russo without having the indictment in their possession, and for the delay in arraigning him. Hoover agreed with an assistant's suggestion that the Justice Department dismiss the charges against Russo and indict him in another federal district to remove the case from Wyzanski. Wyzanski's writings were read in the hope of finding a reason to have him disqualified from hearing the case. Finally, the attorney general and his deputy were told by the FBI: "The Department should endeavor, by whatever means are necessary and available, to have the Russo case set for trial before one of the other judges."

As far back as 1951, the bureau was compiling information about Wyzanski and suggesting to the Justice Department that judge-shopping be employed to keep Wyzanski from hearing Smith Act cases. SAC, Boston, to Hoover, Judge Wyzanski, Jr., Information Concerning, 7/23/51, 62-75474-15. After a lengthy delay (pending the outcome of a Supreme Court case challenging the Smith Act), Federal Judge Bailey Aldrich, not Wyzanski, presided over the Russo case.

28. *See, e.g.*, Edward Bennett Williams main FBI HQ file 62-9886. Attorney Williams and his clients were tailed and overheard in wiretaps and bugs. Hoover's vendetta against Williams included leaking derogatory information to the press and sending a letter of warning to President Lyndon Johnson with a "run-down on Williams' recent activities in defending the country's most notorious hoodlums" after Johnson had attended a Washington Redskins football game with Williams.

29. *See gen.*, Ann Fagan Ginger and Eugene M. Tobin, *The National Lawyers Guild from Roosevelt to Reagan* (Temple University Press 1988).

30. The Executives' Conference to Director, Dissemination of Information by the Bureau Outside the Executive Departments, 10/14/53, 62-53025-NR, first serial after 475 (in addition, information about subversive lawyers was disseminated to the National Conference of Bar Examiners); A.H. Belmont to L.V.

Boardman, visit with U.S. Judge John H. Druffel of Cincinnati, Ohio, July 24, 1957, 7/25/57, 62-27585-NR, first serial after 81; *Age of Surveillance,* pp. 144–146; Harrison Salisbury, "The Strange Correspondence of Morris Ernst and John Edgar Hoover, 1939–1964," *The Nation,* 12/1/84, pp. 575–589 (ACLU general counsel and board member Morris Ernst had a long collaboration with Hoover and the FBI, and he was included on the director's "Special Correspondents List." The bureau maintained tens of thousands of pages of records about the ACLU over the years.)

31. In early 1990 the FBI had informed Congress that it had invoked these exclusions on 88 occasions since the FOIA was amended in 1986. *ACCESS Reports,* Mar. 7, 1990, p. 2.

32. January 25, 1990, Order of Federal Magistrate Russell A. Eliason, *Charns v. U.S. Dept. of Justice,* U.S. Middle District of North Carolina, C-88-175-D (hereafter cited as *Charns I*), p. 24; Tony Mauro, "Striking Gold with the FOIA. How FBI's Court Files Came to Light," *Legal Times,* 9/12/88, p. 6; A. Charns and P. Green, "Perfecting Your Form," *I.R.E. Journal,* May–June 1991, pp. 14–15. A Freedom of Information-Privacy Act file (called a 190 classification file) is opened after every FOIA request that does not involve an "excluded" category of records. The FBI places all records, correspondence, and administrative instructions concerning the request in this file. In the author's 190 file was an FBI "search slip" listing the serial numbers of records that the FBI had located in 1984 in response to his original request for documents. Some of the records on this search slip were then requested by their file number. It was after this request, in 1987, that the FBI located the massive file entitled "Supreme Court" (file 62-27585). *See gen.,* 190-37116.

33. *The Boss,* p. 12; *see infra,* p. 161n84, for a discussion about how the Justice Fortas records were released.

34. *See* 5 U.S.C. 552 (the Freedom of Information Act applies to federal executive agencies. It neither applies to Congress nor to the federal judiciary).

Chapter 1: FBI Spying on the Supreme Court

1. New York *Daily News,* editorial, July 1, 1957. One of the more strident attacks on the Court was written by Rosalie M. Gordon in 1958: *Nine Men against America: The Supreme Court and Its Attack on American Liberties* (Devon-Adair Co.).

2. E.R. Bohner to Acting Dir. Hoover, Assigning a Special Agent to the Supreme Court, 7/29/24, 62-9180-2.

3. Taft to Rush L. Holland, Assist. A.G., 10/21/24, 62-9180-3.

4. Hoover to Mr. Farnum, 8/23/27, 62-14996-3 (Justice Holmes had written to the attorney general from Beverly Farms, Mass., and asked for help).

5. Sacco-Vanzetti–supporter Prof. Felix Frankfurter was picked up in Massachusetts state police wiretaps telling the defense team that he could not approach his friend Justice Louis Brandeis about a stay of execution. Justice Brandeis and Frankfurter had discussed the case, and Brandeis had supported Frankfurter's involvement. Bruce Allen Murphy, *The Brandeis/Frankfurter Con-*

nection (Oxford University Press 1982), pp. 78–82. The petition for writ of *certiorari* was "dismissed on motion of counsel for" Sacco and Vanzetti on Oct. 3, 1927. 275 U.S. 574 (1927).

6. *See, e.g.*, 62-27585-1x through 4, Feb. 1935; June 1935, 62-36032-1.

7. SAC, WFO to Hoover, Julius Rosenberg et al., Espionage-R, 6/23/53, 62-27585-30; Alexander Charns, "FB–Eyed," Durham *Morning Herald*, 8/14/89; "FBI Kept Secret Files on the Supreme Court," New York *Times*, 8/21/89; Alexander Charns, "How the FBI Spied on the Supreme Court," Washington *Post*, 12/3/89. Court employees were not the only ones improperly cooperating with the executive branch. Chief Justice Fred Vinson and Associate Justice Robert Jackson had an *ex parte* discussion with Attorney General Herbert Brownell about calling a special session of Court if Douglas granted a stay of execution to the Rosenbergs. Ronald Radosh and Joyce Milton, *The Rosenberg File: A Search for the Truth* (Vintage Books 1984), p. 403. According to Roy Cohn, the assistant U.S. attorney who prosecuted the Rosenbergs, Cohn not only helped select the judge who would try the Rosenbergs, but he also had improper *ex parte* discussions about the case with the trial judge, Irving Kaufman. Sidney Zion, *The Autobiography of Roy Cohn* (St. Martin's Press 1988), pp. 60–66.

8. D.M. Ladd to Hoover, Julius Rosenberg et al., Espionage-R, 6/25/53, 62-27585-31.

9. Tolson handwritten note on bottom of M.A. Jones to Nichols, Harold B. Willey, Clerk, U.S. Supreme Court Information Concerning, Oct. 14, 1952, 62-60527-31361.

10. The Supreme Court appoints and fixes the compensation of the clerk of court and deputy clerks, who are also subject to removal by the Court. 28 U.S.C.A. Sec. 671 (1948) (amended 1972). Unlike the lower federal courts, in which the marshal of the Court is an employee of the U.S. Marshal's Service (a component of the Department of Justice), the marshal of the Supreme Court is appointed, and may be removed, by the High Court. The marshal, under the supervision of the chief justice, is responsible for hiring assistants and other employees (28 U.S.C.A. Sec. 672 [1948] [amended in 1982]) and for hiring Supreme Court police (40 U.S.C.A. Sec. 13f [1949] [amended in 1982]). The marshal of the Court and the Supreme Court police, with the approval of the chief justice, are authorized to police the Supreme Court Building and grounds. The metropolitan police of the District of Columbia make arrests within the Supreme Court Building and grounds if requested to do so by the marshal of the Supreme Court. 40 U.S.C.A. Sec. 13n (1949) (amended in 1985).

11. Hoover wrote: "It is rather difficult to tell where A.G. stands on Communism. One day he is against it and the next he is either for it or deprecates [*sic*] its existence." Nichols to Tolson, 10/14/46, originally designated DO NOT FILE, but later placed in 62-72944.

12. Summary of information from a confidential informant, War Department, MID 000.24, Communism, 10/30/41, Subject: J. Edgar Hoover (also in FBI files); watches were also kept on Justice Minton's visitors. In February 1955 a professor and four students from Hamilton University visited Associate Justice Sherman Minton. The group was followed into the Supreme Court building by

FBI agents, who asked T. Perry Lippitt, the marshall of the Court, about the visitors. Minton, a New Dealer who was conservative on civil liberties issues, found out about the interview and told Chief Justice Warren. Warren, still on friendly terms with Attorney General Brownell and Hoover, was shown the FBI report about Minton's visitors, parts of which are still classified. Hoover later promised the attorney general that he "could rest assured that from now on no surveillances would be conducted in the Supreme Court Building." Hoover to Tolson et al., 2/15/55, 62-27585-38 and 62-27585-NR 1st after 38. After the incident, unbeknownst to the chief justice or to Attorney General Brownell, Hoover simply ordered agents to ask headquarters for permission before conducting surveillances at the Supreme Court or the Capitol. L.V. Boardman to Director, Surveillances, 2/2/55, 66-4151-229.

13. Records were requested about Arthur Goldberg, but were not received prior to publication of this book. Due to the restrictions of the Privacy Act, FBI records about Justices Brennan and Marshall were not requested.

14. *E.g.*, 62-27585.

15. Harold H. Burton to Hoover, 10/2/39, 62-20429-3X2.

16. R.R. Roach to A.H. Belmont, Justice Harold H. Burton, return to Washington, Aug. 27, 1958, 8/27/58, 62-20429-38.

17. *E.g.*, Hoover to Justice Jackson, 4/2/54, 62-56460-47 (note at bottom of bureau's copy); 77-61449-54 (memo re: Justice Whittaker).

18. *E.g.*, Hoover to Ernest W. McFarland, chief justice of the Arizona Supreme Court, 7/12/68, 62-53025-720; a note on the bureau's copy states that McFarland is on the "Special Correspondents List" and that the SAC "should extend all possible assistance and cooperation to Justice McFarland in matters of mutual interest"; William Friday, former president of the University of North Carolina system, was also on the "Special Correspondents List." Alexander Charns, "The FBI, UNC and Friday: The Southern Part of Hoover," *N.C. Independent,* Sept. 16–29, 1983, pp. 1, 5. Others on this list included then California Governor Warren and Representative Gerald Ford. U.S. District Court Judge John O. Henderson of Buffalo, N.Y., was on "the mailing list to receive the FBI Law Enforcement Bulletin. . . . Judge Henderson is described as a firm supporter and good friend of the FBI." Hoover to Hon. John O. Henderson, 2/13/68, 62-53025-710, note on bureau copy. Judge Henderson had written to Hoover thanking him for the "finest cooperation from the FBI in accomplishing my work." The judge had just "completed the trial" of an organized crime case: "[T]here have been a few occasions when I felt I needed to know some collateral information to assist me in the progress of the case, and I thought it suitable to tell you that I have had the usual splendid cooperation of SAC Neil J. Welch and staff. You may be sure I appreciate the ability to avail myself of these services when required." Henderson to Hoover, 2/9/68, 62-53025-710.

19. FBI correspondence with author. The "Special Correspondents List" continued until at least January 1974, under the directorship of Clarence M. Kelley. Kelley to Rowland Kirks, 1/8/74, 62-56933-81 (note at bottom of bureau copy); 55 Fed. Reg. 49,170 (11/26/90)(describes current bureau mailing lists).

20. SAC, Phil. to Director, [Redacted] Security matter-C, 6/6/50, 62-37356-illegible. The manager of the Stouffer's Restaurant in Philadelphia had been told about this by an accountant friend. The accuser, who had worked at the State Department, was considered to be "overly suspicious and continually distrustful of his fellow employees." Baumgardner to A.H. Belmont, D. Acheson, F. Frankfurter, Information Concerning, 6/15/50, 62-37356-NR. Hoover ordered agents to interview the accuser for information about Frankfurter and Acheson.

21. WFO file 62-6355 by George E. Davis, Dean Acheson, Felix Frankfurter, Information Concerning, 7/14/50, p. 4.

22. Other charges were more reality-bound. Hoover had a memo in his secret office file about Frankfurter's "manipulating changes in Secretaries of War." Memo from E.A. Tamm to Director, Hoover's "Official and Confidential" ("O & C") files, 12/3/40.

23. Hoover to Tolson et al., 1/22/54, 101-2983-4; Alex Charns, "The FBI Connection," Seattle *Weekly,* 7/4/84; "FBI Maintained Close Watch on Justice Douglas," New York *Times,* 7/22/84.

24. James A. Pryde, Chief, Washington state patrol, report to Gov. Arthur B. Langlie, 1/4/54, 101-2983-7.

25. *Id.;* David Caute, *The Great Fear: The Anti-Communist Purge under Truman and Eisenhower* (Simon and Schuster 1979), pp. 317–321; Laura Kalman, *Abe Fortas* (Yale University Press 1990), pp. 149, 150. Lattimore was indicted for perjury after he denied that he had been a "sympathizer or any other kind of promoter of Communism or Communist interests." Ultimately, after years of appeals and a new round of grand jury indictments, the charges against Lattimore were dismissed.

26. Pryde, report to Gov. Langlie, 1/4/54, 101-2983-7.

27. R.D. Auerbach to F.J. Baumgardner, re: Justice William O. Douglas, 1/28/54, 101-2983-7; D.M. Ladd to Hoover, re: Justice William O. Douglas, 2/9/54, 101-2983-18.

28. D.M. Ladd to Hoover, Justice William O. Douglas, 2/9/54, 101-2983-18.

29. A.H. Belmont to L.V. Boardman, [Redacted], 6/1/54, 101-2983-20; Director to SAC, WFO, [Redacted], 6/2/54, 101-2983-NR (Hoover ordering agent to interview Justice Douglas); Alex Charns, "The FBI Connection," Seattle *Weekly,* 7/4/84, p. 26; Allen Weinstein, *Perjury: The Hiss-Chambers Case* (Alfred A. Knopf 1978), p. 87 ("Irving Kaplan . . . figured in Chambers's experience as an underground Communist").

30. Weinstein, *Perjury,* p. 376 (re: character witnesses); A.H. Belmont to L.V. Boardman, Civil Rights Commission, 11/12/57, 62-35016-16, attached memorandum entitled Stanley Foreman Reed (Reed was interviewed by agents in 1949 re: Hiss and "could recall no derogatory information").

31. James J. Kelley, SAC, N.Y., "Personal and Confidential," to Hoover, 4/9/54, 62-37356-NR.

32. SAC Boston to Hoover, 12/4/55, 62-37356-illegible.

33. *E.g.,* in *Gold v. U.S.,* 352 U.S. 985 (1957) a union member's conviction for filing a false non-Communist affidavit was overturned because an FBI agent, while investigating another case, had visited the home of three members

of the jury and asked them if they had received any Communist "propaganda." In *Schware v. Board of Bar Examiners of New Mexico*, 353 U.S. 232 (1957) the Court ruled that a bar applicant who presented evidence of good moral character, but who had been a member of the Communist party for a number of years, was denied due process of law when he was denied the opportunity to take the bar exam for not showing "good moral character." Similarly, in *Konigsberg v. State Bar of California*, 353 U.S. 252 (1957), the bar applicant was suspected of having been a member of the Communist party and for that reason was told that he had not shown sufficiently good moral character to justify his certification to practice law. The Court ruled that membership in the Communist party was not in itself proof of bad character.

34. William Cohen (former law clerk to Justice Douglas) to author, 1/9/90.

35. Tolson to Nichols, 5/23/57, 62-27585-61x.

36. SAC, Cincinnati, to Director, Warren Olney III, Dir. Admin. Office of U.S. Courts, 6/15/60, 62-56933-NR.

37. Memo from [Illegible] to Belmont, 6/5/57, 62-27585-NR, first serial after 81, with handwritten initials of J. Edgar Hoover.

38. For example, Thomas J. Schwab, a Harvard Law School graduate who clerked for the D.C. Circuit Court of Appeals in 1954-55, lost a job offer at the Justice Department because an FBI investigation revealed that he was a member of the National Association for the Advancement of Colored People and other liberal organizations. Warren E. Burger, as head of the Justice Department's Civil Division, offered Schwab a job and then withdrew it after a FBI background check came back detailing Schwab's liberal associations. Author's telephone interview with T. Schwab, 2/13/89; T. Schwab, "My FBI File—A Tragicomedy," Washington *Post*, 5/1/88, C5.

39. Author interview with Dagmar Hamilton, 10/9/88; Weinstein, *Perjury*, p. 499.

40. L.B. Nichols to Tolson, Supreme Court Justice Tom Clark, 5/10/55, 62-72944-381.

41. Author telephone interview with A. O'Donnell, 2/13/89; main FBI files about Justice Clark contain information about Alice O'Donnell's relationship with headquarters. *E.g.*, Legat, London, to Director, Request from Office of Justice Tom C. Clark Supreme Court, Miscellaneous—Information Concerning, 6/30/60 (re: Alice O'Donnell's letter asking for background information about an English justice); Edith Allen, Justice Douglas's secretary, also personally dealt with the FBI on Douglas's behalf. L.B. Nichols to Tolson, re: wiretapping, 12/4/53, 62-12114-2708 (mentioning Edith Allen).

42. The Executives' Conference to Director, Dissemination of Information by the Bureau Outside the Executive Departments, 10/4/53, 62-40772-[?].

43. A.H. Belmont to L.V. Boardman, Allegations of Communist affiliation of father of law clerk to [name of justice redacted], 10/7/57, 62-57585-NR.

44. A.H. Belmont to A. Rosen, Dissemination of Information, 10/21/54 [orig. stamped SECRET], 66-6200-527.

45. In *Jencks v. U.S.*, 353 U.S. 657 (1957), Justice Felix Frankfurter concurred, as did Justices Harold Burton and John Harlan. Justice Clark dissented.

46. William Cohen, professor of Law, Stanford Law School (law clerk to William Douglas during the 1956 term) to author, 1/9/90.

47. 353 U.S. at 681–682 (Justice Clark dissenting).

48. Hoover to Tolson and Nichols, 6/4/57, 94-44896-17.

49. See 66-7225.

50. See, gen., 66-7225 called "Safeguarding Official Records"; see, e.g., Hoover to A.G., H.R. 7915—Legis. Introd. by Cong. Walter to Correct the Jencks Decision, 6/10/57, 66-7225-NR (Hoover suggested that Walter make "additions" to his bill rather than "completely rewrite" it); see, e.g., Q. Tamm to Tolson, S. 2377 (The "Jencks Bill"), 8/20/57, 66-7225-NR, first serial after 1243 ("Recommendation: That no objection be made to the enactment of this bill into law if it passes the Congress.").

51. Palermo v. U.S., 360 U.S. 343, 346 (1959).

52. Pub. L. 85-269, 71 Stat. 595 (1957) (current version at 18 U.S.C.A. Sec. 3500 (1970).

53. In 1959 the Supreme Court ruled in Palermo that the Jencks Act was a rule of criminal procedure that Congress had lawful authority to enact, even though the act effectively limited the ruling in Jencks.

54. 353 U.S. 657 (1957).

55. 354 U.S. 298 (1957).

56. 354 U.S. 363 (1957). The Court reversed and remanded a Foreign Service officer's discharge by the secretary of state because it violated department regulations.

57. 354 U.S. 178 (1957). Watkins's conviction for contempt of Congress for refusal to answer HUAC questions about other persons after testifying about himself was reversed as violative of the Fifth Amendment's due process clause. Watkins was not given a fair opportunity to determine whether he was within his rights in refusing to answer, the "questions under inquiry" by Congress not being clear.

58. 354 U.S. 234 (1957). The attorney general of New Hampshire had acted under a resolution of the state legislature to determine whether there were "subversive persons" in the state and to propose legislation. Prof. Sweezy refused to answer questions about other persons or about the contents of one of his university lectures, arguing that the questions were not pertinent to the inquiry and violative of the First Amendment. The Supreme Court overturned the conviction for contempt as a violation of the due process clause of the Fourteenth Amendment.

59. 341 U.S. 494 (1951).

60. 62-27585-NR after serial 61.

61. Hoover note in 62-27585-65.

62. JEH to DL, 8/15/57, Box 58, David Lawrence Papers, Mudd Manuscript Library, Princeton University, Princeton, NJ.

63. 62-27585.

64. Hoover to W.R. Hearst, 62-27585-76.

65. Fulton Lewis, Jr., Capitol Report, New York Mirror, 7/31/57, filed in 62-57585-A.

66. O'Reilly, Hoover and the Un-Americans, p. 198.

67. Earl Warren, *The Memoirs of Chief Justice Earl Warren* (Doubleday & Co. 1977), p. 325.

68. Cohen to author, 1/9/90.

69. Author interview with former Supreme Court law clerk (relating a story by one of the justices) who requested anonymity; James F. Simon, *The Antagonists: Hugo Black, Felix Frankfurter and Civil Liberties in Modern America* (Touchstone 1989).

70. Warren memorandum for the Conference, 10/7/57, Box 499, JMH Papers, Mudd Manuscript Library. *Yates* and *Jencks* were on the list.

71. 353 U.S. 346 (1957).

72. JMH to WOD, re: No. 162—*Kremen v. U.S.*, 4/24/57, Box 514, JMH Papers.

73. *See, gen.*, 62-27585.

74. Contained in the FBI's files as a cross-reference to Earl Warren.

75. *See, gen.*, bufiles 94-1-5619 and 77-61323; Alexander Charns, "Report Ended Friendship of Hoover, Earl Warren," Durham *Morning Herald,* 11/24/85; "Report on Kennedy Ended a Hoover-Warren Alliance," New York *Times,* 11/29/85.

76. "FBI to Probe Warren on Subcommittee's Request," New York *Times,* 2/17/54.

77. Washington *News,* Feb. 11, 1954, p. 4; L.B. Nichols to Tolson, re: Earl Warren, 2/8/54, 77-61323-5.

78. Callan to Rosen, Earl Warren, Chief Justice, United States Supreme Court, Special Inquiry, 2/15/54, 77-61323-3x.

79. Nichols to Tolson, 2/10/54, 77-61323-9.

80. Callan to Rosen, Earl Warren Special Inquiry, 2/12/54, 77-61323-12.

81. New York *Post,* 2/19/54.

82. L.A. SAC, Malone, to Hoover, re: Nina Warren, 1/26/54, 94-1-5619-196.

83. Olney to Hoover, re: False and Unfounded Charges in Opposition to the Confirmation of Chief Justice Earl Warren, 3/1/54, 77-61323-NR.

84. New York *Times,* 3/2/54.

85. Hoover to Tolson et al., 3/1/57, 77-61449-32.

86. 129 F. Supp. 716, 718 (W.D.MO. 1955).

87. 350 U.S. 551 (1956).

88. Hoover to Whittaker, 3/4/57, 77-61449-33 (note at bottom of letter).

89. G.C. Callan to Rosen, Outstanding Judges, 5/26/58, 62-53025-508.

90. *See, gen.*, 62-53025.

91. Among the others were Judge John A. Danaher, D.C. Circuit Court of Appeals; Judge Irving R. Kaufman, Federal District Court, Southern District of N.Y.; and FBI informer Judge John H. Druffel, Federal District Court, Southern District of Ohio.

92. Author's telephone interview with William Rogers, 11/29/89; Tony Mauro, "Hoover FBI file followed Justice Stewart" *USA TODAY,* 4/20/87, p. 5A.

93. Dwight D. Eisenhower, *The White House Years: Mandate for Change, 1953 to 1956* (Doubleday & Co. 1963).

94. A.H. Belmont to Hoover, Potter Stewart [I]nformation Concerning, 10/6/58, 77-61290-47.

95. Hoover to Tolson et al., 10/6/58, 77-61290-46.

96. *See* HQ file entitled "Federal Judges," 62-53025.

Chapter 2: Wiretapping and Bugging: "Instruments of Tyranny and Oppression"

1. 277 U.S. 438, 475–476 (1928).

2. Hoover's "O & C" files, technical surveillance folder (I thank Athan Theoharis for pointing this out); Alexander Charns, "How the FBI Spied on the High Court," Washington *Post*, 12/3/89, C1.

3. *See The Boss* p. 10.

4. Senate Select [Church] Committee, Final Report, Book III, p. 273, citing the testimony of A.G. Edward H. Levi, 11/6/75.

5. *SWP v. U.S.*, U.S.S.D.N.Y., 73 Civ. 3160, 8/25/86, decision of J. Griesa, p. 85.

6. Prof. Walter E. Dellinger III, law clerk to Justice Black during the 1967 term of Court in a 1989 interview with Lisa Balderson. Black had recalled Clark's comment to Dellinger.

7. *See, gen., Charns I* and *Charns v. U.S. Dept. of Justice*, U.S.M.D.N.C., C-89-208-D (hereafter cited as *Charns II*). Justices Douglas, Black, Frankfurter, Reed, and Stewart were overheard actually speaking and other justices were referred to during the conversations of third parties. Vinson, Fortas, and Warren were overheard speaking on the taps before they went on the bench and were referred to in tapped conversations after they went on the Court.

8. 277 U.S. 438 (1928).

9. 277 U.S. at 455–456.

10. Brief for the U.S., *Olmstead et al. v. U.S.*, Nos. 493, 532, and 533, Oct. Term 1927, pp. 4–5, filed in 62-12114-NR, enclosure 2.

11. 277 U.S. at 471 (Brandeis dissent).

12. 277 U.S. at 464.

13. As Justice Powell noted in his 8-0 opinion (Justice Rehnquist abstaining) in *U.S. v. U.S. District Court*, 407 U.S. 297 (1972), "Historically the struggle for freedom of speech and press in England was bound up with the issue of the scope of the search and seizure power [citation omitted]." *Id.* at 314, 315. Likewise, Chief Justice Taft noted in *Olmstead* that the general warrants were used in England against those who were believed to have engaged in seditious libel against the crown.

14. The solicitor general argued that "the historical background of the Fourth Amendment leaves no doubt but that the adoption of this Amendment was the direct consequence of two abuses practiced by the English Government— the use of general warrants and the use of writs of assistance." After citing the history of the Fourth Amendment, the government brief concluded, and the Court agreed, that the amendment proscribed physical searches and seizures, not wiretapping. Government's brief, pp. 13–18.

15. *U.S. v. U.S. District Court*, 407 U.S. 329, fn 6 (1972)(concurring opinion of Justice Douglas quoting from N. Lasson, *The History and Development of*

the Fourth Amendment to the United States Constitution 51 [1937]). In England in 1763, Lord Camden ruled for the victims of a general search by messengers of the crown, saying: "To enter a man's house by virtue of a nameless warrant, in order to procure evidence, is worse than the Spanish inquisition." 407 U.S. at 329 (Justice Douglas quoting *Huckle v. Money*, 2 Wils. K.B. 206, 207, 95 *Eng.Rep.* 768, 769 (1763)).

16. 407 U.S. at 329, 330.

17. *Katz v. U.S.*, 389 U.S. 347, 352 (1967).

18. 277 U.S. at 474.

19. 277 U.S. at 478.

20. 277 U.S. at 462.

21. 277 U.S. at 470–471.

22. Brief for the U.S., *Olmstead et al. v. U.S.*, p. 41, filed in 62-12114-NR, enclosure 2.

23. "Memorandum re telephone call from Mr. Dodge," 12/28/29, 62-12114-11.

24. *Id.*

25. Hoover to A. G., 2/7/31, 62-12114-33. The bureau's regulations outlawed wiretapping between 1928 and 1931. 62-12114-2593-X

26. Hoover to Mr. Dodge, re: Wire Tapping, 12/31/29, 62-12114-10.

27. Senate (Church) Committee, Final Report, Book III, pp. 277, 388–391; *see*, A.G. Stone to Acting Director Hoover, 5/13/24, cited in Nichols to Tolson, 5/19/50, 62-8782-[illegible], attachment to Nichols blind memo to Dr. Mason; blind memo dated 8/8/50 sent to Dr. Alpheus T. Mason, the authorized biographer of Chief Justice Harlan Stone, from L.B. Nichols, 8/30/50, p. 3, 62-8782-36 (Stone named Hoover acting director of the FBI and instructed him that "the activities of the Bureau are to be limited strictly to investigations of violations of law, under my direction or under the direction of an Assistant Attorney General regularly conducting the work of the Department of Justice.").

28. C.A. Appel to Hoover, telephone tapping incidents, 2/5/31, 66-6200-NR; SAC Frank Cole to Hoover, re: tapping telephone wires in Federal Building, Indianapolis, Ind., 1/5/28, 62-12114-NR.

29. Hoover to Appel, 1/20/28, 62-12114-NR.

30. Blind memo, "Wire Tapping," 6/21/51, 62-12114-2593X, p. 1.

31. *Id.;* Associated Press, "Judge Denounces Tapping of Wires," New York *Times,* 12/3/32; 62-12114-44. In 1932 Federal Judge James A. Lowell, while instructing a jury in a liquor prosecution case, told the jury that phone taps were "a contemptible, vile practice" and that Uncle Sam became a "sneaking cur" instead of "an honorable, upright gentleman."

32. Hoover to Asst. Dir. of Prohibition Unit, memo, 9/5/33, 62-12114-45, citing Appropriations Act for the Dept. of Justice, 72d Congress; *The Boss,* p. 121.

33. The Prohibition bureau was transferred to the Justice Department from the Treasury Department in 1930; Richard Powers, *The Life of J. Edgar Hoover: Secrecy and Power* (The Free Press 1987), pp. 183–185 (hereafter cited as *Secrecy and Power*).

34. Hughes to Hoover, 6/22/33, 62-12114-NR; Werner Hanni to Hoover,

2/21/34, 62-12114-66. The authorization for the taps came from the acting head of the Justice Department's criminal division. By November 1933, Hoover was gearing up for more wiretapping, requesting that agents experiment with various types of devices to find the best ones. Hoover to Tolson, 11/16/33, 62-12114-48. At that time the bureau's regulations limited phone and telegraph taps to those authorized by Hoover himself. Anticipating congressional limits on wiretapping, in February 1934, Hoover ordered all field offices to report any wiretaps installed since January 1933, along with the headquarters authorization letter. Hoover to illegible, memo, 2/12/34, 62-12114-51. Hoover wanted to make sure he had a complete list of all taps "in the event any question arises or any criticism develops," and he ordered all correspondence, requests and authorizations of wiretaps be placed in a separate file. Hoover to file section, 2/14/34, 62-12114-52.

35. *See, e.g.,* 62-12114-85, 86, 87; *see, gen.,* 62-12114.

36. [Name redacted] to Nathan, memo [re: wiretap summary], 3/9/34, 62-12114-106. The increased use of ELSUR in the bureau led to a two-day training program in Chicago to instruct agents from across the country on what to do and where to buy the Western Electric Company receivers, lineman's testing sets, friction tape, pole climbers, wirecutters, clips, condensers, wires, wrenches, pliers, and screw drivers necessary for the job. F.X. Fay to Director, Wire-tap equipment, 5/15/34, 62-12114-285.

37. Hoover to SAC Chicago, 3/17/34, 62-12114-108.

38. H.H. Clegg to File, re: Wire Tapping Dillinger case, 62-12114-116.

39. Don Whitehead, *The FBI Story* (Random House 1956), pp. 104–105.

40. 47 U.S.C. Sec. 605 (1934)(amended in 1988).

41. SAC J.M. Keith to Hoover, 10/9/36, 62-46240-1.

42. The government contends that during this 1936 investigation employees of the judicial branch of government became de facto law enforcement personnel because "it was necessary for the FBI to seek the cooperation of Supreme Court employees . . . to provide information and perform tasks outside the requirements of their employment." Second Llewellyn Declaration, p. 16, in *Charns I.*

43. E.A. Tamm to Hoover, re: W.J. Cox, alleged attempt to sell advance opinions of U.S. Supreme Court, 10/21/36, 62-46240-11. (It is possible that the phone of another suspect at the Court was tapped as well or even a phone at the Court. "A telephone tap was placed on the residence of W.J. Cox and a [two or three sentences redacted]. [A]rrangements are being effected through [half sentence redacted] to keep Cox under surveillance should he apply for leave.") Though Cox worked in the Court building (62-46240-26), the FBI at first listed his employer as the Architect of the Capitol (62-46240-4) but later stated that he was an employee of the Supreme Court (62-46240-28 and 29); E.A. Tamm to the Director, re: W.J. Cox, Alleged attempt to sell advance opinions of the U.S. Supreme Court, 10/24/36, 62-46240-5X ("A surveillance of [Oscar D.] Clarke is being maintained at the request of the Chief Justice.") Clarke was chief librarian in the conference room of the justices of the Supreme Court and had worked at the Court since 1897. 62-46240-14. The FBI concluded that Mr. Clarke "was in no way cognizant of the activities of Messrs. Cox, [redacted name] and [redacted name]. 62-46240-26.

44. E.A. Tamm to the Director, re: W.J. Cox, Alleged attempt to sell advance opinions of the U.S. Supreme Court, 10/22/36, 62-46240-12.

45. Hoover to Chief Justice Hughes, 11/27/36, 62-46240-26.

46. Guy Hottel to Director, re: W.J. Cox, Alleged attempt to sell advance opinions of the U.S. Supreme Court, 12/18/36, 62-46240-29; Chief Justice Hughes to Hoover, 12/3/36, 62-46240-30.

47. E.A. Tamm to the Director, re: W.J. Cox, Alleged attempt to sell advance opinions of the U.S. Supreme Court, 10/17/36, 62-46240-10.

48. *Id.*

49. William O. Douglas, *The Court Years, 1939–1975: The Autobiography of William O. Douglas* (Vintage Books 1981), p. 256. Douglas wrote: "During Hughes's term as Chief Justice, he somehow discovered that our Conference Room was 'bugged.' He made a quick, intensive investigation and learned that two employees of the Court had been enlisted by a District of Columbia policeman to place a bug in the room. He ordered the Marshal to discharge the two employees 'within the hour.' They were fired; the bug was removed; the episode was given no publicity. Who the person or persons behind the policeman were never found out."

50. 302 U.S. 379 (1937).

51. *Id.* at 387.

52. Myron C. Cramer, Major General, The Judge Advocate General, Top Secret Memorandum for the Secretary of War, Subject: Legality of Signal Intelligence Activities, 16 August 1945, p. 7, filed in FBI HQ 62-12114-2261 (citing the opinions of Attorneys General Biddle and Jackson). This memo was declassified on Mar. 20, 1991, by the Office of the Judge Advocate General.

53. E.A. Tamm to the Director, 12/22/37, 62-12114-1305X; *The Boss,* p. 170.

54. *Id.*

55. SAC letter, dated 12/31/37, 62-12114-1329. "It has always been the Bureau's policy during the period in which I have been the Director of the Bureau to utilize telephone taps only in those cases of major importance in which the proper development of the Government's case was impossible without the use of telephone taps. It is significant to note that the Bureau has never attempted to introduce into a Federal Court evidence obtained through the use of a telephone tap."

56. 308 U.S. 338 (1939).

57. E.A. Tamm to the Director, 1/4/40, 62-12114-1834X.

58. *See* Paul A. Sweeney, acting assistant attorney general, Office of Legal Counsel to Hoover, re: Proposed order of the attorney general relating to wiretapping, 7/10/59, 62-12114-3184; press release of Hoover, 3/13/40, 62-12114-1903.

59. Senate (Church) Committee, Final Report, Book III, p. 279.

60. *SWP v. U.S.,* order of Judge Thomas P. Griesa, S.D.N.Y. 73 Civ. 3160 (8/25/86), p. 88; Senate (Church) Committee, Final Report, Book III, pp. 279–280.

61. *See The Boss,* p. 171. Not even the FBI kept a usable index to all wiretaps and bugs until 1966. *See* 54 Fed. Reg. 42,082–42,083 (10/13/89).

62. Author's interview with Edward Scheidt, 10/14/90, Chapel Hill, N.C.

63. *Id.*

64. 316 U.S. 129 (1942). Stone and Frankfurter said they were ready to overrule *Olmstead,* but since the majority of the Court would not, they joined the majority. Murphy dissented and Jackson recused himself.

65. 316 U.S. 114 (1942)(Stone, Frankfurter, and Murphy dissenting. Jackson recused himself). "At trial Government witnesses testified that wire tapping had not furnished clues used in preparing the case." 316 U.S. at 116. The majority of the Court decided the case as a legal "standing" issue of who could object to the introduction of illegally seized evidence.

66. *Id.* at 123 (Stone and Frankfurter dissenting).

67. Thomas G. Corcoran technical surveillance folders, Hoover's "O & C" files. The author was directed to the "O & C" files for ELSUR information about Justice Douglas by Athan Theoharis in 1988. Summaries of conversations (Thomas G. Corcoran), President's Secretary's Files (hereafter cited as PSF), Apr.–Aug. 1946, box 337, Harry S. Truman Papers, Harry S. Truman Presidential Library, Independence, MO.

68. Clifford, *Counsel to the President,* p. 190.

69. *The Boss,* pp. 244–247.

70. As Truman aide Harry Vaughan noted, in theory the attorney general is the boss of the director of the FBI. In practice, Hoover was the head of an independent agency. Ovid Demaris, *The Director: An Oral Biography of J. Edgar Hoover* (Harper's Magazine Press 1975), p. 107.

71. Kai Bird and Max Holland, "Truman and Corcoran: The Tapping of 'Tommy the Cork,' " *The Nation,* 2/8/86, pp. 141–142; *The Boss,* pp. 244–245; *But see* Demaris, *The Director,* p. 109. In a 1972 interview, Vaughan wrongly stated that the Corcoran wiretap was ordered by President Roosevelt because he was "suspicious of him." Vaughan also said that the wiretap reports were "dull," concerning things like "whether Mrs. Corcoran gets her hair fixed" and that when he showed the reports to President Truman, Truman told him to tell the FBI to turn the taps off.

72. Memorandum of 11/15/45, technical summaries, "O & C" files; *The Boss,* note, p. 247.

73. *Supra* note 72.

74. *The Boss,* pp. 245–246; Clifford, *Counsel to the President,* p. 67 (Vaughan's relationship with Truman).

75. Oral history (hereafter cited as OH), Harry Vaughan, p. 24, HST Library.

76. *The Boss,* p. 245.

77. *See* Technical summaries, Pritchard to Frankfurter, 9:35 PM, 5/8/45, "O & C"; Hoover letter to James Vardaman, "P & C" by special messenger, 8/17/45, with "Detailed Study requested of Mr. Gurnea of the Source of Leaks to Press Re: Hopkins-Stalin Conferences in Moscow." 7/31/45, p. 87, FBI Folder "H," box 168, PSF, HST Papers; *The Boss* at 245.

78. *The Boss,* p. 245.

79. Clifford, *Counsel to the President,* p. 190.

80. "Chief Justice Harlan Stone of Supreme Court is Dead," *New York Times,* 4/23/46, p. 1.

81. Technical surveillance summaries, 4/22/46, "O & C"; summaries of conversations (Thomas G. Corcoran), Apr.–Aug. 1946, box 337, PSF, HST Papers.

82. Diary folder 1946, April 21st, Sunday–April 25th, Thursday, Eben A. Ayers Diaries, box 16, Ayers Papers, HST Library.

83. New York *Times*, 4/24/46, p. 28.

84. But it was Black's refusal to recuse himself in the 1945 *Jewell Ridge Coal Corp. v. Local 6176, United Mine Workers*, 325 U.S. 161 (1945), case that precipitated Jackson's fury. The case was argued by Crampton Harris, who two decades before had briefly been Black's law partner in Alabama. William H. Rehnquist, *The Supreme Court* (William Morrow and Co.1987), pp. 65–68. Justice Murphy wrote the majority opinion in favor of the union's position, and he was joined by Black, Douglas, Rutledge, and Reed. Justice Jackson wrote the dissenting opinion, joined by Chief Justice Stone and Associate Justices Roberts and Frankfurter. The coal company petitioned the Court for a rehearing and asked that Justice Black recuse himself from the case because of his former law partner's participation. Instead of summarily denying the petition as was customary, Jackson wrote an opinion, joined by Frankfurter, which did not directly question Black's failure to recuse himself, but was clearly a jab at Black.

85. United Press International, "Jackson-Black Feud May Bring Congressional Probe of Court," Washington *News,* summer 1946, located in FBI Headquarters file 62-27585-Appendix.

86. CO Summary, 3:10 PM, T. Corcoran to Ernest Cuneo, 4/28/46, Hoover's "O & C."

87. Technical surveillance summaries, 4/28/45, 3:10 PM, "O & C."

88. Technical surveillance summaries, 4/29/46, 8:15 PM, "O & C."

89. Truman had called Hughes and asked to speak with him in person. Telephone memo of Matthew Connelly, 10:00 AM, 2/29/46, White House Telephone Office, box 3, HST Papers. Hughes's appointment was set for 3:00 PM. President's Appointments, Daily Sheets, 4/29/46, box 83, PSF, HST Papers.

90. President's Appointments, Daily Sheets, box 83, PSF, HST Papers. According to Truman, Hughes told him Fred Vinson was "best fitted" for the job. Truman to Joe Short, 12/19/51, "Supreme Court of the U.S.," folder OF 41A, Endorsements, box 198, HST Papers. On the other hand, Hughes told his biographer, Merlo Pusey, that he had recommended Justice Jackson. Merlo Pusey to Truman, 4/24/52, "Supreme Court of the U.S.," folder, OF 41A, Endorsements, box 198, HST Papers.

91. Truman had already met with Postmaster General Robert E. Hannegan, chairman of the Democratic National Committee. John W. Snyder, director of the Office of War Mobilization and Reconversion, and Richard B. Keech, White House administrative assistant, also discussed the vacancy with Truman. Felix Blair, "Truman to Name Member of Court as Chief Justice," New York *Times,* 4/29/46, A1.

92. I. Brant to Truman, 4/29/46, "Supreme Court file," folder 1, box 221, PSF, HST Papers.

93. Technical surveillance summaries, 4/30/46, 10:40 PM, "O & C."

94. Hoover to Harry Vaughan, aide to Pres. Truman, 5/1/46, "O & C."

95. Associated Press, "Bridges Demands Politics Ban on Supreme Court Members," Washington *Post*, 5/1/46.

96. [Typed Appointments for] Thursday, May 2, 1946, "11.30 [AM]—Justice Owen Roberts," White House Telephone Office, box 3, HST Papers.

97. Justice Roberts' Memo on Supreme Court, longhand, "Supreme Court File," folder 1, box 221, PSF, HST Papers.

98. CO summary, 5/2/46, 8:35 PM, Hoover's "O & C."

99. Simon, *The Antagonists*, pp. 158–159.

100. Technical surveillance summaries, 5/1/46, "O & C."

101. *Id.*

102. Douglas also asked his brethren to lobby for him. He asked Justice Murphy, the Court's only Catholic, to talk to Father White, dean of the Catholic University Law School, about contacting the White House in opposition to a Jackson appointment. Murphy refused, and Douglas said there were other ways to get it done. According to Murphy, Douglas was trying to line up Catholic and labor opposition to Jackson. Joseph P. Lash, *From the Diaries of Felix Frankfurter* (W.W. Norton & Co. 1975), p. 301 (Tuesday, Nov. 19, 1946).

103. Technical surveillance summaries, 1945, "O & C."

104. WOD to Truman, 2/23/46, WOD folder, General File, box 306, PSF, HST Papers.

105. Robert A. Carp and C.K. Rowland, *Policymaking and Politics in the Federal District Courts* (University Tennessee Press 1984), pp. 66–67.

106. Truman to Joe Short, 12/19/51, "Supreme Court of the U.S." folder, OF 41A, Endorsements, box 198, HST Papers; Associated Press, "Bridges Demands Politics Ban on Supreme Court Members," Washington *Post*, 5/1/46; Henry J. Abraham, *Justice & Presidents: A Political History of Appointments to the Supreme Court* (Oxford University Press 1985), p. 240 (hereafter cited as *Justices and Presidents*); Frances Howell Rudko, *Truman's Court: A Study in Judicial Restraint* (Greenwood Press 1988), p. 29.

107. The article was about the Jewell Ridge Coal Corp. memorandum, written by Justice Jackson with Frankfurter's concurrence, critical of Black's failure to recuse himself in the case. Rudko, *Truman's Court*.

108. Technical surveillance summaries, 5/19/46, 6:22 PM, "O & C."

109. Technical surveillance summaries, 5/21/46, "O & C."

110. *See infra*, n113; *see supra*, p. 150n90, for the varied and somewhat inconsistent recollections of Truman, Hughes (via Merlo Pusey), and Tom Clark. *See also* Eben A. Ayers (Assis. Press Sec. to Truman), Ayers Diaries, 12/2/47, box 16, E.A. Ayers Papers; OH Robert G. Nixon, p. 259, HST Library; and former Justice Owen Roberts' Memo on the Supreme Court, "Supreme Court File," box 221, PSF, HST Papers.

111. Technical surveillance folder, Hoover's "O & C" files; summaries of Conversations (Thomas G. Corcoran), April–June, 1946, Box 337, PSF, HST Papers.

112. White House Telephone Office, Typed cover sheet for 5/31/46 and the President's Telephone Memorandum, 5/31/46, box 3, HST Papers.

113. Clifford, *Counsel to the President*, p. 70 (about Vinson's relationship with Truman); OH Tom C. Clark, pp. 52–54, HST Library.

114. Jackson sent a vicious letter to the House and Senate Judiciary committees and made it available to the press. It was an attack on Justice Black and a rehashing of their feud, which he called a "declaration of war" between the justices. Jackson's letter ended with a threat to make his Jewell Ridge opinion look "like a letter of recommendation by comparison" should any justice refuse to recuse himself in a similar situation in the future. *Justices & Presidents;* Lash, *From the Diaries of Felix Frankfurter,* pp. 263–264. The wiretaps on Corcoran provided Hoover and Truman with the uninhibited reactions of prominent New Dealers to Jackson's public outburst.

115. White House Telephone Office, President's Telephone Memorandum, 6:25 PM., 6/11/46, box 3, HST Papers.

116. This memo was released to the author by the FBI in a letter dated July 22, 1988, five months after filing the FOIA lawsuit. It appears that it was derived from a wiretap or bug. This memo was prepared on pink paper (earlier blue paper was used), which identified it as not to be serialized, those records being prepared on white paper. These "Do Not File" records were either to be retained in Hoover's office or to be destroyed. This "Do Not File" procedure was instituted by Hoover in 1940 to prevent memos authorizing break-ins and other illegalities from becoming part of the regular FBI central records system. For an excellent description of the origins and development of Hoover's "Do Not File" system, *see* Athan G. Theoharis, ed., *Beyond the Hiss Case: The FBI, Congress and the Cold War* (Temple University Press 1982), pp. 21–60; *The Boss,* pp. 11–12.

117. Athan G. Theoharis, "In-House Cover-up: Researching FBI Files," in Theoharis, ed., *Beyond the Hiss Case,* pp. 21–22.

118. *Id.*

119. *See, gen.,* Second Declaration of Special Agent Angus B. Llewellyn, 3/21/90, pp. 11–14, *Charns I; The Boss,* pp. 257–261; *see, e.g.,* Senate (Church) Committee, Final Report, Book III, p. 343.

120. The Executives Conference to Tolson, 7/31/57, AG's memo re: the use of terms restricting the avail. of unclassified files, docs. records and reports, 66-7225-1233. "Certain mail involving highly secretive techniques in the security field such as technical or microphone surveillances and other secretive sources of information is marked 'JUNE.' This designation is primarily a routing device. . . . The 'JUNE' system was instituted to keep such information from the personal knowledge of employees. . . . the designation 'JUNE' is strictly for routing purposes, and need not be taken up in detail with the Department."

121. *Id.*

122. *The Boss,* pp. 11–12. In 1942 Hoover had set up a system of records that were not to be indexed to the central records system or serialized. These records of illegal FBI break-ins were captioned "Do Not File." Though these files were also to be destroyed regularly, the New York field office did not destroy all of its "surreptitious entries" files.

123. Author's phone conversation with DeLoach, 6/28/90, and letter from DeLoach to author, 7/31/90.

124. Author interview with Edward Scheidt, 10/14/90.

125. *United States v. Coplon,* 185 F.2d 629 (2nd Cir. 1950), and *Coplon v. United States,* 191 F.2d 749 (D.C.Cir. 1951).

126. Author interview with Scheidt, 10/14/90.

127. *E.g.,* Nichols to Tolson, 2/27/51, 62-12114-2565; Ladd to Hoover, 1/10/52, 62-12114-2589; *e.g.,* 82nd Congress, H.R. 406, H.R. 479, H.R. 1947, 83rd Congress, H.R. 9011, 84th Congress, H.R. 76, H.R. 4276, H.R. 4513, H.R. 4728, Cong. Index, C.C.H.; Senate (Church) Committee, Final Report, Book III, p. 284.

128. Belmont to D.M. Ladd, Wire Tapping Bill H.R. 479, 1/29/51, 62-12114-2548X (H.R. 479 was identical with H.R. 9929 introduced by Keating in the 81st Congress).

129. F.J. Baumgardner to A.H. Belmont, Wire Tapping Legislation, 5/17/51, 62-12114-2567 (quoting the *Congressional Record,* 2/14/51).

130. *See* D.M. Ladd to Hoover, National Security Problems, 12/12/50, 66-6200-239. Ladd suggested that a number of national security problems that might be handled "through appropriate legislation." One of the seven areas of concern included "the use in evidence of information obtained through interception of radio or wire communications."

131. L.B. Nichols to Tolson, Judge Jerome Frank, 6/21/51, 62–12114-2593-X.

132. A.H. Belmont to D.M. Ladd, H.R. 4404, Wiretapping, 7/2/51, 62-12114-2574; H.R. 1947 introduced by Congressman Celler on 1/23/51.

133. Senate (Church) Committee, Final Report, Book III, p. 280.

134. D.M. Ladd to Hoover, Derogatory Data on Certain Federal Judges for Possible Use "Off the Record" in connection with Proposed Wire Tapping Legislation, 5/19/53, 62-12114-2699.

135. *Id.* (allegations against the Federal judges ranged from "associated with numerous organizations regarded as Communist fronts" to being a heavy drinker to opposition to the HUAC to being a "woman chaser").

136. Hoover to Tolson et al., 2/2/54, 62-12114-2752; H.R. 9011 (introduced by Celler on 2/5/54, and referred to the House Judiciary Committee on which Keating served); 82nd Congress, Cong. Index, C.C.H.

137. L.B. Nichols to Tolson, Proposed Wire Tapping Legislation, 1/16/54, 62-12114-2756.

138. Senate (Church) Committee, Final Report, Book III, p. 284.

139. See ch. 9; *see, gen.,* 62-12114.

140. 347 U.S. 128 (1954).

141. Senate (Church) Committee, Final Report, Book III. *E.g.,* an agent in the early 1940s had installed a bug in a New York City hotel; the occupant returned to find the agent standing in his living room. The agent claimed to be checking a rug that needed replacing and walked out the door. Later the hotel manager complained to the agent that he had to buy a new rug for the tenant. Author interview with Edward Scheidt, 10/14/90 (story told to him by another agent). I thank Athan G. Theoharis for identifying the target of this bugging as Harry Bridges, president of the International Longshoremen's Union.

142. Senate (Church) Committee, Final Report, Book III, pp. 296–297; *SWP v. U.S.* at 90–91.

143. Senate (Church) Committee, Final Report, Book III, p. 297.

144. 316 U.S. 129 (1942).
145. 365 U.S. 505 (1961).
146. Bench memo from HL to Justice Harlan, *Silverman v. U.S.*, undated, box 119, JMH Papers.
147. 365 U.S. at 512–13.

Chapter 3: Gavelgate: G–Men in the Conference Room

1. 277 U.S. 438, 485 (1928).
2. *U.S. v. Black*, 282 F.Supp. 35, 37 (1968). The Court in *U.S. v. Baker*, 262 F.Supp. 657 (1966), held that Baker established no standing with regard to the Levinson and Sigelbaum ELSUR.
3. "The Serv-U Man," *Newsweek*, 10/7/63; author interview with Edward Scheidt, 10/14/90.
4. Author interview with Bubba Fountain, former congressional page, 10/9/90, Durham, N.C.
5. "The Serv-U Man," *Newsweek*, 10/7/63.
6. *Id.*
7. *Black v. U.S.*, 389 F. Supp. 529, 537 (D.C. 1975).
8. *The Boss*, p. 346.
9. For a record of the FBI's surveillance of and interest in Edward Bennett Williams, see HQ 62-98896.
10. *U.S. v. Black*, 282 F.Supp. 35, 38 (1968).
11. Fred B. Black, Jr., v. U.S., Petition for a writ of *certiorari*, O.T. 1965, No. 1029 (2/16/66), at 12a.
12. *Id.* at 18.
13. *Id.* at 19.
14. *Id.* at 37.
15. Brief for the United States in Opposition to Petition for a Writ of Certiorari to the U.S. Court of Appeals, D.C. Circuit, 4/18/66.
16. Lister to JMH, 4/25/66, box 266, JMH Papers.
17. Michael Smith to E.W., memo, 4/25/66, *Black v. U.S.* Conference Memos file, Earl Warren Papers, Manuscript Division, Library of Congress, Washington, D.C.
18. Rehnquist, *The Supreme Court*, p. 288.
19. Anthony Lewis, *Gideon's Trumpet* (Vintage Books 1966), p. 39.
20. Generally, after *cert* is granted, oral arguments are heard. Later the justices meet in conference to vote on the case. The chief justice, if he is in the majority, assigns the decision to himself or one of the associate justices, who then writes a proposed opinion and circulates it among the justices. Dissenting opinions are also circulated, and informal lobbying takes place, positions shift, and compromises are proposed. The final Court opinion is read aloud in the courtroom, and the printed ruling is distributed by the clerk's office. Bernard Schwartz, *The Ascent of Pragmatism: The Burger Court in Action.* (Addison-Wesley 1990), p. 13.
21. In response to the author's letter with questions about the *Black* case,

Justice Fortas, and Hoover, Justice Marshall wrote back, in part: "I have no intention whatsoever of discussing my term as Solicitor General with anybody under any circumstances." Justice Marshall to author, 1/28/91.

22. Hoover to Katzenbach, Robert G. Baker, Fraud Against the Government, Conflict of Interest, 8/24/65, Fred Black folder, Hoover's "O & C."

23. Gale to DeLoach, Fred B. Black, Jr., Anti-Racketeering, 5/20/66, Fred Black folder, Hoover's "O & C."

24. *Id.*

25. Katzenbach to Hoover, 5/31/66, pp. 1–2, Fred Black Folder, Hoover's "O & C" files.

26. *See* A.H. Belmont to Tolson, Special Investigative Techniques, 9/28/65, 62-12114-3398. As early as September 1965, Katzenbach was concerned about the Long investigation. "The AG apparently feels that he is on solid ground in approving microphones and wiretaps in national security cases, but he is fearful of the Long Committee and attorneys such as Edward Bennett Williams with reference to the use of microphones in the organized crime field. . . . '[I]n light of the present atmosphere I believe that efforts in the immediate future' should be confined to national security."

27. Senate (Church) Committee, Final Report, Book III, p. 342.

28. David J. Garrow, *The FBI and Martin Luther King, Jr.* (Penguin Books 1981), p. 149 (hereafter *The FBI and King*).

29. *The FBI and King*, p. 138; *Age of Surveillance*, p. 255.

30. *The FBI and King*, p. 150.

31. Senate (Church) Committee, Final Report, Book III, p. 308.

32. *Id.* at 309.

33. *Id.* at 309.

34. *Id.* at 310.

35. Author's telephone interview with Nicholas Katzenbach, 10/2/89.

36. *The Boss*, p. 378.

37. Kennedy denied he had knowledge of bureau bugging practices. Fred P. Graham, "Robert Kennedy Aided Buggings," New York *Times*, 12/11/66, A1.

38. *See Black v. U.S.*, 389 F.Supp. at 532 (1975). The eavesdropping did occur during the time Black was being investigated and during the time the tax case was being presented to the grand jury. *Black v. U.S.*, 385 U.S. 26, 27 (1966).

39. On May 23, to beat the filing of the *Black* memo disclosing the bugging to the Court, Assistant FBI Director J.H. Gale paid a visit to Senator Long to explain the reason for bugging Black. Long thanked Gale for the briefing and said that he "had no desire to hurt the FBI or hold hearings on the FBI and he would figure out something with respect to handling his critics," who would probably be calling for hearings about FBI eavesdropping practices due to the *Black* case revelations. Gale to DeLoach, 5/23/66, Fred Black folder, Hoover's "O&C" files. Apparently, the FBI also paid a visit to the Supreme Court that same day. Justice Douglas's appointment book for May 23, 1966 at 3:00 PM shows an appointment with "Mr. Casper—FBI." The appointment book does not record what the meeting was about. J.J. Casper was head of the FBI's Training

Division. After the *Black* ruling, Casper advised other bureau officials of the anticipated effects of the ruling on "future cases of a similar nature." 62-12114-3469.

40. Government Memorandum in *Black v. U.S.,* 5/24/66, Fred Black Folder, Hoover's "O & C" files.

Chapter 4: A "Sniveling Liberal" Justice
Makes the Best FBI Informer

1. J. Edgar Hoover, *Masters of Deceit* (Henry Holt 1958), pp. 199–200.

2. M.A. Jones to DeLoach, Mrs. Hugo L. Black Meeting with the Director, 8/25/65, 62-90518-15.

3. *Justices & Presidents,* p. 263.

4. Hoover to Tolson, 4/2/58, 62-27585-NR first after 103.

5. Hoover to Douglas, 12/11/44, 94-33476-6; Douglas to Hoover, 6/18/45, 94-33476-7.

6. Douglas to Hoover, 11/30/49, 94-33476-15; L.B. Nichols to W.A. Murphy, 12/27/49; W.A. Murphy to Clyde Tolson, 1/24/50, 94-33476-18; Alexander Charns, "The FBI Connection" Seattle *Weekly,* 7/4/84, p. 26.

7. D.M. Ladd to Hoover, Justice William O. Douglas, 2/9/54, 101-2983-18.

8. 341 U.S. 494.

9. 94-33476-NR, first serial after 23.

10. 101-2983-18, p. 7.

11. L.B. Nichols to Tolson, Justice William O. Douglas, 5/3/55, 94-33476-27.

12. *Id.*

13. L.B. Nichols to Tolson, 4/25/55, 94-33476-28.

14. D.M. Ladd to Hoover, Justice William O. Douglas, 2/9/54, 101-2983-18.

15. *E.g.,* "[Douglas] has an inexhaustible fund of dirty stories which the judges themselves appreciate but they do not like to have him tell such stories at the podium at the banquet when their ladies are present there. [T]he justice did tell a quite filthy story to the banquet group which had perhaps 75 to 100 ladies present." SAC, SF, to Director, 9th cir. Judicial Conference, Portland, Oregon, 7/13/61, Information Concerning, 7/21/61, 94-33476-NR, p. 2, as well as W.C. Sullivan to D.J. Brennan, re: William O. Douglas, Sup. Ct. Justice, 11/20/62, stating that "Supreme Court Justice Douglas recently became separated from his wife and may marry a 22-year old girl employed by the Agency for International Development, whom he has been seeing for some months." The rest of the page is censored by the FBI for privacy reasons, i.e., use of FOIA exemption b6.

16. SAC, SF, to Hoover, re: Well-arranged data on radical activities in Alameda County District Attorney's Office, Oakland, Ca., 8/17/38, 61-7559-3038.

17. Warren to Hoover, 4/15/37, 62-28882-41.

18. *See, e.g.,* Hoover to Communications Section, Cooperation with Governor Earl Warren, 6/20/52, 94-1-5619-126. Informal cooperation with Warren began in the 1940s (*e.g.,* McCabe to Rosen, Gov. Earl Warren of California, 11/1/47, 62-85287-2) and predated the "Responsibilities Program." The Executives' Conference to Director, Dissemination of Information by the Bureau Outside the Executive Departments, 10/14/53, 62-53025-NR. Two days prior to the

meeting between Hoover and a committee of governors appointed by the Executive Committee of Governors' Conference, at which the "Responsibilities Program" was "initiated," Warren told the FBI that he "felt it would be an excellent idea for the Director to see the Governors. He felt it would be no difficulty in winning the Governors over to [the FBI's] views." Tolson to L.B. Nichols, Governors' Conference, 2/10/51, 62-93875-80. The "Responsibilities Program" was not Warren's idea, but he jumped on the bandwagon. It was started by the FBI as an alternative to state Un-American investigations, for Hoover preferred the FBI to be the lead agency in rooting out subversives. The formal "Cooperation with Gov. Earl Warren" program was an offshoot of the "Responsibilities Program." *See, e.g.*, A.H. Belmont to D.M. Ladd, Responsibilities of the FBI in the Internal Security Field, Cooperation with Gov. Earl Warren, 7/14/51, 62-93875-409.

19. Alexander Charns, "How JFK Report Split Warren and Hoover," San Francisco *Examiner*, 11/30/85.

20. Hoover to Communications Section, Cooperation with Gov. Earl Warren, 7/14/51, 94-1-5619-100.

21. *See, gen.*, 94-1-5619.

22. *See, e.g.*, McCabe to Rosen, re: Gov. Earl Warren, 11/1/47, 62-85287-2.

23. 62-93875-2190.

24. *See, e.g.*, Army intelligence documents in 100-7660.

25. *See, e.g.*, Hoover to AG, List of Names Protesting your Appointment to the Supreme Court, 8/9/49, Supreme Court file, Confirmation Memorandum etc. folder, box 119, Tom Clark Papers, HST Library.

26. Hoover to Tolson and Nease, 6/5/58, 62-72944-396.

27. 357 U.S. 116 (1958).

28. 357 U.S. at 139–140, fn. 2 (Clark was joined by Burton, Harlan, and Whittaker in his dissent).

29. Clark to Hoover, 11/30/59, 62-72944-402.

30. Hoover to Tolson, Mohr, and DeLoach, 5/22/62, 62-72944-NR.

31. H.G. Foster, SAC, NY, to redacted, 4/14/60, 62-72944-403.

32. After the ABA conference in 1957, the FBI was at the beck and call of Justice Clark and his wife as they traveled to other parts of Europe. The FBI legal attache in Rome arranged for a special tour for the Clarks, guided by Italian police. The FBI legal attache in Paris obtained theater tickets. On his return to the United States, Clark thanked "Dear Edgar": "Mary and I just returned and the prints of the Queen Mary pictures were a hearty welcome home. It was thoughtful of you to send them. In London Mr. Nichols took excellent care of us—furnishing cars etc. Mr. Cimperman [special agent in charge of the FBI legal attache in London] . . . was very helpful. He wrote agents in other European capitals and each was very thoughtful. In Paris we saw Brookings and Doyle, Cammarota in Venice and Miss Schoenberger in Madrid. The agents were away so she came to meet us. While we had arranged for a car at each spot (through the American Express) it was certainly good to see a friendly face in these foreign parts. You will be pleased to know that your people in Europe are all up to the high standards of the Bureau. I heard good reports on all sides. Please thank "Nick" [Louis Nichols] for me. Hope to see you soon and

that your summer leaves you in good shape." Clark to Hoover, 9/12/57, 62-72944-390.

Justice Clark was not the only one at the Court to benefit from FBI attentions. When cars had not been provided for the justices at an ABA meeting in London, Louis Nichols arranged for them. "I think our actions will pay dividends," he wrote Hoover. The director was less optimistic. "How," he wrote, "by more help from the U.S. Supreme Court!" (Nichols to Tolson, Supreme Court, 8/2/57, 62-27585-NR, second serial after 82x4). Hoover was told that Justice Harlan had appreciated the FBI courtesies extended to him while he was in London and hoped that he might someday return the favor. "I abhor his double talking," Hoover roared back to his assistants (Nichols to Tolson, 8/28/57, NR). Nevertheless, favors to the Supreme Court justices continued. FBI personnel in London, Rome, Madrid, and Paris received commendations from Hoover for providing personal favors to Justice and Mrs. Clark. Earl Warren and his wife received similar favors while vacationing in Europe.

33. FBI noted that Clark's "decisions on the Supreme Court have been more favorable to law enforcement than most of the court." J.F. Malone to Mohr, FBI Academy Graduation 1960, 5/4/60, 62-72944-404.

34. Clark to Hoover, 10/10/60, 62-72944-421.

35. Ungar, *The FBI*, p. 287.

36. *See* Fred Black folder, Hoover's "O & C" files.

37. OH, Larry Temple, tape #1, p. 5, Lyndon B. Johnson Presidential Library, Austin, TX.

38. OH, Tom Clark, LBJ Library.

39. Marvin Watson to LBJ, 2/11/66, 9:10 p.m., Abe Fortas folder, WHCF Name File, box 195, LBJ Library.

40. OH, Tom C. Clark, p. 152, HST Library.

41. OH, Tom Clark, LBJ Library.

42. Author interview with Robert Hamilton, former law clerk to Clark, Austin, TX, 6/20/90. Once Justice Clark ushered a friend into his chambers and, apparently without thinking, let slip the outcome of a decision not yet announced publicly.

43. OH, Ramsey Clark, LBJ Library.

44. Tony Mauro, "Hoover FBI file followed Justice Stewart," *USA Today*, 4/20/87, p. 5A; Alex Charns, "FBI Tapped Phones Snared Potter Stewart," Durham *Morning Herald*, 4/28/87, p. A2; *The Boss*, p. 303.

45. Norman Dorsen, "John Marshall Harlan," in Leroy Friedman and Fred Israel, *The Justices of the United States Supreme Court, 1789–1969* (Chelsea House 1969), vol. 4, p. 2805.

46. *Justices & Presidents*, p. 259. Two previous FBI background checks on Harlan requested by the attorney general and completed by the bureau in 1951 and 1953 were favorable. The day after Eisenhower nominated Harlan to the Supreme Court, Hoover scrawled a note for Tolson to "get [him] a summary" of information from FBI files about Harlan. Evidently, Hoover had received no advance notice of the nomination. It was Hoover's practice to order FBI files searched after he was notified or otherwise learned of a

potential nominee. Nothing "derogatory" was located in the files about Harlan, and so Hoover sent him a congratulatory letter. No additional investigation of Harlan was requested by the attorney general after Harlan's nomination, presumably due to the fact that Harlan was already on the federal bench and had already gone through two background investigations and a Senate confirmation for his former position. Main HQ file about John M. Harlan, 11/9/54, 94-48173-43.

47. Author telephone interview with Quinlan J. Shea, Jr., former director of the Office of Information and Privacy, U.S. Justice Department, 9/26/88.

48. Arthur Daley, New York *Times*, 5/1/62.

49. The retirement of Justices Felix Frankfurter and Charles Whittaker gave President John F. Kennedy two appointments. For a time, the president had considered nominating black federal appeals Judge William Henry Hastie to the High Court. Hoover reacted by preparing a memo for Attorney General Robert Kennedy that connected Judge Hastie with subversive organizations (O'Reilly, *Racial Matters*, p. 327; *but see*, E.A. Tamm to the Director, re: William Henry Hastie, 2/13/39, 62-53025-NR, Doc. 104, stating that a 1935 applicant investigation revealed "nothing unfavorable"). The ultimate appointees, Deputy Attorney General Byron White and liberal Secretary of Labor Arthur Goldberg, were well known, personally and professionally, to the Kennedys and would face no opposition in the Senate (*Justice & Presidents*, pp. 272–274). Both were nominated to the High Court in 1962. One conservative and one liberal justice took the place of two conservatives and created a voting block made up of Warren, Black, Douglas, Brennan, and Goldberg on criminal law issues.

50. Robert A. Caro, *The Years of Lyndon Johnson: The Path to Power* (Vintage Books 1983), p. 451.

51. Kalman, *Abe Fortas*, p. 293 (quoting an anonymous justice).

52. M.A. Jones to DeLoach, Abe Fortas, 3025 N Street, N.W., Wash. D.C., 5/11/64, 101-1605-19 (Assistant Attorney General Miller had referred to Fortas and others as "sniveling liberals" and "the Director commented concerning these individuals, 'What a bunch of screwballs!' "); *see also* DeLoach to author, 3/12/91. Hoover "may have had some feelings" that Fortas was pro–criminal defendant.

53. W.V. Cleveland to Gale, Abe Fortas, Special Inquiry—White House, 7/21/65, 161-2860-48; M.A. Jones to DeLoach, Abe Fortas, 3025 N Street, N.W., Wash. D.C., 5/11/64, 101-1605-19 (Fortas "was reportedly a member of a clique in the old A.A.A. which included Alger Hiss, Lee Pressman and John Abt. Fortas has served as Defense Counsel for individuals and organizations whose loyalty has been in question. These include Owen Lattimore, Dr. Edward U. Condon, the Joint Anti-Fascist Refugee Committee and the American Council on American-Soviet Friendship").

54. M.A. Jones to DeLoach, Abe Fortas, 3025 N Street, N.W., Wash. D.C., 5/11/64, 101-1605-19.

55. *See, gen.*, FBI WFO references to Abe Fortas released in *Charns II*.

56. Nat Hentoff, "Profile of Justice William Brennan," *The New Yorker*, 3/12/90, p. 62.

57. *See* 28 U.S.C.A. Sec. 453 (1948) (oaths of justices and judges), 28 U.S.C.A. Sec. 454 (1948) (practice of law by justices and judges a "high misdemeanor"), and 28 U.S.C.A. Sec. 455 (1948) (disqualification of justice or judge) for Justice Fortas's improprieties. Hoover, Tolson, and DeLoach arguably violated 28 U.S.C.A. Sec. 518 (1966) (attorney general and solicitor general shall "conduct and argue suits and appeals in the Supreme Court") and 28 U.S.C.A. Sec. 519 (1966) (attorney general "shall supervise all litigation to which the United States, an agency, or officer thereof is a party"). In addition, the FBI's contact with Fortas arguably was an attempt to violate the principle of separation of powers inherent in the Constitution as well as being an improper *ex parte* contact with a justice in which evidence was presented that was intended to be passed on to the Court. This also gave the appearance of impropriety.

58. DeLoach to author, 3/12/91.

59. *Justice & Presidents*, p. 283.

60. DeLoach to Tolson, 7/19/65, 161-2860-37.

61. Born in Claxton, Ga.

62. William Sullivan with Bill Brown, *The Bureau: My Thirty Years in Hoover's FBI* (Pinnacle Books 1979), p. 61 (hereafter cited as *The Bureau*).

63. Ungar, *FBI*, pp. 287–288; *The Bureau*, p. 61.

64. *The Bureau*, p. 61.

65. Biography of Cartha D. DeLoach, Assistant to the Director, F.B.I., 7/10/68, Vol. XIII, FBI Document Supplement, Part XIX; Cartha D. DeLoach, Name file, Memo for the President, 4/8/65, LBJ Library (memo arguing against placing DeLoach on the V.A. Hospital Committee because he "has been an Administration informant on the activities of veterans organizations" and this would "surface him"); O'Reilly, *Racial Matters*, pp. 207–210.

66. DeLoach to author, 3/12/91.

67. *The Bureau*, pp. 68–70, 235; *Fortas*, pp. 137–140 (for a description of Fortas's role).

68. Hoover to Tolson, Belmont, DeLoach, and Sullivan, 5/19/65, 161-2860-XX.

69. M.A. Jones to DeLoach, Abe Fortas, 3025 N. Street, N.W., Wash. D.C., 5/11/64, 101-1605-19 ("Fortas turned over to our Washington Field Office on 1-10-64, a transcript of the tape-recorded interview between [the remainder of the paragraph is redacted citing the (b)(7)(C) privacy exemption.])

70. Hoover to Marvin Watson, 7/21/65, 161-2860-49.

71. AF to LBJ, 8/19/65, File Pertaining to Abe Fortas and Homer Thornberry (hereafter File re: AF–HT), box 1, WHCF, LBJ Library.

72. Laurence Stern, "Fortas Calmly Faces Senate Questioners," Washington *Post*, 8/6/65.

73. "Senate Confirms Fortas after 20-Minute Debate," Washington *Evening Star*, 8/12/65.

74. White House memo, 10/7/65, File re: AF–HT, box 1, WHCF, LBJ Library.

75. *Abe Fortas*, p. 312 (citing an anonymous source).

76. *Id.* at 408–440; *Justice & Presidents*, pp. 283–284.

77. Valenti to Fortas, 1/29/66, Abe Fortas folder, box 195, WHCF, LBJ Library.

78. Abe Fortas to Earl Warren, memorandum re: disqualification in *Black v. U.S.*, 6/10/66, Earl Warren Papers, Manuscript Division, Library of Congress, Washington, DC. Fortas offered no explanation for his disqualification, though it probably had to do with his short-lived representation of Bobby Baker. It is unusual for a justice to cite a reason for recusing himself.

79. Hoover to Katzenbach, Fred B. Black, Jr. Anti-Racketeering, 6/3/66, Fred Black folder, Hoover's "O & C," copies to the solicitor general and others at Justice, and with a 6/7 cover letter to Marvin Watson, special assistant to LBJ.

80. Byron White to Earl Warren, 6/11/66, folder 1962-1974, container #358, Earl Warren Papers. Justices White and Marshall declined to comment about the *Black* case.

81. Conference case list for 6/1/66 and 6/10/66, Earl Warren Papers. Warren was to write the Court's response.

82. Conference log in *Black v. U.S.*, William O. Douglas Papers, Manuscript Division, Library of Congress, Washington, D.C.; E.W. Memo to Conference, 6/10/66, box 266, JMH Papers.

83. *Black v. U.S.*, 384 U.S. 983 (June 13, 1966).

84. DeLoach to Tolson, 6/14/66, Fred Black folder, "O & C" files; James Rowan, "FBI files show justice violated court secrecy," Milwaukee *Journal*, 1/21/90, A1; Tony Mauro, "Fortas Took Loyalty to LBJ into Chambers," *Legal Times*, 2/3/90; 1. Alexander Charns, "Gavelgate," *Southern Exposure* 18 (Fall 1990): 8–11. The DeLoach and Hoover memos about Fortas reporting on the *Black* case were released to Athan Theoharis and to the author of this book by letters dated on the same day in December 1989. Theoharis had asked for all of Hoover's "official and confidential" files, and the author requested all records concerning the U.S. Supreme Court including those found in Hoover's "O & C" files. The FBI's letter to the author said that it was providing him with a copy as a "courtesy" as they were aware of his interest in the Supreme Court. Later the FBI maintained the memos were not responsive to the lawsuits of *Charns II*.

85. *Id.*, Hoover's "O & C" files, Fred Black folder.

86. *Id.*

87. Cartha D. DeLoach to author, 7/31/90.

88. Biography of Cartha D. DeLoach, Assistant to the Director, F.B.I., 7/10/68, Vol. XIII, FBI Document Supplement, Part XIX; *The Boss*, pp. 35, 45.

89. Author interview (1990) with a former newsman who requested anonymity. For a story about DeLoach's modus operandi when someone crossed J. Edgar Hoover, *see, e.g.*, Nicholas Von Hoffman, *Citizen Cohn* (Bantam Books 1988), pp. 336–339.

90. DeLoach to Tolson, 6/14/66, Fred Black folder, Hoover's "O & C" files.

91. Sullivan, *The Bureau*, p. 60; *Abe Fortas*, p. 306 (noting Fortas's antipathy for RFK).

92. Black leather [untitled] folder [contains a manuscript of a book about the Kennedys], box 13, Oct. '89 accession papers, Abe Fortas Papers, Manuscripts and Archives, Sterling Memorial Library, Yale University, New Haven, CT. These papers are closed to the public until January 1, 2000. The author received permission from Mrs. Fortas to conduct his research.

93. See DeLoach to Tolson, 6/14/66, p. 2, and Hoover memo for personal files, 10:15 AM, 6/14/66, p. 1, both in Fred Black folder, "O & C" files.

94. *See* Fred Black folder, Hoover's "O & C" files.

95. DeLoach to Tolson, 6/14/66, Fred Black folder, "O & C" files. James E. Haggerty, Sr., who practiced in Detroit, Michigan, had represented Hoffa. He died in the mid-1960s. Michael Haggerty, his grandson, said that he was not aware that his grandfather had been bugged. Michael Haggerty telephone interview with author, 12/31/90.

96. DeLoach to Tolson, 6/14/66, Fred Black folder, "O & C" files. Hoffa's Nashville lawyer, Z.T. Osborn, Jr., hired an investigator to work on Hoffa's case. The FBI had already entered into an agreement with this investigator to serve as an informant. The investigator-informant was wired by the FBI with a body recorder and picked up the conversations of Hoffa and his attorney. *Osborn v. U.S.*, 385 U.S. 323 (1966). Fortas voted with the majority to uphold the lawyer's conviction for attempting to bribe jurors. Fortas recused himself in Hoffa's related conviction for attempting to bribe jurors. *Hoffa v. U.S.*, 385 U.S. 293 (1966).

97. Fortas voted with the majority of the Court in *Hoffa v. U.S.*, 387 U.S. 231 (1967) to vacate Hoffa's conviction for mail and wire fraud because the FBI had overheard Hoffa in illegal bugs. The Court sent the case back to the trial court for a hearing to determine whether any of the evidence was tainted. Fortas had recused himself earlier when other interested organizations requested that the Court allow them to file friend of the Court briefs. *Hoffa v. U.S.*, 386 U.S. 940, 951 (1967).

98. At oral argument on March 1, 1966, Justice Fortas "asked whether [Solicitor General Marshall] could provide . . . information as to the practices followed by the Federal Bureau of Investigation" during interrogations. By a letter dated March 2 and after consultation with the FBI, Marshall wrote to the Court about the FBI's practice. Marshall to John F. Davis, Clerk, Sup. Ct., Box 530, JMH Papers; "Cases No. 759, 760, 761, 584—Miranda, et. al.," box 5, Abe Fortas Papers.

99. Cartha D. DeLoach to author, 11/13/90.

100. *Id.* DeLoach said that Hoover "appreciated" Fortas's work in getting the Court to make reference to the professionalism of the FBI in the *Miranda* ruling. Even with the accolade, Hoover did not support the decision because he apparently believed it would shackle the hands of less professional local lawmen. Senator Robert C. Byrd (D–West Virginia) even called Hoover and asked for the FBI to prepare a "little speech" for him to deliver on the Senate floor "hitting that ruling." Hoover commented that the ruling "will hit the local authorities harder than the Federal authorities, but I would get him up some notes on this." Hoover to Tolson, DeLoach, Wick, 6/16/66, 62-27585-NR, serial before 214. Even so, when the FBI was concerned about the public fallout of the *Black* ruling in July 1966, a suggestion was made to call attention to "the praise that we get" from "members of the present Supreme Court." The three examples given were *Miranda* and recent speeches given by Justices Clark and Douglas. J.J. Casper to Mohr, Supreme Court's Remarks Praising FBI, 7/5/66, 62-27585-219.

101. According to White House telephone records, Fortas called LBJ at 9:29 AM on 6/14/66. The subject of the call was not noted. Claudia Anderson, archivist, LBJ Library to author, 5/24/90. Fortas's Eastern Airlines flight to Jacksonville was scheduled to leave Dulles at 10:15 AM on 6/14/66. Will Wilson to Hoover, Louis Wolfson, 4/15/69, 72-1882-[illegible].

102. Hoover memo for personal files, June 14, 1966, Fred Black folder, "O & C" files.

103. Fred Black folder, "O&C" files.

104. *See also* T.J. McAndrews to Gale, Carmine Tramunti, a.k.a., et al., Interstate Transportation in Aid of Racketeering—Gambling, 12/7/65, 62-27585-NR, serial before 209. "In a ruling handed down December 6, 1965, the . . . Supreme Court reversed the decisions of the District and Second Circuit Court of Appeals in a contempt of court conviction of Al Harris, who fronted for Tramunti, a leader in the Thomas Luchese 'family' of La Cosa Nostra, in a huge dice game being operated nightly in the Miami, Florida, area during early 1963. . . . The liberal element of the Supreme Court has struck another blow against law enforcement and the drive against organized crime . . . [with their] 'fear of reprisal' doctrine." The bureau was concerned that this ruling "could well have an effect on a number of our more important cases in the field of organized crime in which immunity is an issue, primarily our case against Chicago 'commission' member, Sam Giancana. . . . With regard to the Giancana case, the Department has made a preliminary observation, in light of this reversal, that, while Giancana's contempt citation is a civil matter, on which the above-discussed decision does not touch, the Court may in the future return a ruling adverse to the Government because of the introduction of the 'fear of reprisal' doctrine."

105. *The Boss*, pp. 341–342; *Secrecy and Power*, pp. 359–360.

106. On June 17 at 9:45 AM, Ramsey Clark had phoned Justice Black at his Court chambers. R. Clark Daily Calendar, box 72, Ramsey Clark Papers, LBJ Library. On June 18 at 11:45 AM, Justice Fortas phoned Ramsey Clark at his Justice Department office. At 12:37 PM that same day, Marvin Watson talked to Clark on the phone. That same day, less than an hour after Clark met with Attorney General Katzenbach at 2:35 PM, he got together with DeLoach. R. Clark Daily Calls, box 111, Ramsey Clark Papers. (There is no record about the content of these meetings and calls, and Ramsey Clark did not respond to the author's written request about these matters.) On June 19 Justice Fortas made two morning calls to President Johnson, and the next day Johnson phoned Fortas at 8:18 AM. Box 7, President's Daily Diary, LBJ Library.

107. The White House Central files at the LBJ Presidential Library had no file about the *Black* case and the file about the Supreme Court has no written record (not classified or otherwise not open to the public) of Fortas talking to Johnson about a pending case.

108. Abe Fortas, Secretary McNamara, General Wheeler, Undersecretary Ball, Clark Clifford, Walt Rostow and George Christian all had lunch. By 2:45 PM, only Clifford and Fortas were with the president; apparently they stayed at the White House until 3:50 PM. It cannot be ascertained from the diary cards

whether Fortas was alone with Johnson that afternoon. Diary Card, 6/21/66, box 7, LBJ's Daily Diary, 6/21/66, both in LBJ Library. Fortas is not mentioned in the White House diary backup for 6/21/66; by letter to James O. Eastland, chairman of the Senate Judiciary Committee, 9/13/68, Clifford wrote that Fortas had participated in White House meetings about Vietnam. "Inasmuch as I maintained no record and have no precise recollection of these deliberations, I am unable to furnish the Committee with specific details. I am sure that on none of these occasions was there discussed with Justice Fortas, or in his presence, any matter pending before the Supreme Court, or, indeed, any other judicial matter." Nominations of Abe Fortas and Homer Thornberry, Hearings before the Senate Judiciary Committee, 90th Cong., 2d. Sess., p. 1363.

109. LBJ's Daily Diary, 6/21/66, box 7, LBJ Library.

110. WH telephone office, 6/21/66 folder, box 28, LBJ Library.

111. LBJ telephone operator's notes.

112. LBJ's Daily Diary.

113. James Rowan, "FBI Files Show Justice Violated Court Secrecy," Milwaukee Journal, 1/21/90, A1.

114. Id.

115. See, gen., Fred Black folder in the October 1989 accession papers, Abe Fortas Papers. The press release about the wiretapping commission is not in the Fred Black folder.

116. The Boss, p. 391.

117. Id. Less than an hour after Fortas left the White House on June 21, Marvin Watson wrote two memos to the president. These memos remain classified. Marvin Watson chronological file, box 38, LBJ Library.

118. Rowan, "Justice Violated Secrecy," Milwaukee Journal, 1/21/90, p. A20. There are two classified memos from Marvin Watson to the president during the late afternoon of June 23, 1966. Marvin Watson chronological file, box 38, LBJ Library.

119. LBJ telephone operator's notes.

120. WH telephone office, 6/23/66, box 29, LBJ Library.

121. Nicholas Katzenbach to author, 7/10/90.

122. Id.

123. Memo for the president, 6/15/66, from Robert Kintner, WHCF, Cabinet Papers, Box 6, LBJ Library.

124. Katzenbach to author, 7/10/90.

125. DeLoach to Tolson, re: Use of Microphones in Internal Revenue Cases, 6/28/66, Fred Black folder, Hoover's "O & C."

126. Who's Who in American Law, 3d ed. (Marquis Who's Who, Inc. 1983), p. 129.

127. DeLoach to Tolson, re: Use of Microphones in Internal Revenue Cases, 6/28/66, Fred Black folder, Hoover's "O & C" files; see, Fortas to LBJ, re: Sheldon S. Cohen and Mitchell Rogovin, 12/21/64, "OO—White House, 5. Personnel, a. Official—Vol. III" folder, box 9, Abe Fortas Papers.

128. Sheldon Cohen to Marvin Watson, Judicial-Legal Matters, Box 1, LBJ Papers, LBJ Library (response to LBJ's memo was also included here).

129. *The Boss,* p. 387.

130. *Id.* at 389–390.

131. DeLoach to Tolson, re: Fred Black case, 7/11/66, Fred Black folder, Hoover's "O & C" files.

132. Box 72, Ramsey Clark daily calendar, LBJ Library; *but cf.,* Prof. Owen M. Fiss, Yale Law School, to author, 1/17/91 ("The call from Ramsey Clark that you mentioned would have been taken as part of my duties as law clerk, and thus not a subject I would like to discuss, out of respect for the confidentiality of the relationship with the Justice, but in truth I have no recollection of it").

133. LBM [Lewis B. Merrifield] memo to Douglas re: supplemental memo for U.S., 9/26/66, William O. Douglas Papers, Manuscript Division, Library of Congress; Fred Graham, "FBI had sanction in eavesdropping," New York *Times,* 7/14/66, A1; *The Boss,* p. 392.

134. *See* Fred Black folder, Hoover's "O & C" files; *The Boss,* pp. 387–390.

135. "FBI: Day in Court," *Newsweek,* 7/25/66.

136. *SWP v. U.S.,* J. Griesa opinion, pp. 99–100.

137. Hentoff, "Profile of Brennan," *The New Yorker,* 6/12/90, pp. 61–62; Bob Woodward and Scott Armstrong, *The Brethren* (Avon Books 1979), p. 86.

138. Hentoff, "Brennan," *The New Yorker,* 6/12/90, pp. 61–62.

139. Woodward and Armstrong, *The Brethren,* p. 86.

140. *Id.*

141. Quoting 100-391697-281, part of FBI file on Vern Countryman, H. Hubert Wilson Papers, Box 1, Mudd Manuscript Library.

142. *See* Ch. 1 herein.

Chapter 5: Justice Douglas and the Parvin Foundation

1. M.A. Jones to Wick, re: Justice William O. Douglas, 8/3/66, 94-33476-57.

2. James Simon, *Independent Journey* (Harper & Row 1980), p. 383.

3. *Id.;* N.P. Callahan to Hoover, criticism in the *Congressional Record* of Douglas's recent marriage, 7/19/66, 94-33476-NR.

4. William O. Douglas files 1966, box 414, JMH Papers.

5. DeLoach to Tolson, [redacted] Antiracketeering (Las Vegas), Justice William O. Douglas, Civil Rights Matters (Conference with Deputy AG Ramsey Clark), 8/3/66, 94-33476-NR. Ramsey Clark's daily calendar for 8/1/66 reflects the following note: "9:00 Justice Fortas/home: 332-2455/or in his chambers." Ramsey Clark daily calendar, 7/15/66 to 8/5/66, box 72, LBJ Library.

6. DeLoach to Tolson, *supra* note 5.

7. Ramsey Clark said he did not recall DeLoach talking to him about Justice Douglas. Telephone call from author, 10/3/89.

8. Author's telephone interview with Ramsey Clark, 8/2/88.

9. C.D. DeLoach to Tolson, re: John Francis Drew Anti-Racketeering (Las Vegas), Justice William O. Douglas, U.S. Supreme Court, Civil Rights Matters, 8/3/66, 62-12114-NR.

10. M.A. Jones to Wick, Justice Douglas, 8/3/66, 94-33476-57.

11. J.J. Casper to Mohr, Justice Clark visit to FBI Academy, 8/17/66, 62-72944-439.

12. Hoover memorandum for Tolson, Mohr, Casper, and Wick, 8/19/66, 9:42 AM, 62-72944-NR.

13. DeLoach to Tolson, 9/12/66, Fred Black folder, "O & C" files.

14. Id.

15. MES to Warren, 6/6/66, Supreme Court file: conference memos, Earl Warren Papers; Michael Smith was not aware of any lobbying about the Black case by Justice Fortas. Smith to author, 5/31/90.

16. Cdr supplemental memo to Justice Clark, Black v. U.S., 25 May 1966, box B212, Tom Clark Papers, Rare Books and Special Collections, Tarlton Law Library, University of Texas Law School (hereafter cited as Clark Papers, Tarlton/Univ. Texas).

17. BCS to Warren, 9/15/66, Supreme Court file: conference memos, Earl Warren Papers.

18. Nimetz to JMH, 9/15/66, box 277, JMH Papers.

19. Telephone memorandum (telephone operators' logs), 9/12/66, (6:18 PM, 10:30 PM, 1:42 PM, and 4:45 PM), LBJ Library.

20. Ramsey Clark daily calls 1966, Ramsey Clark Papers. Justice Byron White had called and talked to Clark on 9/21/66 at 10:37 AM. On 9/22/66 Ramsey Clark returned Fortas's call at 11:18 AM. At 11:35 AM that same morning DeLoach talked to Clark on the phone. Later that afternoon Clark also met with Attorney General Katzenbach twice and talked to Solicitor General Marshall twice and talked on the phone to Marvin Watson.

21. Ramsey Clark daily Calls (9:40 AM), 10/3/66, box 111, Ramsey Clark Papers.

22. Ronald J. Ostrow, "Vegas-Linked Fund Pays Justice Douglas," Los Angeles Times, 10/16/66.

23. Id.

24. Douglas, The Court Years, p. 257.

25. Justice Douglas, Black v. U.S., on petition for rehearing, October 1966, Douglas Papers; Douglas, The Court Years, p. 257; Arthur Sparrow, unpublished article on the Fred Black case, University of North Carolina at Chapel Hill, May 1990.

26. Fortas to Douglas, 10/20/66, Douglas Papers.

27. Douglas, The Court Years, p. 257.

28. Id.

29. Brennan to Douglas, handwritten note, undated, container 1396, Douglas Papers. Peter L. Strauss, law clerk to Justice Brennan during the 1965 term of Court, believed that "it would be inappropriate to discuss the confidential matters [about the Court, Justice Fortas, and the Black case]." Strauss to author, 5/24/90. Former Brennan law clerk Owen Fiss felt similarly: Owen M. Fiss to author, 1/17/91. In response to the author's written questions about the Black case, Fiss wrote: "Over the years, I have treated my clerkship with Justice Brennan as a highly confidential relationship and have not submitted myself to any interviews. . . . I am afraid therefore that I cannot help you."

30. Douglas, *The Court Years*, p. 257.
31. Douglas to Parvin, 10/18/66, Final Report by the Special Subcommittee on H. Res. 920 of the Committee on the Judiciary, H.R., 91st Cong., 2nd Sess., Sept. 17, 1970, p. 907.
32. Defendant's Ninth Status Report, *Charns II*.

Chapter 6: Return of *Fred B. Black, Jr., v. United States*

1. Fred P. Graham, "Robert Kennedy Aided Buggings," New York *Times*, 12/11/66, pp. A1, 24.
2. Hoover to Acting AG, Albert B. Parvin, 10/26/66, 94-33476-NR; Hoover to Marvin Watson, 10/26/66, 94-33476-58. The bulk of these letters are redacted under law enforcement exemption claims.
3. *See* WOD to Fortas and WOD to Johnson, correspondence between 2/26/64 and 10/22/64, about a Center for the Study of Democratic Institutions project, White House Folder #7 (Request for the President—favors, etc.), Abe Fortas Papers.
4. Los Angeles *Times*, 10/19/66.
5. Final Report by the Special Subcommittee on H. Res. 920 of the Committee on the Judiciary, H.R., 91st Cong., 2nd Sess., Sept. 17, 1970, p. 907 (hereafter Final Report on the Impeachment Resolution).
6. Douglas to Warren, 10/31/66, Final Report on the Impeachment Resolution, pp. 192–195.
7. Tom Clark to each justice, proposed disposition in *Black v. U.S.*, 10/20/66, container 1396, Douglas Papers; John M. Harlan to each justice, proposed dissent in *Black*, 10/18/66, container 1396, Douglas Papers; Flood Box 5, No. 1029 *Black v. U.S.* folder, and Flood Box 1, No. 245 *Davis v. U.S.* folder, Abe Fortas Papers.
8. *See* Agenda for the conference, Friday, 11/4/66, Douglas Papers; *see, gen.*, Fred Black folder, "O & C." During the October 3 and 14, and November 3 conferences, Fortas took notes about the case of *Davis v. U.S.*, which was handled together with *Black v. U.S.* after October 20, 1966. October Term 1966 Conference Notes for *Davis v. U.S.*, Abe Fortas Papers; compare with *Black v. U.S.* case summary of Douglas, Douglas Papers, which notes that Fortas was "not voting." Douglas also uses a designation "NP," which apparently means "not participating"; Justice Hugo Black "assiduously maintained" his conference notes, but just before his death he ordered that these notes be destroyed (*Hugo LaFayette Black: a Register of His Papers in the Library of Congress* [Manuscript Division, Library of Congress, 1982], p. 5). Justice White wrote that his papers "are not available for research at this time." White to author, 4/22/91. It was rare for a justice who had recused himself on a case to leave the conference room when that case was discussed.
9. Fred Black folder, accession materials, Abe Fortas Papers (e.g., the preparation of the blind memo entitled "BLACK"); Douglas Papers (Fortas talked Douglas out of writing an opinion about the powerful forces trying to knock him out of the case). *See, gen.*, Fred Black folder, Hoover's "O&C"; (DeLoach tells Tolson and Hoover that Fortas said he was going to expose Robert

Kennedy); *but see,* in response to the author's 8/17/90 letter to Justice William J. Brennan, Jr., concerning Justice Fortas and the *Black* case, Justice Brennan wrote: "I regret that I have no information regarding Justice Fortas and the *Black* case."

10. "Technical and Microphone Surveillances" folder, Abe Fortas Papers.

11. BLACK memo, Fred B. Black [secret] folder, Box 12, 1989 accession papers, Abe Fortas Papers; undated, edited draft of Justice Harlan's dissent, *Black,* O.T. 1965, No. 1029, with undated two page blind memorandum entitled *Black,* box 266, JMH Papers.

12. Undated, edited draft of Justice Harlan's dissent, *Black,* O.T. 1965, No. 1029, with undated two page memorandum entitled *Black,* box 266, JMH Papers.

13. Agenda for the conference, Friday, 11/4/66, Douglas Papers; Clark memo to all justices, *Davis v U.S.* and *Black v U.S.,* Oct. 20, 1966, container 1396, Douglas Papers.

14. Justice Black's memorandum for the conference, 10/20/66, No. 245, *Davis v. U.S.,* A209, Clark Papers, Tarlton/Univ. Texas.

15. To accept a case for the Court's discretionary review (the issuance of the writ of *cert*), at least four justices must vote to grant the writ at a confidential *cert* conference. The overwhelming majority of the cases heard by the Court each year arrive by way of *cert.* In contrast, for those cases involving the original jurisdiction of the Supreme Court under Article III, Section 2, of the Constitution, appellants have a technical right of appeal, but the case is reviewed only if the question presented is of a "substantial federal nature." Henry J. Abraham, *Freedom and the Court: Civil Rights and Liberties in the United States* (Oxford University Press, 5th ed., 1988), p. 7 (hereafter cited as *Freedom and the Court*).

16. JMH memorandum to the Conference, *Black v. U.S.,* No. 1029, O.T. 1965, circulated 10/18/66, box 266, JMH Papers.

17. Clark to all justices, *Davis et al. v. U.S.,* No. 245, *Black v. U.S.,* No. 1029, container 1396, Douglas Papers. According to David Wigdor, assistant chief, Manuscripts Division of the Library of Congress, no case file concerning *Black v. U.S.* was located in the Brennan Papers. Wigdor to author, 1/7/91. Mike Klein, reference librarian at the Manuscripts Division, said that no *Davis et al. v. U.S.* case file was located in response to the author's request to conduct research using Justice Brennan's papers. Author's telephone interview with Klein, 12/26/90. Evidently, Justice Brennan did not retain these files at the Court, as he had requested that the Library of Congress send the files to the Court so he could go through them before he would agree to grant the author access to them.

18. Clark's typewritten addition to the third printing of the opinion, box A209, Clark Papers, Tarlton/Univ. Texas.

19. Black to Clark, 10/28/66, box A209, Clark Papers, Tarlton/Univ. Texas. Justice Black destroyed his conference notes and kept no case file folder on the *Black* or *Davis* cases. Justice Black did maintain files indexed as "intracourt memoranda" and "opinions of other justices." *See Black: A Register,* pp. 5, 71–73.

20. C.D. DeLoach to Tolson, re: Conversation with Justice Fortas—[redacted] Matters; Black Case, 10/25/66, 62-12114-NR.

21. *Id.* DeLoach wrote an addendum to his memo: "Justice Fortas did not in any manner give me any information to which I was not entitled. He did not violate ethics in any manner. The above supposition—and that is all it is—was strictly on my part. On the few occasions that I have interviewed Justice Fortas, he has never furnished me 'any inside information.' Neither have I asked for such information. This memorandum was written merely because of the Director's interest in the Black case. This memorandum is naturally an 'informal' type memorandum and the contents should be maintained in strict confidence."

22. David Wigdor wrote that "[a]fter an examination of the case files for 1965, 1966, and 1967 it appears that the Brennan Papers do not contain a file dealing with this case. Justice Brennan's docket book for 1965 has a page for the *Black* case, but the page is empty of any entries beyond the title." Wigdor to author, 1/4/91.

23. Conference Memo Scorecard, *Black v. U.S.,* No. 1029, Douglas Papers.

24. *Black v. U.S.,* 385 U.S. 26 (1966). With regard to *Davis,* the Court denied *cert,* so that the bugging question "might be fully explored at the new trial, as suggested by the Solicitor General."

25. Statement of J. Edgar Hoover, *FBI Law Enforcement Bulletin,* Sept. 1952, p. 1, quoted in *Irvine v. California,* 347 U.S. 149–150 (1954) (Frankfurter dissenting).

26. Justice Clark's October 20th proposed opinion in *Davis and Black* ended differently: "Mr. Justice White and Mr. Justice Fortas took no part in the consideration and decision in . . . *Black v. United States.*

27. Black was acquitted of tax evasion at his new trial. He later sued the FBI for the illegal bugging and was awarded close to a million dollars. An appeals court overturned the amount of the award.

Chapter 7: Paint It *Black*

1. Abe Fortas Poetry re: cases (written on the bench) folder, box 1, Abe Fortas Papers. Permission to quote the first two paragraphs of this poem was granted by Judith Ann Schiff, chief research archivist, Manuscripts and Archives, Yale University Library, New Haven, CT.

2. J.J. Casper to Mohr, Wiretapping; Technical Surveillance, 11/14/66, 62-12114-3469.

3. *Id.*

4. *Id.* "*Question:* Does the *Black* decision in effect demand that any possible illegal Government activity which may have prejudiced the accused be disclosed to the trial court? *Answer:* Yes." The memo goes on to say that if "the illegality prejudiced much of the evidence as to make conviction doubtful, prosecution will be declined."

5. In 1972 the Court resolved the major legal issues about eavesdropping on domestic "national security" targets. The *U.S. v. U.S. District Court* rebuke to the Richard Nixon–John Mitchell warrantless wiretapping was issued by the

Court on June 19, 1972, just two days after the Watergate burglary and bugging. The Court ruled that the president had no constitutional authority to wiretap domestic subversives without a warrant.

6. Senate (Church) Committee, Final Report, Book III, pp. 305–306.

7. *Id.* at 306.

8. *See, e.g., id.* at 306, 307, n. 123.

9. C.D. DeLoach to Tolson, re: Ramsey Clark, acting AG, Declassification of documents pertaining to microphones and wiretaps, administrative matters, 10/5/66, 62-12114-NR. After DeLoach talked to Ramsey Clark, he "called Marvin Watson at the White House and explained to him the matter of declassification and that the memorandum of August 17, 1961, which Bobby Kennedy had signed, was hereby declared declassified."

10. 12/11/66, 62-12114-3514.

11. Fred P. Graham, "Robert Kennedy Aided Buggings," New York *Times,* 12/11/66, A1. Hoover was displeased with Acting Attorney General Ramsey Clark in this regard as well, writing to him that he had "noted with increasing concern the apparent tendency of the Department to place this Bureau in an embarrassing position in cases which involve revelation of usage of electronic devices." Hoover to Clark, 11/28/66, 62-12114-NR.

12. Hoover to Marvin Watson, 11/17/66, 62-98896-NR, first serial after 33. Hoover informed the president that Bobby Baker's defense attorney, Edward Bennett Williams, had succeeded in convincing Federal Judge Oliver Gasch to allow the press to read some of the summaries of these microphone surveillances.

Chapter 8: The FBI versus the Supreme Court, Jimmy Hoffa, and Privacy

1. *U.S. v. Clay,* 430 F.2d 165, 167–168 (5th Cir. 1970). The quote concerns the wiretap log of taps on Martin Luther King. Former world champion boxer Cassius Clay (Muhammad Ali) had been convicted the year before of violating Selective Service laws by refusing induction into the armed forces.

2. *Hoffa v. U.S.,* 382 U.S. 1024 (1966) (*cert granted* in No. 794 Sixth Cir. on issue of "secret informer" on 1/31/66); *Hoffa v. U.S.,* 385 U.S. 293 (1966) (attempted bribery of jurors in the so-called Test Fleet trial was affirmed despite government use of secret government informer in Nos. 32–35); *Hoffa v. U.S.,* 386 U.S. 940, 951 (1967) (*rehearing denied* in No. 432 6th Cir.); *Hoffa v. U.S.,* 389 U.S. 859 (1967)(*cert denied* in No. 432 6th Cir.); *Hoffa v. U.S.,* 387 U.S. 231 (1967) (convictions for mail and wire fraud and conspiracy vacated and remanded to district court for proceedings concerning electronic surveillance in No. 1003); *Hoffa v. U.S.,* 390 U.S. 924 (1968)(*cert denied* in No. 912 6th Cir.); *Hoffa v. U.S.,* 394 U.S. 310 (1969)(convictions vacated and remanded to district court for hearing re: electronic surveillance in Nos. 546 and 895 along with *Giordano v. U.S., Clay v. U.S.,* and eleven other similarly situated cases. Hoffa's cases were from the Sixth Circuit [No. 546] and the Seventh Circuit [No. 895]).

3. Dan E. Moldea, *The Hoffa Wars: Teamsters, Rebels, Politicians and the Mob* (Paddington Press Ltd. 1978), p. 173 (hereafter *The Hoffa Wars*).

4. Herbert Miller to Fortas, 7/29/64, box 6, Abe Fortas Papers.

5. *Abe Fortas*, p. 216; Fortas to Davis III, 5/19/64, "White House, 4. Politics, c. Contributions" folder, box 9, Abe Fortas Papers.

6. *The Hoffa Wars*, p. 26.

7. In at least one later Hoffa case, Hoffa's lawyers filed papers saying that their client "waived" any ethical conflict that Fortas might have had in ruling on his case.

8. DeLoach to Tolson, 6/14/66, Fred Black folder, Hoover's "O & C" files.

9. *The Hoffa Wars*, pp. 140–141.

10. Fred J. Cook, "Anything to Get Hoffa," *The International Teamster*, Mar. 1967 (reprinted from *The Nation*, 2/20/67), p. 27, 62-12114-3532.

11. *Osborn v. U.S.*, 385 U.S. 323 (1966).

12. Conference notes in *Osborn v. U.S.*, Abe Fortas Papers.

13. *Id.*

14. *Id.*

15. *Id.*

16. *Osborn v. U.S.*, 385 U.S. 323, 340 (1966).

17. Oct. Term 1966, Nos. 32–35, Abe Fortas Papers.

18. *Id.*

19. *Hoffa v. U.S.*, 385 U.S. 293 (Dec. 12, 1966).

20. *See supra*, ch. 4, p. 58.

21. 87 S.Ct. 421 (1966)(Warren dissenting).

22. *Id.* at 422.

23. Conrad D. Kranwinkle [law clerk] to EW, re: *Hoffa, et al.*, Nos. 32–35, 12/7/66, Earl Warren Papers.

24. Nimetz to Harlan, 1/7/66, *Hoffa*, O.T. 1965, Nos. 32–35, box 27, JMH Papers.

25. Cook, "Anything to Get Hoffa," p. 27, 62-12114-3532.

26. *Id.*

27. *Id.* at 23; A. Rosen to DeLoach, James Riddle Hoffa *et al.*, obstruction of justice, etc., 2/8/67, 62-12114-NR.

28. In another Hoffa case, forty FBI special agents had been assigned to follow and photograph Hoffa in Chattanooga in 1964. While still in private practice, Fortas had joked that the Justice Department had not sent him the photographs of Hoffa along with the internal memo about the prosecution. Herb Miller to Fortas, 7/29/64, White House—Departmental Problems folder, box 10, Oct. '89 accession papers, Abe Fortas Papers.

29. L.M. Walters to Felt, James Riddle Hoffa etc., 2/4/67, 62-12114-NR, second serial after 3508.

30. *Id.*

31. 87 S.Ct. 1583 (1967)(7th Cir. case).

32. *Hoffa v. U.S.*, 387 U.S. 231 (1967).

33. *U.S. v. Hoffa et al.*, 402 F.2d 380, 383–385 (7th Cir. 1968).

34. *U.S. v. Hoffa et al.*, 402 F.2d 380, 383–385 (7th Cir. 1968).

35. 388 U.S. 41 (1967).

36. *Id.* at 60.

37. *Katz v. U.S.*, 389 U.S. 347, 365 (1967)(Black dissenting).

38. *Id.* at 364.

39. J.J. Casper to Mohr, Eavesdropping and Wiretapping *Berger v. New York* (6/12/67), 6/15/67, 62-12114-3566.

40. *Id.*

41. *Id.*

42. That Justice Clark's son served both as deputy and acting attorney general did not cause Justice Clark to recuse himself from participating in Justice Department cases, even controversial cases like *Black v. U.S.*, for which he had written the majority opinion, but had not signed. To avoid the appearance of impropriety, Justice Clark probably should have recused himself in the *Black* case, especially since his son was the Justice Department's liaison with the FBI on the case.

43. *Justices & Presidents*, pp. 288–289.

44. O'Reilly, *Racial Matters*, p. 327.

45. G. Kenneth Reiblich, Summary of October 1967 Term, 88 S.Ct. 153–160 (1968).

46. The Court had not held that warrantless federal wiretapping was unconstitutional. Abraham, *Freedom and the Court*, p. 180: "[W]iretapping . . . is *not* unconstitutional—or at least the Supreme Court has never so held it." Abraham argues that some types of wiretapping are unconstitutional today— warrantless non-national security wiretapping, for instance.

47. 389 U.S. 347 (1967).

48. *See* AF to PS, 11/30/67, AF folder, box 531, JMH Papers (Fortas said he agreed with White).

49. Fortas to Stewart, 11/30/67, Abe Fortas folder, Box 531, JMH Papers.

50. 389 U.S. at 358, f.n. 23.

51. Bruce A. Murphy, *Fortas: The Rise and Ruin of a Supreme Court Justice* (William Morrow and Co. 1988), p. 82.

52. *See, e.g.*, Plaintiff's Index II to Records Claimed as Non-Exempt Filed in Opposition to Defendant's Second Partial Summary Judgment Motion, pp. 25–31, *Charns II* (WFO 100-17493, 9/30/47: Robert Miller phoned Abe Fortas about a "legal matter of great urgency." The FBI claimed that part of this conversation was exempt under the FOIA, as it pertained to grand jury matters. Index II at 28.)

53. *Abe Fortas*, p. 144.

54. *Coplon v. U.S.*, 191 F.2d 749 (D.C.Cir. 1951), *cert. denied*, 342 U.S. 926 (espionage conviction overturned where conference between defendant and attorney was wiretapped by the government).

55. Edward Condon to Abe Fortas, FBI MI [microphone] Summary, Washington, D.C., 9/3/48, MI-8926; Plaintiff's Index II, p. 31, *Charns II.*

56. *E.g.*, ELSUR index cards, Plaintiff's Index II, p. 13, *Charns II.* The government claims that Justice Fortas was neither the target of the surveillance nor heard talking. On two electronic surveillances, one in Chicago and one in

Atlanta, the government claims that it cannot determine if Fortas was the subject. The bureau to this day claims that the records of these conversations are classified due to national security concerns. There is no indication that Fortas knew that he had been picked up by FBI eavesdropping.

57. AF to PS, 11/24/67, Abe Fortas folder, box 531, JMH Papers.

58. 389 U.S. 347, 359 (1967).

59. 389 U.S. 347, 360 (1967). Justice Marshall did not participate in the case due to his former position as Solicitor General.

60. Fred M. Vinson, Jr., Assistant AG, Crim. Div., to Director, FBI, Eavesdropping and Wiretapping, 1/23/68, 62-12114-3607. "In footnote 23 in *Katz*, the Court specifically stated that its decision involved no question as to whether prior judicial approval of electronic surveillance was required in situations involving the national security."

61. See 62-12114 entitled "Wiretapping" which is the FBI headquarters' subject file. It covers the years from the 1920s to the present day.

62. 12/28/67, Box 301, JMH Papers.

63. *Kolod v. U.S.*, 390 U.S. 136, 137 (1968).

64. 390 U.S. 136 (1968).

65. *Id.* at 137.

66. Belmont to J.H. Gale, Edward Bennett Williams, 5/5/65, 62-98896-31.

67. Alschuler Folder, Abe Fortas Papers. Lucille Loman clerked for Justice Douglas during World War II (Douglas, *The Court Years*, p. 415), and Margaret Corcoran, Tommy Corcoran's daughter, clerked for Justice Black during the 1966 term (Woodward and Armstrong, *The Brethren*, p. 88).

68. Alschuler to Fortas, bench memo in *Hoffa v. U.S.*, No. 546, OT 1968, dated 11/29/68, box 41, Abe Fortas Papers.

69. 394 U.S. 165 (1969).

70. *See, gen.*, Murphy, *Fortas.*

Chapter 9: Death of the Earl Warren Court

1. Nominations of Abe Fortas and Homer Thornberry, Hearings before the Senate Judiciary Committee, 90th Cong., 2d., July 11, 12, 16–20, 22, and 23, 1968, p. 166 (hereafter Senate Hearings on Fortas, which also encompasses Part 2, Sept. 13 and 16, 1968).

2. *See* SAC, Atlanta, to Director, FBI, Abe Fortas–U.S. Supreme Court, FOIPA Request, 1/3/85, 190-37116-45X. ("Atlanta is unable to determine if Abe Fortas overheard 1/15/65 and Justice Fortas overheard 1/19/66 on an ELSUR installation at SCLC is identical with Abe Fortas" because of the court order issued by Federal Judge John Lewis Smith, Jr., requiring "all logs and transcripts relating to Attorney General authorized electronic installations at the Headquarters of the Southern Christian Leadership Conference (SCLC) have been forwarded to the Bureau for sealing in the National Archives.")

3. Hoover (personal letter by special messenger) to Burger, 5/22/69, 77-54996-19 (note at bottom of bureau copy notes Burger's ties to the agency and that "Judge Burger is on the Special Correspondents List and is known to the

Director on a first-name basis"). (The FBI released only a small portion of Burger's "Departmental Applicant" file to the author because of a claim that the balance of file would constitute an invasion of Burger's privacy rights); *U.S. News & World Report*, 6/2/69, p. 32; *see, gen.*, Bernard Schwartz, *Ascent of Pragmatism*, p. 8; *Justices & Presidents*, p. 298.

4. Abe Fortas, *Concerning Dissent and Civil Disobedience* (Signet Books 1968), pp. 122–123.

5. Pub.L. 90-351, Title III, §802, 82 Stat. 112 (1968).

6. 18 U.S.C.A. Sec. 2510 *et seq.* (1968)(amended in 1986).

7. *U.S. v. U.S. District Court*, 407 U.S. 297 (1972).

8. Other crimes included are bribery of public officials, sports bribery, illegal betting, jury tampering, obstruction of justice, racketeering, interstate transportation of stolen property, counterfeiting, bankruptcy fraud, drug offenses, extortion and conspiracy, among others. 18 U.S.C.A. Sec. 2516(1)(a)–(g)(1968) (amended in 1990).

9. *Congressional Quarterly Weekly Report*, Vol. 26, No. 9, 3/1/68, p. 392.

10. *See* 62-12114.

11. Jones to Bishop, S. 917 Safe Streets and Crime Control Act, 3/28/68, 62–12114–NR; J.H. Gale to DeLoach, Electronic Surveillance Section of "Law Enforcement and Criminal Justice Act" submitted by U.S. Sen. John McClellan, 3/9/68, 3/11/68, 62-12114-NR.

12. J.H. Gale to DeLoach, Electronic Surveillance Section of "Law Enforcement and Criminal Justice Act" submitted by U.S. Sen. John McClellan, 3/9/68, 3/11/68, 62-12114-NR *inter alia* serials located in 62-12114 which is the FBI subject file entitled "Wiretapping."

13. A. Rosen to DeLoach, Proposed Statutory Prohibition on Manufacture or Interstate Shipment of Eavesdropping Devices, 2/7/67, 62-12114-NR. On 12/21/66 Senator James O. Eastland "provided the Bureau with a draft of the bill for the control of 'eavesdropping.'" Eastland's bill would allow ELSUR in criminal and national security cases upon judicial warrant.

14. J.H. Gale to DeLoach, Wiretapping and Electronic Eavesdropping, 3/16/67, 62-12114-3544 (Hoover instructed that a copy of this letter be sent to Attorney General Ramsey Clark).

15. FBI, NY, to Director, [Name redacted] information concerning, 4/4/67, 62-12114-NR (Governor Nelson Rockefeller said he "did not see how the FBI can get the job done without wiretapping," that he is "for wiretapping" and Hoover "cannot openly take this same position as it would be contrary to that held by the Attorney General"). For e.g., M.A. Jones to Wick, "The Great Wiretapping Controversy: Three-Part Article Appearing in Various Newspapers by Edward J. Mowery," Information Concerning, 5/15/67, 62-12114-NR (Mowery was on Hoover's Special Correspondents List, and his articles praised the FBI's use of ELSUR and criticized the "Supreme Court for giving aid and comfort to the criminal by its unwarranted excessive concern with the 'constitutional' rights of criminals").

16. *Congressional Quarterly Weekly Report*, Vol. 26, No. 29, 7/19/68, pp. 1842–1844; James G. Carr, *The Law of Electronic Surveillance* (Clark Boardman Co. 1977), pp. 23–24.

17. M.A. Jones to Wick, Senator Edward V. Long (D–Missouri) Appearing on WTTG Television 9:30 P.M., Sunday, 5/7/67, 5/8/67, 62-12114-NR. In talking about the legislation, Long publicly praised Hoover who, he said, in response to his subcommittee's investigation of wiretapping, "had men there right away, explaining what the FBI does and what it has been doing over the years." Long reiterated that he had no plans to call Hoover to testify before his subcommittee on the issue of electronic spying.

18. Donner, *Age of Surveillance*, p. 256.

19. *Id.;* Hoffman, *Citizen Cohn*, pp. 332–339.

20. J.H. Gale to DeLoach, 3/11/68, 62-12114-NR, *supra* note 12.

21. *Id.* DeLoach was ordered to call Senator McClellan and ask that the "requirement for . . . serving . . . an inventory on an individual named in an application for an electronic surveillance order which has been *denied* by a judge be eliminated as unnecessary and undesirable." Despite FBI opposition, the final version contained this notice provision. 18 U.S.C.A. Sec. 2518(8)(d)(1968) (amended in 1986).

22. 18 U.S.C.A. Sec. 2511(3)(1968)(amended in 1986).

23. Athan G. Theoharis, "Misleading the Presidents. Thirty Years of Wire Tapping," *The Nation*, 6/14/71, pp. 744–750.

24. Hoover to Deputy A.G., Eavesdropping and Wiretapping, H.R. 13275, 10/20/67, 62-12114-3587.

25. J.H. Gale to DeLoach, Electronic Surveillance Section of "Law Enforcement and Criminal Justice Act" submitted by U.S. Sen. John McClellan, 3/9/68, 3/11/68, 62-12114-NR. Hoover noted his concurrence in a hand-written notation at the end of the memo.

26. 407 U.S. 297 (1972). Six years later, Congress passed the Foreign Intelligence Surveillance Act (FISA), 50 U.S.C.A. Sec.s 1801–1811 (1978), which regulates "electronic surveillance" for the purpose of collecting foreign intelligence that concerns a "foreign power" or "agents of a foreign power" and provides for a warrant procedure through a secret proceeding before a U.S. Foreign Intelligence Surveillance Court. The statute allows the attorney general to authorize electronic surveillances only against foreign powers if an "emergency situation exists."

27. J.H. Gale to DeLoach, Electronic Surveillance Section of "Law Enforcement and Criminal Justice Act" submitted by U.S. Sen. John McClellan, 3/9/68, 3/11/68, 62-12114-NR.

28. Carr, *Law of Electronic Surveillance*, p. 24 (date of signing); J.A. Califano, Jr., Special Assist. to Pres., to Fortas, 6/19/68, "Safe Streets Act" folder, box 12, Oct. '89 accession papers, Abe Fortas Papers, where Fortas criticized some of the wiretapping portions of the law.

29. *Congressional Quarterly Weekly Report*, Vol. 26, No. 29, 7/19/68, p. 1842.

30. Murphy, *Fortas*, pp. 300–302.

31. Kalman, *Abe Fortas*, p. 323.

32. *Id.*

33. OH, Ramsey Clark, transcript, p. 19, LBJ Library.

34. *See, e.g.,* Senate Hearings on Fortas, Pt. 2, pp. 1286–1304, 1308–1309.

35. C.D. DeLoach to Tolson, Justice Abe Fortas, Scheduled Confirmation by U.S. Senate as Chief Justice of Supreme Court, 7/8/68, 161-2860-61.

36. *Id.* One apparent purpose of the call was to have FBI protection at the Senate, as Fortas had been verbally assailed by a member of the American Nazi Party as he entered the hearing room in 1965.

37. DeLoach to Fortas, 2/16/67, "D" folder general, box 1, 1989 accession papers, Abe Fortas Papers. *See, e.g.,* Carolyn Agger Fortas to DeLoache [*sic*], 1/13/69, 161-2860-72: Mrs. Fortas sent her condolences to DeLoach about the death of an agent who helped investigate the theft of her jewelry (which is not an offense of which the FBI has investigatory authority) the summer before. The letter was sent to DeLoach's home address, not FBI headquarters. It should also be noted that the bureau's note at the bottom of its copy of Hoover's response does *not* contain any derogatory information about Justice or Mrs. Fortas. Bureau "enemies" would be identified as such in a note.

38. DeLoach to author, 11/13/90.

39. *See* White House "EYES ONLY" Memo from Larry Levinson to Jim Gaither, 8/17/68, File pertaining to Abe Fortas and Homer Thornberry, Chronological File, 8/3/68–8/17/68, WHCF, LBJ Library. Deke DeLoch [*sic*] was the "point of contact with Lou Nichols (V.P. of Schenley)" who is a former FBI assistant director. A handwritten notation at the top-right corner of the memo says: "File Fortas." DeLoach was to contact Nichols on behalf of the Fortas nomination. DeLoach said that he did not recall "ever discussing Justice Fortas with the late Louis B. Nichols." DeLoach to author, 11/13/90.

40. Senate Hearings on Fortas, p. 104.

41. Kalman, *Abe Fortas,* pp. 333–334; Murphy, *Fortas,* pp. 381–386.

42. C.D. DeLoach to Tolson, Justice Abe Fortas, Nomination for Chief Justice of the Supreme Court, Inquiry by Office of Senator Robert P. Griffin (Republican-Michigan), 9/23/68, 161-2860-68. By an anonymous letter dated September 22, 1968, the Senate Judiciary Committee was tipped off that it should look into Justice Fortas's association with Louis Wolfson. Kalman, *Abe Fortas,* p. 356.

43. DeLoach to Tolson, Justice Abe Fortas, Nomination for Chief Justice of the Supreme Court, Inquiry by Office of Senator Robert P. Griffin (Republican-Michigan), 9/23/68, 161-2860-68.

44. *Id.*

45. Senate Hearings on Fortas, Pt. 2, Sept. 13 and 16, 1968, pp. 1293–1298; OH Paul Porter, pp. 33–37, LBJ Library; Robert C. Albright, "Senate Rejects Fortas Cloture by Wide Margin," Washington *Post,* 10/2/68, A-1; Kalman, *Fortas,* pp. 497–507.

46. OH Paul Porter, pp. 33–37, LBJ Library.

47. Senate Hearings on Fortas, pp. 1306–1308.

48. Kalman, *Abe Fortas,* p. 322.

49. Senate Hearings on Fortas, p. 1368, citing *Keyishian v. New York Board of Regents,* 385 U.S. 589 (1967), and *U.S. v. Robel,* 389 U.S. 258 (1967).

50. *See The Brandeis/Frankfurter Connection.* Justices Louis Brandeis

and Felix Frankfurter had both engaged in partisan politics while on the bench.

51. Clifford, *Counsel to the President*, p. 215.

52. Douglas to Fortas, 6/14/65, and Fortas to Johnson, 6/15/65, folder "White House—Correspondence with Individuals," box 9, Oct. '89 accession papers, Abe Fortas Papers.

53. Goldberg to Fortas, 2/2/65, box 11, Oct. '89 accession papers, Abe Fortas Papers.

54. Interim Report Sensitive Case, Baltimore District, Intelligence Div., IRS, re: Robert G. Baker, 1/29/65, Robert G. Baker folder, box 13, Oct. '89 accession papers, Abe Fortas Papers.

55. *See, gen.,* Conference lists during 1966, AF Papers.

56. *Justices & Presidents*, p. 43.

57. Note at bottom of Hoover to Mitchell congratulatory letter, 12/12/68, 94-64578-1.

58. Lyle Denniston, Washington *Evening Star*, 12/31/68, A-1, 94-64578-A.

59. *Id.*

60. *Id.*

61. See *Justices & Presidents*, p. 296.

62. *Boykin v. Alabama*, 395 U.S. 238 (1969).

63. *Spinelli v. U.S.*, 393 U.S. 410 (1969). Justice Marshall disqualified himself in this case. White concurred. Black, Fortas, and Stewart dissented. Fortas, after reciting the grand purpose of the Fourth Amendment, concluded that the FBI agent's affidavit was constitutionally sufficient. "A policeman's affidavit should not be judged as an entry in an essay contest. It is not 'abracadabra.'" 393 U.S. at 438. This case was argued in October 1968 and the opinion was issued on January 27, 1969.

64. *Tinker v. Des Moines*, 393 U.S. 503, 506 (1969).

65. *Brandenburg v. Ohio*, 395 U.S. 444 (1969).

66. *Street v. New York*, 394 U.S. 576 (1969). Warren, Black, White, and Fortas dissented. Fortas had originally voted with the majority in a concurring opinion but later changed his mind. "I have concluded that it is fair to say that the conviction was for the conduct of publicly burning the flag and not for the words used." Fortas memo to the Conference, 3/19/69, JMH Papers. The majority found that Street was punished for his words *and* the flag burning.

67. *Gregory v. City of Chicago*, 394 U.S. 111 (1969).

68. *Shuttlesworth v. City of Birmingham*, 394 U.S. 147 (1969).

69. 394 U.S. 165 (1969).

70. Lister bench memo for JMH, *Ivanov v. U.S., Butenko v. U.S.*, 2/26/68, box 337, JMH Papers.

71. White memo to the Conference, 3/17/69, box 498, JMH Papers.

72. Justice Marshall sent a memo to the Conference on June 11, 1968, stating that "the minutes of the Department of Justice's ad-hoc committee reveal that I attended a meeting at which the *Ivanov* and *Butenko* cases were discussed and a decision made not to disclose the bugging. I am therefore disqualified in these cases." JMH Papers.

73. My account of this incident is based upon Warren's *Memoirs of Chief Justice*, pp. 337–342, and Douglas's *Court Years*, pp. 258–260.

74. Justice Fortas participated in this ruling.

75. Author interview with Dagmar Hamilton, 6/20/90; Simon, *Independent Journey*, p. 443.

76. Prof. William A. Reppy, Jr., law clerk to Douglas during the 1967 term of Court, telephone call to author, 4/30/90.

77. *In re: Heutsche v. U.S.*, 414 U.S. 898 (1973). In August 1973 Justice Douglas asked former Justice Abe Fortas, who was then in private law practice, to investigate whether the FBI had wiretapped calls he had made from the state of Washington to the Supreme Court when he had dictated his opinion ordering a temporary cessation of the U.S. bombing in Cambodia. Fortas contacted Acting Deputy Attorney General William Ruckleshaus, who informed FBI Director Clarence Kelley. The FBI concluded that "[t]here is absolutely no support to the allegation that an FBI Agent is involved in this matter. It appears this is merely speculation on the part of Justice Douglas without any basis in fact whatsoever." Because Fortas was involved, the bureau "felt some inquiry should be made." A check of the phone booth from which Justice Douglas made his calls to the Court uncovered no evidence of "interception devices." No security check was conducted of the phones at the Supreme Court. 139-4370.

78. S.A. [redacted name] to SAC, WFO, Wire Intercepts & Bugging U.S. Supreme Court, 6/26/74, 66-3491-NR, doc. 16, attachment 5 to the seventh declar. of Angus B. Llewellyn, *Charns II*. The FBI suggested that the Secret Service be employed to makes "sweeps to discover bugs and wire intercepts" at the Court. In recent years there have been unsubstantiated and discredited allegations that the phones of liberal federal judges were tapped on orders of the FBI in an attempt to find a reason to force them off the bench. Leonard Gates, a former Cincinnati Bell telephone installer, claimed that he had placed wiretaps on the phones of three federal judges in the Southern District of Ohio during the 1970s and 1980s. According to Gates, the taps were installed on orders from the phone company and were requested by the bureau. The FBI and the phone company denied any part in this alleged wiretapping. Gregory Flannery, "Tappers' Probe Meant to Oust Federal Judge," Mt. Washington (Ohio) *Press*, 1988; G. Flannery to author, 12/21/89.

79. Murphy, *Fortas*, pp. 549–551.

80. Wolfson served nine months in prison for his convictions related to Continental Enterprises. He was also convicted relative to Merritt-Chapman & Scott and was given an eighteen-month sentence that was overturned on appeal. He was retried twice, and after two mistrials Wolfson pleaded no contest to the charges. Kalman, *Abe Fortas*, p. 359. Kalman suggests that Wolfson may have been rewarded for his assistance to the Justice Department about Justice Fortas. William Bittman, Wolfson's attorney, did not respond to the author's request for an interview.

81. Wilson to Hoover, Louis Wolfson, 4/14/69, 72-1882-1 (notations on this memo show that DeLoach and Tolson received a memo about Wilson's allegations).

82. A. Rosen to DeLoach, Louis Wolfson Name Check Matter, 4/15/69, 72-1882-2.

83. Author telephone interview with William Lambert, 12/26/90; Mike Leary, "A Reporter's path to the Fortas story," Philadelphia *Inquirer*, 12/2/90, I-1, 4. William Lambert received the IRS tip about Fortas approximately one week before Nixon was elected president in 1968. Lambert said that he received the information after he had asked about LBJ "cronies". The Nixon administration did not leak the information to him.

84. *Supra* note 83.

85. *Id.; see* author's interview with Will Wilson, 6/19/90.

86. Lambert said that he had no notes showing the dates he spoke with Will Wilson, but he puts the date of their first meeting at late March or early April 1969. Will Wilson's source for his "reliable information" about Wolfson and Fortas may have been Bittman, Lambert, or both.

87. Author's telephone interview with William Lambert, 12/26/90. But, according to Will Wilson, his primary source of information about Fortas and Wolfson was Wolfson's attorney, Bittman, though Lambert provided him with some information. Author's interview with Will Wilson, 6/19/90.

88. Author interview with William Lambert, 12/26/90.

89. Author's interview with Will Wilson, 6/19/90.

90. Morganthau was later placed on Nixon's enemies' list.

91. Author interview with Will Wilson, 6/19/90.

92. Author interview with Will Wilson, 6/19/90.

93. DeLoach to author, 11/13/90.

94. Hoover to Tolson et al., 4/23/69, 161-2860-NR after 75.

95. *Id.*

96. DeLoach to author, 11/13/90, 3/12/91.

97. *Id.*

98. Hoover memo for Tolson et al., 4/23/69, 94-33476-NR, first serial after 59; Alexander Charns, "How the FBI Spied on Supreme Court Justices," *News and Observer* (Raleigh, N.C.), 12/10/89, J1.

99. Hoover's handwritten note on the margin of a Washington *Post* newsclip was "Someone in D.J. certainly leaked this." John P. MacKenzie, "Wolfson Airs Fee to Fortas. $20,000 Set as Annual Fee, He Tells FBI," Washington *Post*, 5/15/69, A-1, 72-1882-73.

100. William Lambert, "Fortas of the Supreme Court: A Question of Ethics," *Life*, 5/9/69; Murphy, *Fortas*, p. 556.

101. A. Rosen to DeLoach, Louis E. Wolfson, Information Concerning, 5/7/69, 72-1882-48.

102. *Id.*

103. A. Rosen to DeLoach, Abe Fortas, Justice, Supreme Court, Obstruction of Justice, Unlawful Practice of Law, Bribery, 5/8/69, 72-1882-52.

104. *Id.*

105. *Id.*

106. Papers Delivered to the Chief Justice [about Justice Fortas and Wolfson] Personal and Confidential. For the Eyes Only of the Chief Justice, from Attorney

General John Mitchell, delivered 5/12/69, container 353, Earl Warren Papers (hereafter cited as Wolfson Affidavit Papers).

107. Abe Fortas to William Lambert, 4/23/69, attachment to "Wolfson-Fortas Matter" from Will Wilson to Hoover, Louis E. Wolfson; Abe Fortas; Obstruction of Justice; Conflict of Interest; Unlawful Practice of Law; Bribery, 5/21/69, 72-1882-65, hereafter cited as "DOJ Wolfson-Fortas Chronology."

108. Wolfson Affidavit Papers.

109. Rogert Shogun, *A Question of Judgment: The Fortas Case and the Struggle for the Supreme Court* (Bobbs-Merrill Co. 1972), p. 211. Levitt did not respond to the author's letter to him.

110. *Abe Fortas*, p. 321.

111. Shogun, *A Question of Judgment*, p. 211.

112. Wolfson Affidavit Papers.

113. Shogun, *A Question of Judgment*, p. 211.

114. "DOJ Wolfson-Fortas Chronology," p. 29.

115. *Id.* Wilson had provided Hoover with a detailed chronology titled "Wolfson-Fortas Matter." This chronology was evidently not provided to Warren. The title of the memo indicates that Fortas was being investigated for possible criminal prosecution even *after* he resigned from the Court. *See* FBI memo entitled "Telephone Calls. Period Checked 1/1/66 to 12/31/67," which was released to the author by the Securities and Exchange Commission (SEC) with a cover letter signed by Edward A. Wilson, FOIA officer, 3/25/85. A notation for 6/1/66 recorded "Incoming Justice Fortas' office dictated message to staff—unable to come (I believe this concerned the dedication of the new headquarters of the SEC at 500 North Capitol Street)" and a notation dated 9/26/66 was recorded as "Outgoing Justice Fortas 1207."

116. WFO Report, Louis E. Wolfson; Abe Fortas, 5/27/69, 72-1882-71, pp. 3–4. The former SEC chairman told agents that he did "not recall any contact directly or indirectly by Abe Fortas" with himself or any of his employees about Louis Wolfson.

117. "DOJ Wolfson-Fortas Chronology."

118. Wolfson Affidavit Papers.

119. Will Wilson, A.A.G., to Hoover, re: Louis Wolfson, 4/15/69, 72-1882-3 [illegible], p. 2.

120. Kalman, *Abe Fortas*, pp. 370–371.

121. *Id.* at 368.

122. Wolfson Affidavit Papers.

123. Douglas, *The Court Years*, p. 358; Simon, *Independent Journey*, p. 396.

124. Kalman, *Abe Fortas*, p. 368.

125. MacKenzie, "Wolfson Airs Fee to Fortas," Washington *Post*, 5/15/69, A-1, 72-1882-73.

126. *Id.*

127. Fortas to Warren, 5/14/69, container 353, Earl Warren Papers.

128. A year after Fortas left the Court, Hoover wrote to Fortas, objecting to a speech that Fortas made in which he mentioned that the FBI had informers on U.S. campuses. Fortas replied that in "every speech that I have made in which I

have talked about the danger of police presence on campuses . . . I have noted my complete respect for the F.B.I. which, as you may recall, I have elsewhere demonstrated." Fortas also wrote that he is "not one of those who denigrates the F.B.I.; that on the contrary, I have the greatest respect for its method of operations." Fortas ended by saying: "I assure you, Mr. Director, of my continuing esteem." Fortas to Hoover, 11/12/70, 161-2860-78; Kalman, *Abe Fortas,* pp. 378–379.

129. *See, e.g.,* Hoover to Burger, 5/22/69, 77-54996-19.

130. John Ehrlichman, *Witness to Power: The Nixon Years.* (Simon and Schuster 1982), p. 117; *see* Woodward and Armstrong, *The Brethren,* p. 18; *see also* the FBI's "77" departmental applicant file on Warren E. Burger.

131. Hoover memo to Tolson and Sullivan, 7/26/62, 77-54996-17 (Judge Burger inviting Hoover to speak at a Convocation of the University of Minnesota to counteract the recent appearance on campus of Benjamin Davis, "a high official of the Communist Party in the United States").

132. 349 U.S. 331, 75 S.Ct. 790 (1955). Warren E. Burger, assistant attorney general, is the only government lawyer listed in the opinion.

133. Kalman, *Abe Fortas,* pp. 141–143.

134. L.B. Nichols to Tolson, 3/29/55, 62-53025-NR (part of the "Federal Judges" file).

135. The FBI redacted the names when it provided the record.

136. Kalman, *Abe Fortas,* p. 143 (citing transcripts of the oral argument).

137. Ehrlichman, *Witness to Power,* p. 113.

138. Sullivan, *The Bureau,* p. 205.

139. O'Reilly, *Racial Matters,* p. 325; *but cf.,* Richard M. Nixon, *The Memoirs of Richard M. Nixon,* vol. 1 (Warner Books 1978), p. 70.

140. Sullivan, *The Bureau,* p. 196.

141. *Id.* at 205.

142. During Nov. 1969, Hoover formalized a new program called "INLET" to pass on "high-level intelligence data in the security field" directly to the White House and the Attorney General. This included information about demonstrations, disorders and political adversaries. Theoharis and Cox, *The Boss,* pp. 407–408.

143. *See* Carp and Rowland, *Policymaking and Politics in the Federal District Courts,* pp. 56–57.

144. *See, e.g.,* Hoover memo to Tolson et al., 1/11/71, 62-56733-61 (concerning the use of Chief Justice Burger's administrative prerogative to hire past or present FBI employees as court administrators to further political goals).

145. Buchanan memo for the president, 5/26/69, President's Handwriting File, May 1969, WHSP—President's Office Files, Nixon Presidential Materials Project, National Archives and Records Administration, Alexandria, VA (hereafter Nixon Project).

146. William Safire to H.R. Haldeman, re: Presentation of Supreme Court Appointments, 5/20/69, Box 177, Staff Members and Offices Files of H.R. Haldeman, Nixon Project.

147. Sullivan, *The Bureau,* p. 59 (Sullivan called the FBI's investigation of Nixon appointee Carswell as "puny" and compared it unfavorably to the thor-

ough FBI investigation of a judicial nominee favored by Senator Edward Kennedy whom the Johnson White House wanted to scuttle).

148. O'Reilly, *Racial Matters*, p. 327.

149. *See, e.g.,* Hoover to Sen. Sam J. Ervin, Jr., 11/7/62, 94-46685-10. The note at the bottom of the bureau's copy stated: "Sen. Ervin has spoken out strongly on civil rights legislation and the integration issue. He is very sympathetic toward the Bureau and during contacts with him . . . Sen. Ervin has been most complimentary of the Director." Sen. Eastland is also described in an FBI file by the Crime Records Division as "a strong advocate of 'White Supremacy.' " O'Reilly, *Racial Matters*, p. 327.

150. *See, e.g.,* WFO 161-2419 (special inquiry re: Abe Fortas); O'Reilly, *Racial Matters*, p. 327.

151. Krogh Memo for Ehrlichman, re: Supreme Court nominations, 9/24/71, Nixon Project.

152. *Id.*

153. See HQ 77-74002.

154. HQ 77-74002-21.

155. HQ 77-74002-23.

156. Mohr to J.J. Casper, re: George Edward Slaughter, ITSMV (interstate trans. of stolen motor vehicle); CGR–Murder (crime on gov't. reserv.)(Ft. Bragg, N.C.), Request from Hon. Clement F. Haynsworth, Jr., Chief Judge, U.S. Circuit Court of Appeals, Fourth Cir. for Information Concerning Interviews and Confession, 7/26/66, 77-74002-35.

157. Hoover memo to Tolson, DeLoach, and Gale, 2:28 PM, 7/1/69, 77-74002-NR (notation at bottom "all copies destroyed").

158. Hoover to Mitchell, Clement F. Haynsworth, Judge, Fourth Circuit Court of Appeals, 7/1/69. Hoover's "O&C" files (copies to Gale and DeLoach were destroyed).

159. W.V. Cleveland to Gale, Clement F. Haynsworth, Jr., George H. Carswell, Supreme Court Nominees, 2/26/70, 77-74002-41.

160. Mitchell said on "Meet the Press" that he "felt the background checks by the FBI and other sources were complete in every way." M.A. Jones to Bishop, Appearance of Attorney General on "Meet the Press," NBC, Sunday, 11/2/69, 11/3/69, 94-64578-20; Eve Edstrom, "Nixon Nominates Haynsworth to Supreme Court," Washington *Post*, 8/19/69, A-1. Ron Ziegler, White House press spokesman, said "no political clearance" from congressional leaders was involved in the decision. In May (regarding the Burger nomination) President Nixon said that there would not be any clearances with senators, the Republican National Committee, or the American Bar Association on Supreme Court appointments. Nixon said he would follow the custom of clearing circuit court and district court appointments with home state senators of nominees. Ernest F. Hollings (D–South Carolina) recommended Haynsworth; Strom Thurmond (R–South Carolina) recommended Donald S. Russell.

161. The New York Times, *The Watergate Hearings: Break-in and Cover-up* (Bantam Books 1973), p. 762.

162. W.V. Cleveland to DeLoach, 10/15/69, 77-74002-39 (Mollenhoff asked

for a "fast, off-the-record check of property owned" by Senator Birch Bayh "located in Cleveland Park, D.C.").

163. Haynsworth Case memo, box 125, Staff Members and Office Files of H.R. Haldeman, Nixon Project; Harry S. Dent memo to the Attorney General, 10/27/69, box 125, Staff members and Office files of H.R. Haldeman, Nixon Project: "Members of my staff have been working with Clark Mollenhoff to learn more about Bayh's Indiana financial dealings and his contacts with organized labor."

164. Dent memo, p. 2, Nixon Project.

165. The column was entitled "Security Clearances—Hard and Soft."

166. *Justices & Presidents*, p. 15.

167. W.V. Cleveland to Gale, re: Haynsworth and George Harrold Carswell, Supreme Court Nominees, 2/26/70, 77-74002-41.

168. *Id.*, One paragraph of the memo was redacted under FOIA exemption b7c, to protect a third person's privacy. The redaction apparently is a discussion of allegations against Carswell that the Baltimore and Miami FBI offices determined to be false and about an inquiry into allegations made by Professor John Lowenthal before the Senate Judiciary Committee.

169. *Justices & Presidents*, p. 15.

170. William E. Timmons memo to the president, re: Judge Carswell, 3/25/70, "Administratively Confidential," Nixon Project.

171. *Justices & Presidents*, pp. 16–17.

172. *Id.* at 19.

Chapter 10: Impeach Douglas! Remember Haynsworth and Carswell

1. H. Res. 93. A Resolution Authorizing the Committee on the Judiciary to Conduct Studies and Investigations Relating to Certain Matters within its Jurisdiction (concerning Associate Justice William O. Douglas), First Report by the Special Subcommittee on H.Res. 920, Committee on the Judiciary, House of Representatives, 92d Cong., 2nd Sess., June 20, 1970, pp. 28, 43–44 (hereafter Report on H.Res. 93).

2. *Charns II*, Defendant's Brief in Opposition to Plaintiff's Second Rule 56(f) Motion and Defendant's Reply to Plaintiff's Opposition to Defendant's Second Motion for Partial Summary Judgment, p. 6.

3. *See, e.g.,* Emil P. Moschella, Chief, FOI–PA Section, Records Management Division, FBI, in a letter to the author (with attachments), 12/13/88, acknowledged that the FBI Washington Metropolitan Field Office (WMFO) had eleven pages of classified electronic surveillance records that picked up Justice Douglas on seven occasions and that the New York Field Office (NYFO) had two pages of classified ELSUR records (Douglas's name was only mentioned in this ELSUR); *Charns II*, Tenth Declaration of Angus B. Llewellyn, II(9) ("With regard to ELSUR information, Justice Douglas was not the target of the surveillance. His name was mentioned or his voice was overheard and made a matter of public record in monitored conversations of other individuals"). In addition, the FBI has over 200 pages of classified Washington Field Office

records, presumably from wiretaps or bugs, about which the Justice Department refuses to release even the file number. *See, e.g., Charns II,* Plaintiff's Index II to Records Claimed as Non-Exempt Filed in Opposition to Defendant's Second Partial Summary Judgment Motion and in Support of Plaintiff's Rule 56(f) Motion, pp. 181–187 (which reflect 223 pages claimed as exempt under the FOIA.) A number of FBI documents about Justice Douglas were referred to other government agencies for consultation because the information originated with other agencies. A number of these referrals are still pending as this book goes to press. *See, e.g., Charns II,* at pp. 49, 50, 59–62, 118 *inter alia.* Of course, in the wiretaps on Thomas Corcoran, Justice Douglas had been overheard numerous times (Hoover's "O & C" files). *See, e.g.,* Defendant's Ninth Status Report, Declaration of [CIA employee] Katherine M. Stricker, June 1991, pp. 23–26, *Charns II.* Douglas was apparently picked up by CIA electronic surveillances and/or informers in 1960, 1963, and 1971.

Douglas was not the only justice overheard, as was stated in chapter 1. The so-called 17 Kissinger wiretaps on reporters and administration officials, designed to locate leaks, had apparently snared Justice Stewart. *See* Report of the Special Master, 2/14/91, *Charns I,* pp. 28–29. The target of the ELSUR made a call to "Justice Potter Stewart, who was not a target or otherwise involved. . . . This information merely involves times for appointments and a 'possible article to be written about' a remark made by Kingman Brewster (president of Yale University who had questioned whether any black revolutionary could receive a fair trial in America)." *See* Senate (Church) Committee, Final Report, Book III, p. 345 and p. 346, fn, citing a letter from Hoover to Haldeman, 6/25/70, about an associate justice of the Supreme Court who was overheard on one of the wiretaps talking about reviewing a manuscript written by one of the ELSUR targets. One year earlier, on 6/25/69, Hoover sent Kissinger a letter about Justice Douglas, which the FBI still claims is classified and which may contain information obtained from ELSURs. *See,* 94-33476-NR, Doc. 61, Tenth Declar. of Llewellyn, *Charns II.*

4. The FBI claims the ELSUR log concerning John Mitchell is still classified. Emil Moschella, chief, FOI–PA Section, FBI, to author, 8/9/90. After the Watergate break-in, Martha Mitchell on at least two occasions called the FBI after she had been drinking and accused them of tapping her phones. *E.g.,* L.H. Martin to Cleveland, Mrs. Martha Mitchell, wife of former Attorney General John N. Mitchell, Information Concerning, 94-64578-115.

5. James Angleton to director, FBI, attn: Sam Papich [FBI's liaison to the CIA], re: Hunter Report # 4946, 3/21/66, 105-69845-18139; Defendant's Ninth Status Report, *Charns II,* Declaration of Katherine M. Stricker, CIA Information Review Officer, June 1991. Pursuant to *Charns II,* the CIA forwarded the Project Hunter transmittal cover letter as "information pertaining to William Orville Douglas," but claimed that two pages of attachments were exempt under (b)(1), (b)(3) and (b)(6). John H. Wright, CIA, to author, 12/28/90.

" 'Project Hunter' was the cryptonym given by the FBI to the receipt of information from the CIA's New York mail intercept program." The CIA opened and copied letters to and from the USSR between 1956 and 1973 and gave the FBI 57,846 of these letters or summaries of their contents. While the purpose of the project was "counterespionage information," the FBI "specifically requested information on numerous individuals and organizations in the antiwar, civil rights, and women's movements, and on such general categories as 'government employees' and 'protest organizations.' " Senate (Church) Committee, Final Report, Book III, pp. 624, 634. *See also,* "Rattling Skeletons in the CIA Closet," *Time,* 1/6/75, pp. 44–46 (claiming that Justice Douglas was "among the targets of CIA surveillance").

6. Ehrlichman, *Witness to Power,* p. 122.

7. Editorial by Alice Widener, "What About Activities of Douglas," *Commercial Appeal* (Memphis), 5/14/69.

8. *See* Director to Assistant Attorney General, Criminal Division, re: Albert B. Parvin et al., 5/27/69, 94-33476-NR (responding to letter dated 5/23/69 and oral request).

9. Ehrlichman to Nixon, 5/23/69, Nixon Project.

10. *E.g.,* see the 1954 investigation of Justice Douglas and the "colony of communist sympathizers" in LaPush, Washington, ch. 1 herein, and note also that warrantless wiretaps on Thomas G. Corcoran from 1945 to 1948 picked up Justice Douglas's conversations. Technical Surveillance Folder, "O & C." *See also* James Angleton to Director, FBI, attn: Sam Papich [FBI's liaison to the CIA], re: Hunter Report # 4946, 3/21/66, 105-69845-18139 (mail opening).

11. Ehrlichman, *Witness to Power,* p. 122.

12. Author interview with Will Wilson, 6/19/90.

13. *Id.;* Nomination of Gerald R. Ford to be the Vice President of the U.S., Hearings before the Committee on the Judiciary, House of Representatives, 93d Cong., 1st Sess., 1973, pp. 641, 670–671 (hereafter 1973 House Hearings on Gerald Ford). (According to Ford, Wilson brought the blind memo on 12/12/69, about a month after Haynsworth's nomination had been voted down.)

14. 1973 House Hearings on Gerald Ford, pp. 589, 612–619; J.J. McDermott to Jenkins, Request from Les Whitten re Source of Data on Supreme Court Justice William O. Douglas, 1/29/75, 94-33476-NR; Jack Anderson and Les Whitten, "FBI Data Said Slipped to Rep. Ford," Washington *Post,* 2/3/75, D-11, 94-33476-NR.

15. Compare the H.Res. 93 findings with Rep. Ford's speech.

16. Author interview with Will Wilson, 6/19/90.

17. 1973 House Hearings on Gerald Ford, p. 34.

18. *Id.* at 35–36.

19. *Id.* at 38.

20. *Id.* at 43.

21. *Id.* at 41.

22. Report on H. Res. 93, pp. 28, 43–44.

23. Douglas, *The Court Years,* p. 364.

24. Report on H. Res. 93, pp. 49–53.

25. William E. Timmons [White House director of congressional relations], to John Ehrlichman, 4/15/70, Nixon Project.

26. Handwritten notes on Action Memorandum from Staff Secretary to B. Harlow, D. Rumsfeld, Moynihan, R. Ziegler, B. Krogh, S. Blair, re: log no. 3713, 4/16/70, Nixon Project.

27. Daniel P. Moynihan to White House Staff Secretary, subject: Log No. 3713, 4/24/70, Nixon Project.

28. Timmons to Ehrlichman, 5/7/70, Nixon Project.

29. Nixon to Celler, 5/15/70, WHCF, Nixon Project.

30. Hoover Memorandum for Tolson, DeLoach et al., 6/5/70, 94-33476-NR, also in 62-27585 and 164-00-215.

31. *See* A. Rosen to DeLoach, *State of Illinois v. William Allen*, 3/31/70, 63-0-26873. The Supreme Court held that a disruptive defendant may be removed from the courtroom under certain circumstances. Hoover wrote at the bottom of this memo: "The Supreme Court is beginning to see the light of day."

32. Hoover Memorandum for Tolson et al., 9/28/70, 62-27585-NR, doc. 521, Exhibit 17, U.S.S.C., part III, *Charns I.*

33. Extremists Attack the Courts, 4/17/70, 62-117775-65.

34. Hoover Memorandum for Tolson et al., 9/28/1970, 62-27585-NR, doc. 521, Exhibit 17, U.S.S.C., part III, *Charns I.*

35. Senate (Church) Committee, Final Report, Book III, p. 923, and Book II, pp. 111–112.

36. Senate (Church) Committee, Final Report, Book III, p. 926; Athan Theoharis, *Spying on Americans: Political Surveillance from Hoover to the Huston Plan* (Temple University Press 1978), pp. 13–39.

37. Sullivan, *The Bureau*, pp. 251–254; Senate (Church) Committee, Final Report, Book III, pp. 933–936.

38. Senate (Church) Committee, Final Report, Book III, p. 932.

39. *Id.* at 931.

40. *Id.* at 942.

41. *Id.* at 927, 938.

42. *Id.* at 958.

43. Theoharis, *Spying on Americans,* pp. 32–33.

44. Theodore H. White, *Breach of Faith: The Fall of Richard Nixon* (Dell Publishing Co. 1975), pp. 439–440 (reproducing the articles of impeachment in Appendix A).

45. Senate (Church) Committee, Final Report, Book III, p. 4.

46. *Id.* at 735.

47. *Id.* at 681, 962–963.

48. Gerald Gold, ed., *The White House Transcripts* (Bantam Books 1974), p. 814.

49. Simon, *Independent Journey,* pp. 409–411.

Chapter 11: From Burger to Rehnquist: Court Administration from the Right

1. Hoover memo for Tolson et al., 1/11/71, 62-56733-61.

2. 90 S.Ct., Summary of October 1971 term, p. 193.

3. *Memoirs of Richard Nixon,* pp. 523–524.

4. DeLoach to Tolson, 6/14/66, Fred Black folder, Hoover's "O & C" files. DeLoach said that Powell occasionally "had been naive and a little weak."

5. *Justices & Presidents*, p. 309. In 1972 Powell wrote the *U.S. v. U.S. District Court* decision, which held that it was a violation of the Fourth Amendment to wiretap domestic radicals without a judicial warrant. Nominations of William H. Rehnquist and Lewis F. Powell, Jr., Hearings before the Committee on the Judiciary, U.S. Senate, 92d Cong., 1971, pp. 463–467 (hereafter 1971 Rehnquist hearings).

6. *Justices & Presidents*, pp. 307–309.

7. *E.g.*, in 1971, Rehnquist, as assistant attorney general, worked closely with the FBI to respond to questions posed by Senator Sam Ervin's Senate Judiciary Subcommittee on Constitutional Rights concerning the issue of government invasion of privacy to protect the bureau's political information gathering. J.P. Mohr to Tolson, Senate Judiciary Subcommittee on Constitutional Rights, Sam J. Ervin, Jr. (D.-North Carolina), Chairman, 3/12/71, 94-46685-NR, first serial after 24. Rehnquist also testified before the subcommittee. The bureau was worried because the requested information "could open a Pandora's box" that ultimately could "open the door to questioning FBI investigative procedures and policies." T.J. Smith to E.S. Miller, Request for Information by Senate Subcommittee on Constitutional Rights, 11/24/71, 94-46685-NR. Before and after Rehnquist left the Justice Department to join the Supreme Court, the FBI misled Ervin's committee about the extent of the bureau's surveillance of citizens. *See* Alex Charns, "FBI Had Sam Ervin Wondering," Durham *Morning Herald*, 5/17/87, A2.

8. Richard Kluger, *Simple Justice: The History of Brown v. Board of Education and Black America's Struggle for Equality* (Vintage Books 1977), p. 609, fn.

9. *Id.*

10. William H. Rehnquist, *U.S. News & World Report*, 12/13/57, p. 75. At the Court, Rehnquist's article had been treated with amusement by the justices and the clerks. Chief Justice Earl Warren had commented to William Douglas that his three clerks during the 1956 term of Court had not agreed with any of his decisions that year. William Cohen (former clerk to Douglas during the 1956 term) to author, 1/9/90.

11. Kluger, *Simple Justice*, pp. 605–609. Rehnquist claimed, in a letter to the Senate Judiciary Committee, that he was writing Justice Jackson's opinion, not his own. Kluger comes to the conclusion that the memo reflected Rehnquist's views at the time, not Justice Jackson's. *See also* Herman Schwartz, *Packing the Courts: The Conservative Campaign to Rewrite the Constitution* (Charles Scribner's Sons 1988), p. 113.

12. 1971 Rehnquist hearings, p. 184.

13. William H. Rehnquist to Senator James O. Eastland, chairman of the Senate Judiciary Committee, 11/20/71, 1971 Rehnquist hearings, p. 489.

14. Judge Hardy to Eastland, 1971 Rehnquist hearings, p. 486.

15. *Id.* at 491.

16. Hearings before the Committee on the Judiciary on the Nomination of Justice William Hubbs Rehnquist to be Chief Justice of the United States, U.S. Senate, 92d Cong., 2d Sess., July 29, 30, 31, and August 1, 1988, pp. 984–1077

(testimony of James Brosnahan, Melvin Merkin, Charles Pine, Sidney Smith and Manuel Pena), compiled in Roy M. Mersky and J. Myron Jacobstein, Vol. 8, *The Supreme Court of the U.S.: Hearings and Reports on Successful and Unsuccessful Nominations of Supreme Court Justices by the Senate Judiciary Committee, 1916–1972* (William S. Hein & Co., Inc. 1975) (hereafter *Compilation of Senate Judiciary Committee Hearings*); Schwartz, *Packing the Courts,* p. 114.

17. *Time,* 8/11/86, p. 14.

18. James Brosnahan telephone interview with David Birman, 1986; Alex Charns and David Birman, "Scrutiny of Nominees Varied with Ties to FBI," Durham *Morning Herald,* 9/16/86, A2; David Birman, "FBI Abuses with the Federal Judiciary: Some Illustrations," unpublished paper submitted to Professor Walter Dellinger, Duke University Law School, 1/6/87, pp. 22–24.

19. The FBI investigation in 1962 and subsequent investigations in 1971 and 1986 concluded that voter harassment had occurred, but that Rehnquist had not been involved. *Compilation of Senate Judiciary Committee Hearings,* vol. 12, p. viii.

20. Nomination of William H. Rehnquist, Report from the Committee on the Judiciary together with Individual Views, Individual Views of Messrs. Bayh, Hart, Kennedy and Tunney, Sen. Exec. Report 92-16, 92d Cong., 1st Sess., p. 8, *Compilation of Senate Judiciary Committee Hearings.*

21. *Id.* at 13.

22. *Id.* at 42.

23. Director to Attorney General, Lewis Franklin Powell, Jr., William Hubbs Rehnquist, Justices, Supreme Court of the United States, 10/29/71, 62-27585-NR (citing "FBI Queries Possible Opponents of Two Supreme Court Nominees," Washington *Post,* 10/29/71, A1. The memo said that the agents who conducted the interviews in question denied asking about opposition to the confirmations.

24. *Justices & Presidents,* p. 316.

25. E.g., John Ehrlichman to Dwight Chapin, 2/28/70, Executive files, FG 17-5, FBI, box 3, WHCF, and Dwight L. Chapin to John Ehrlichman, 1/16/71, both in Nixon Project.

26. Woodward and Armstrong, *The Brethern,* pp. 87–88.

27. *Id.*

28. Ehrlichman, *Witness to Power,* p. 133.

29. Woodward and Armstrong, *The Brethern,* p. 348.

30. Gold, ed., *White House Transcripts,* p. 457.

31. Hoover memo for Tolson et al., 1/11/71, 62-56733-61; Theoharis and Cox, *The Boss,* p. 407.

32. Hoover memo for Tolson et al., *supra* note 31.

33. *Id.*

34. Schwartz, *Ascent of Pragmatism,* p. 8. Chief Justice Burger's lobbying on behalf of the Court extended to the White House. After Justice Douglas resigned in November 1975, Burger wrote President Gerald Ford a three-page "confidential" letter, listing a number of "specifications" for a Supreme Court nominee, and he offered to "pursue these points in more depth" if Ford desired. Burger emphasized that the age of the nominee was a "crucial factor" and that

the Court had been "crippled" since 1969 due to the battles over nominees as well as Douglas's illnesses. Burger to Ford, 11/10/75, folder "Supreme Court—Vacancy General," Philip Buchen file, box 62, Gerald Ford Presidential Library, Ann Arbor, MI.

35. During 1988 and 1989 former Chief Justice Burger, through Supreme Court public information officer Toni House, declined to be interviewed by the author.

36. *See* Schwartz, *Ascent of Pragmatism,* pp. 12–14.

37. "Kirks Named U.S. Courts Aide," Washington *Evening Star,* 6/8/70, A2, located in bufile 77-53317.

38. *Id.* Burger's "close friend," retired U.S. appeals court judge Alfred P. Murrah, was named director of the Federal Judicial Center.

39. Hoover to Kirks, 6/30/67, 62-97344-18 (note on bureau copy).

40. Callan to Rosen, re: Rowland Falconer Kirks, 6/17/52, 62-97344-NR.

41. FBI records released to date do not reflect any other information about this plan to hire former FBI agents as court administrators.

42. Hoover to Tolson et al., 12/2/70, 62-56933-60. The names of the judges in the FBI record are deleted on privacy grounds.

43. *Id.*

44. Demaris, *The Director,* p. 333.

Epilogue

1. In 1974 then Director Clarence Kelley had an "informal lunch" with Supreme Court law clerks. In recommending that Kelley take up the clerks' offer for lunch, bureau officials wrote that the clerks are "cream of the crop" lawyers and that many go on to hold key positions in private firms and in government. G.E. Malmfelt to Franck, Request for the Director to Appear at Informal Lunch with Law Clerks to the Justices of the U.S. Supreme Court, 1/31/74, 62-27585-287. In 1980 Chief Justice Burger talked to a number of FBI National Academy students on a Saturday. William Webster to Chief Justice Burger, 11/20/80, 62-27585-301. In 1983 Justice Sandra Day O'Connor spoke with FBI supervisors as a part of an FBI lecture series. William Webster to Justice O'Connor, 11/17/83, 62-27585-305.

2. *See* SAC, WFO airtel, to Director, re: Leaks to Newspapers, United States Supreme Court, 6/28/74, 62-116144-1, p. 2.

3. W.M. Mooney to Jenkins, U.S. Supreme Court Selection Board, Request for FBI Assistance, August, 1975, 8/6/75, 62-27585-290.

4. *E.g.,* K.T. Boyd to Colwell, Technical Security Assessment for the Chief Justice, U.S. Supreme Court, 1/3/84, 62-27585-306.

5. David E. Pitt, "Tampa F.B.I. is Said to Have Helped Steinbrenner," New York *Times,* 8/10/90, A1:B10. Allen McCreight, special agent in charge of the Tampa FBI office, denied a number of the allegations made by former agents concerning favors provided to Steinbrenner, but he did admit that agents had been occasionally invited to use Steinbrenner's box at Tampa Stadium as part of "longstanding F.B.I. policy to maintain effective liaison with business leaders in the community."

6. *E.g.*, from 1970 to 1976, the FBI provided "applicant-type investigations" of law clerks to judges of the U.S. Court of Appeals in the D.C. Circuit as well as the D.C. District Courts when requested by judges. Hoover arranged this as a favor to Federal Judge Edward Tamm, a former FBI official: 62-53025-259. "Liaison" has long entailed a public relations function for the bureau. After a federal judge, his law clerk, and secretary were taken on a tour of the Cincinnati FBI office, the head agent wrote to Hoover that the "Sixth Circuit Court of Appeals is certainly not as strong a court as it was a few years ago, but we hope to make the most of it through effective liaison." SAC, Cinci., to Hoover, Harvey Phillips, Judge, U.S. Sixth Cir., 10/15/63, 62-53025-578. To encourage this type of "liaison" activity with federal judges, Hoover sent out a letter to all offices in 1962, discussing the "outstanding success" of "personal contacts with such key individuals": 3/13/62, SAC Letter No. 62-17, (F) Visits to FBI Offices by Federal Judges, 62-53025-NR. "Liaison" with federal judges begins at their confirmation. FBI Director William S. Sessions sends a congratulatory letter to all federal judges when "bufiles contain no information to preclude this letter." *E.g.*, Sessions to Hon. Malcolm Howard, Judge of the U.S.D.C., E.D.N.C., 3/15/88, 62-53025-889 (bureau note at bottom of bureau copy of letter).

7. Legat London to Director, ATTN Liaison Unit, Liaison Matter, 8/22/85, 62-27585-NR serial after 307. "Two carpets from P & O Carpets were selected by, and set aside for, Chief Justice Warren Burger when he recently visited London in conjunction with the American Bar Association meeting here. [FBI] Legat London was asked to expedite delivery."

8. SA XX to SAC, WFO, Liaison with Sources of Bureau cases, 6/5/81, WFO 66-3491.

9. *Id.*

10. 54 Fed. Reg. No. 197, p. 42068 (Oct. 13, 1989).

11. Ann Mari Buitrago and Leon Andrew Immerman, *Are You Now or Have You Ever Been in the FBI Files? How to Secure and Interpret Your FBI Files* (Grove Press 1981), p. 27.

12. SAC, S.F., to Hoover, Liaison with Clerk, Circuit Court of Appeals Ninth Circuit, 3/4/59, 66-6200-1050. "Liaison was established with Mr. Paul O'Brien, Clerk, of the Ninth Circuit . . . and his [redacted name] to comply with instruction in referenced SAC letter." O'Brien said that while he and his clerks would be "cooperative" they could not keep track of bureau cases alone and suggested this procedure: the FBI case agent should notify the S.F. office of appeals. "San Francisco will send a letter to the Clerk of the Ninth Circuit. . . . By so doing, the Clerk's Office can be alerted regarding the appeal or pending appeal, and the San Francisco liaison agent's name will be placed upon the docket card which is made up by the Appeal Court Clerk's Office at the time the appeal is received. From this point on, all briefs and official communications in the Circuit Court will be furnished [to] the S.F. Office and forwarded to the Bureau."

13. *E.g.*, [Redacted name] to SAC, WFO, United States Supreme Court Liaison Program, 5/5/72, 66-3491; [Redacted name] to SAC, WFO, United States Supreme Court Liaison with Sources of Bureau Cases, 2/3/77, 66-3491.

14. *E.g.*, 62-53025.

15. SAC, S.F., to Director, Liaison with Federal Judges (80-695), 7/31/81, 62-53025, first serial after 868 (the instructions for photo processing for this "Special Project" were: "Develop and print for selection of best pose for multiple prints from one selected by Hon. Marilyn Patel, USDC, San Francisco"); SAC, L.A., to Director, attn: Photographic Processing, U.S. District Court Judges at Court House, 7/20/88, 62-53025-NR.

16. 55 Fed. Reg. 49,168 (Nov. 26, 1990); Flanders to Bailey, Procedure for Responding to Requests for Information from the Federal Judiciary, 3/10/80, 62-53025-864X2.

17. Herbert Mitgang, "The F.B.I.'s War on Spies in the Stacks," New York *Times*, 6/26/88, Week in Review section.

18. SAC, Phil., to Director, CISPES, IT–El Salvador, 3/6/84, 199-612-233, reproduced in a Center for Constitutional Rights pamphlet entitled "Amendment I (1991)," which is undated; editorial, "The F.B.I. Confesses," New York *Times*, 9/17/88, A14.

19. *See, e.g.*, Philip Shenon, "Black FBI Agent Talks of Years of Harassment on Job," New York *Times*, 8/12/90, A14. Black agent Donald Rochon settled his lawsuit for discrimination and harassment for one million dollars. *But see* "FBI Appoints Hispanic to Post in New Mexico," News & *Observer* (Raleigh, N.C.), 3/9/91, A6. The FBI agent who led 310 other Hispanic agents in suing the bureau for race discrimination was named Special Agent in Charge of the FBI in New Mexico, a job he sought.

20. Associated Press, "FBI Chief Holds Talks on Bias," News & *Observer*, (Raleigh, N.C.), 4/6/91, A3.

21. Angus Mackenzie, "FBI discourages dissent, frowns on nonviolence," *In These Times*, 12/16–22/87, p. 5.

22. Robert Morgan to author, 12/14/89.

23. As an example, Morgan said that with his informant money he could "infiltrate" and "affect" the governor's office or the North Carolina Supreme Court just as the FBI could do on a national level. Robert Morgan telephone interview with author, 12/18/89.

24. Jim McGee, "Syria Said to Help Neutralize Terrorist Threat," Washington *Post*, 3/3/91, A1, A26–27. "The FBI oversaw a massive information collection effort from their agents, local police detectives and various federal agencies." President Ronald Reagan's 1981 Executive Order 12333 concerning intelligence activities is still in effect. It relaxed post-Watergate restraints on collection and dissemination of intelligence information.

25. *See, e.g.*, "ACLU challenges FBI on Arab interviews," News & *Observer*, (Raleigh, N.C.), 1/29/91, A4: The ACLU challenged the FBI's tactic of interviewing Arab-American leaders about potential terrorist threats related to the Persian Gulf war as not truly voluntary and argued that refusal to be interviewed might be docketed in an uncooperative person's FBI file. David Johnston, "F.B.I. Increases Its Attempts to Block Any Terrorist Acts," New York *Times*, 1/20/91: The FBI said that due to Iraqi threats the bureau was expanding its counterterrorism measures "like electronic eavesdropping and other information col-

lected here and abroad on suspected terrorists." But the FBI's program, "including interviews with Arab-American leaders, have inflamed fears that the Justice Department has responded to the crisis by reverting to the style of J. Edgar Hoover."

26. *See, gen.,* Executive Order No. 12333, promulgated by Ronald Reagan in 1981, which loosened many of the domestic intelligence restraints established during the Jimmy Carter presidency. Theoharis and Cox, *The Boss,* p. 255.

27. The burden of justifying the withholding of law enforcement records was relaxed by the 1986 amendments. In addition, certain categories of records were excluded, as opposed to exempted, from the provisions of the FOIA. These excluded records fall into three main categories: (1) ongoing criminal investigations, (2) informants, and (3) classified foreign intelligence, counterintelligence, or international terrorism matters. 5 U.S.C. Sec. 552(c)(1), (c)(2), and (c)(3)(1986). The bureau may "treat the records as not subject to the [FOIA]." 5 U.S.C. Sec. 552(c)(1).

28. *See, gen.,* Schwartz, *Ascent of Pragmatism.*

29. Alexander Charns, "How the FBI Spied on the High Court," Washington *Post,* 12/3/89, C1.

30. William Baker, assistant director, FBI, *Nightline* (ABC), 10/16/91.

31. *Nightline* (ABC), 10/16/91.

32. Neil A. Lewis, "Judge's Backers Seek to Undercut Hill," New York *Times,* 10/13/91, A8.

33. Andrew Rosenthal, "White House devises counterattacks on Hill," *News & Observer* (Raleigh N.C.) (N.Y. Times News Service), 10/14/91, A1, A6.

34. Currently, the U.S. Marshals Service, a component of the Justice Department, is primarily responsible for protection of the federal judiciary. The Marshals Service has a Court Security Division and Threat Analysis Division. "Domestic Terrorism. Prevention Efforts in Selected Federal Courts and Mass Transit Systems," GAO Report to the Chairman, Subcommittee on Civil and Constitutional Rights, Committee on the Judiciary, House of Representatives, June 1988, p. 24. There is a separation of powers problem in giving the judiciary too much policing authority.

35. According to the Administrative Office of the U.S. Courts, the Judicial Conference of the United States has already established a Committee on Court Security, which consists of nine federal judicial officers. *Id.,* p. 100.

36. *E.g.,* H.R. 50, 101st Cong., 1st Sess. (1989) (called the "Federal Bureau of Investigation First Amendment Protection Act of 1989").

Selected Bibliography:
Primary Sources

Archives

Tom C. Clark Papers, Tarlton Law Library, University of Texas, Austin
Gerald R. Ford Presidential Library, Ann Arbor, Michigan
Abe Fortas Papers, Sterling Memorial Library, Yale University, New Haven, Connecticut (by special permission. The Fortas Papers are closed to the public until 2000.)
Lyndon B. Johnson Presidential Library, Austin, Texas
Library of Congress, Manuscript Division, Washington, D.C.
    Hugo L. Black Papers
    William J. Brennan, Jr. Papers
    William O. Douglas Papers
    Earl Warren Papers
Mudd Manuscript Library, Princeton University, Princeton, New Jersey
    John M. Harlan Papers
    David Lawrence Papers
    H. Hubert Wilson Papers
    ACLU Papers
Nixon Presidential Materials Project, National Archives and Records Administration, Alexandria, Virginia
Harry S. Truman Presidential Library, Independence, Missouri

FBI Documents

Headquarters (HQ)
HQ subject files
    62-27585 ("U.S. Supreme Court")
    62-53025 ("Federal Judges")
    62-12114 ("Wiretapping")
    62-56933 ("Admin. Office of U.S. Courts" [AOUSC])
    62-40772 ("House Appropriations Committee" portions re: the Sup. Ct.)
    62-53439 ("U.S. Marshal's Service-General" portions re: the Sup. Ct.)

62-46240 ("Leaks in the Sup. Ct. U.S.")
66-7225 ("Safeguarding Official Records")
62-116144 ("Leaks to Newspapers Sup. Ct. U.S.")
94-1-32555 ("Judicial Circuit Conferences")
66-2554 (FBI "Executives Conference")
190-13741 (FOIA Request File of Israel Shenker)
190-37116 (FOIA Request File of author)
Washington Field Office (WFO) subject file
66-3491 (WFO Liaison with Supreme Court)
HQ main files re: Supreme Court justices (* = Wash. Field Office and "see references")
William O. Douglas*
Earl Warren*
Hugo Black*
Tom C. Clark*
Robert H. Jackson
Stanley F. Reed
Frank Murphy
Felix Frankfurter*
Abe Fortas
Potter Stewart
Oliver Wendell Holmes, Jr.
John M. Harlan (II)
Harlan F. Stone
Benjamin N. Cardozo
Harold H. Burton
Fred M. Vinson
Sherman Minton
Charles E. Whittaker
Joseph McKenna
Willis Van Devanter
James C. McReynolds
William Howard Taft
James F. Byrnes
Charles Evans Hughes
Louis D. Brandeis
HQ main files re: federal judges
Clement H. Haynsworth, Jr.
J. Skelly Wright
John J. Parker
Carl McGowan
Luther M. Swygert
Charles E. Wyzanski, Jr.
J. Waties Waring
Edward A. Tamm
George C. Edwards, Jr. (blind memo only)

HQ files of Court workers
  Rowland F. Kirks, Dir. AOUSC
  Harold B. Willey
  Philip H. Crook
  T. Perry Lippitt
J. Edgar Hoover's "Official & Confidential" files (62-116606)
  Fred Black folder
  Thomas H. Corcoran technical surveillances
  Clemont Haynsworth
  John Mitchell
HQ main files re:
  John N. Mitchell
  Sam J. Ervin, Jr.
  Allard Lowenstein
  Edward Bennett Williams*
  Chauncey Eskridge (Chicago files)

Federal Litigation

Alexander Charns v. U.S. Dept. of Justice, U.S.M.D.N.C., Civ. 89-208-D and
  88-175-D
Paul M. Green v. FBI et al., U.S.E.D.N.C., 89-699-Civ.-5-BR

Interviews and Correspondence

Associate Justice William J. Brennan, Jr., letter, 1990
James Brosnahan (former AUSA), telephone interview by David Birman, 1986
Special Agent Bill Carter, FBI HQ, telephone interview, 1990
Ramsey Clark, telephone interviews, 1988, 1989
William Cohen (former law clerk to Justice William O. Douglas), letter, 1990
Walter Dellinger (former law clerk to Justice Hugo Black), interview in Durham,
  N.C., 1989, by Lisa Balderson
Cartha D. DeLoach, telephone interview and letters, 1990, 1991
Rufus L. Edmisten (former aide to Senator Sam Ervin and Deputy Chief Counsel
  of the Senate Watergate Committee), telephone interview, 1987
George C. Edwards, Jr. (Senior Judge, Sixth Circuit Court of Appeals), letters,
  1988
Bubba Fountain (former congressional page), interview in Durham, N.C., 1990
Stephen Goodman (former law clerk to Justice William Brennan), telephone
  interview, 1990
Eugene Gressman (former law clerk to Justice Frank Murphy), telephone interview,
  1987
Harold Gross (assistant to Senator Alan Cranston), telephone interview by
  David Birman, 1986
Dagmar Hamilton (editor of Justice William Douglas's autobiography), interviews,
  Durham, N.C., Austin, Tex., 1990

Robert Hamilton (former law clerk to Justice Tom Clark), interview Austin, Tex., 1990
Toni House (Supreme Court public information officer), telephone interviews, 1988, 1989
Diana Huffman (staff director, Senate Judiciary Committee), telephone interview, 1990
Nicholas Katzenbach, telephone interview 1989; letter, 1990
William Lambert (journalist), telephone interview, 1990
Associate Justice Thurgood Marshall, letter, 1991
Richard Kleindienst, telephone interview, 1989; letter, 1990
Robert Morgan (former member of Senate Select Committee on Intelligence), letter, interview in Raleigh, N.C., 1990
Former Supreme Court Law Clerk (anonymous), 1990
Former Special Agent, FBI (anonymous), 1983
Alice O'Donnell (former secretary to Justice Tom Clark), telephone interview, 1989
William A. Reppy, Jr. (former law clerk to Justice William O. Douglas), letter and telephone interview, 1990
William Rogers, telephone interview, 1989
Edward Scheidt (former FBI special agent in charge, N.Y. field office), interview in Chapel Hill, N.C., 1990
Thomas J. Schwab (former law clerk at the D.C. Circuit Court of Appeals), telephone interview and letter, 1989
Quinlan J. Shea, Jr. (former director, Department of Justice, Office of Information and Privacy), telephone interview, 1988
Michael E. Smith (former law clerk to Chief Justice Earl Warren), letter, 1990
Abraham D. Sofaer (former law clerk to Justice William Brennan), letter, 1990
Peter L. Strauss (former law clerk to Justice William Brennan), letter, 1990
Nina Totenberg (NPR reporter covering the Court), telephone interview, 1988
Frank Wilkinson (activist in the National Committee to Abolish the House Un-American Activities Committee), interview, 1989
William Wilson (former assistant attorney general, Criminal Division), interview in Austin, Tex., 1990
Associate Justice Byron White, letter, 1991

Oral Histories

Lyndon B. Johnson Presidential Library, Austin, Texas
    Ramsey Clark
    Tom Clark
    Clark Clifford
    Abe Fortas
    Arthur Goldberg
    Thurgood Marshall
    Paul Porter
    Larry Temple
    Earl Warren

Mudd Manuscript Library, Princeton University, Princeton, New Jersey
    William O. Douglas
Harry S. Truman Presidential Library, Independence, Missouri
    David E. Bell
    Kenneth M. Birkhead
    David Bruce
    J.F. Carter
    Tom Clark
    Clark M. Clifford
    Ed D. McKim
    Robert G. Nixon
    Harry H. Vaughan

Index

A Note on the Author

ALEXANDER CHARNS received his J.D. from the University of North Carolina and his B.A. from the University of California, Berkeley. He practices law in Durham, North Carolina, and is a research affiliate of the Institute for Southern Studies. His articles have appeared in the Washington *Post,* the New York *Times,* the San Francisco *Examiner,* and many other publications. Research for *Cloak and Gavel* included eight years of Freedom of Information Act requests and four years of litigation with the Federal Bureau of Investigation.